The Enlightened Enterprise

The Enlightened Enterprise

Walking the Path of the Conscious and High Performing Organization

Christian M. Ellis

SelectBooks, Inc.
New York

This edition published by SelectBooks, Inc.
For information address SelectBooks, Inc., New York, New York.

First Edition

ISBN 978-1-59079-208-7

Cataloging-in-Publication Data

Ellis, Christian M.

The enlightened enterprise : walking the path of the conscious and high performing organization / Christian M. Ellis. — 1st ed.

p. cm.

Includes bibliographical references and index.

Summary: "Offers blueprint for how an enterprise can achieve a new level of consciousness and fundamentally change the nature of its operations to unleash superior capability, productivity, and value creation"—Provided by publisher.

ISBN 978-1-59079-208-7 (pbk. : alk. paper)

1. Organizational effectiveness. 2. Organizational change.
3. Organizational behavior--Psychological aspects. 4. Value. I. Title.

HD58.9.E44 2011
658.4'01--dc22

2010022589

Manufactured in the United States of America
10 9 8 7 6 5 4 3 2 1

This book is dedicated to my wondrous sons:
Keyvan *and* **Hogan**
May they fully experience the flow of life
and walk their own paths in joy, fulfillment, and abundance.

CONTENTS

ACKNOWLEDGMENTS xi

WALKING THE PATH xiii

INTRODUCTION—A PERSONAL REALITY 1

CHAPTER 1 *The True Spirit of the Enterprise* 17

CHAPTER 2 *The Virtue of Value Creation* 39

CHAPTER 3 *The Flowing Fields of Energy* 71

CHAPTER 4 *The Elegant Chaos of Co-evolution* 95

CHAPTER 5 *The Qualities of Productive Activity* 131

CHAPTER 6 *The Conditions for Collaboration* 165

CHAPTER 7 *The Harmony of Healthy Relationships* 187

CHAPTER 8 *The Path of the Enlightened Participant* 217

CHAPTER 9 *The Currents of Consciousness* 247

CLOSING—A COLLECTIVE OPPORTUNITY 271

ENDNOTES 275

INDEX 277

ABOUT THE AUTHOR 289

ACKNOWLEDGMENTS

The author would like to thank the following individuals for their wisdom, belief, support, guidance, and insight: Donna Anderson, Lisa Ellis, Alice Ellis, Thomas Ellis, Darryl Carlson, Dr. Sara Mangat, Carolee Mann, Ted Perkins, Bill Gladstone, Robert Sibson, Mike Norman, and my eternal friend and mentor, Peter LeBlanc.

WALKING THE PATH

If you want to be a leader,
you must learn to walk the Path.
Stop trying to control,
let go of fixed plans.
And eliminate coercive acts.
By not *doing, nothing lacks,*
and the world will govern itself.

The more rules you make,
the less virtuous people will be.
The more weapons you have,
the less secure people will feel.
The more commands you give,
the less self-reliant people will act.

As a wise leader, you will say:
I let go of the law
and people become honest.
I let go of structure
and people become encouraged.
I let go of beliefs
and people become serene.

Through the art of letting go,
harmony reigns.
Through the practice of simplicity,
the more tranquility flows.
Through awakening to self-direction,
everyone gains.
And goodness for all grows.

Composite translation adapted by C.M. Ellis
Adapted from the *Tao Te Ching, Verse 57*, by Lao-tsu

Introduction— A Personal Reality

For the past twenty years I have worked as a consultant focused on helping organizations of all sizes and types improve their effectiveness. During this time, I have had the good fortune of serving clients in every region of the country and working closely with diverse groups of people at all levels of the enterprise to help them improve their ability to contribute to the overall success of their organizations. I have worked in major metropolitan areas with large, multi-national companies. I have worked in rural areas with manufacturing facilities and family-owned businesses. I have worked in towns and cities of all sizes with organizations at every stage in their life cycle. I have had the privilege of working with commercial organizations, non-profit and not-for-profit institutions, hospitals and medical systems, universities, and professional sports franchises and leagues. A colleague once said to me that my travel itinerary looked like the concert schedule of a washed-up lounge singer.

I recall a time several years ago when *in a single week* I spent a night at a local motel in rural Tennessee (next to a very noisy cow barn and chicken coop that had been converted into a diner) in order to meet with an appliance manufacturer the next day, then flew to Manhattan and stayed at a five-star hotel to meet with a large multi-national consumer products company on Park Avenue, and then the following day traveled to southern Maine to meet with a sixth-generation family-owned business where we had a lobster boil in an employee's garage after an all-day meeting.

That week was not too dissimilar from every other week in my life as a consultant. Yet, for a few reasons that week in particular is still vivid in my memory. I remember the pride the people showed in making quality washers and dryers, many of whom had not had a good paying job before. I remember how the sandwich and diet soda I ordered from room service in New York after a long evening of travel cost more than my entire stay in Tennessee. I can still remember the beautiful blueberry fields that mingled with the cozy New England neighborhoods on my drive to the lobster boil. More than anything else, though, what I remember from that week, and from the hundreds of other weeks on the road, is the myriad of personalities and workplaces that mirror the wondrous diversity of our great society. It has truly been a pleasure meeting the good people of this country who care so much about doing a good job and contributing to the success of their organizations. Over the years I have learned as much from them—*and probably more*—than they have learned from me.

The diversity of workplaces and of the people that participate within them makes the world of organizations beyond interesting, both inspiring and tragic at the same time, never dull, and often humorous. I recall a chief operating officer of a technology company who would flush with crimson, start breathing heavily, and then pout in the corner of the meeting room when he did not get his way. I recall a chief executive of a major entertainment organization whose jovial personality on television was entirely opposite from his near-psychotic rage and profanity-laden rants that were commonplace behind closed doors.

I recall an operations supervisor who came to a project team meeting covered in blood because on his way to work he had field-dressed a deer killed by a car (and he stored some of the more tasty organs in the office refrigerator). And then there was the general manager of a customer service center who exuded stillness, presence, and excellence, and role-modeled these organization values in everything he did, contributing to an amazingly efficient and satisfying workplace. And I remember a head of human resources who understood the operations and financials of his organization well-enough that he was more influential than any other executive on the leadership team. I remember the bench scientist who came out of his shell to passionately lead the implementation of a new database management process, even while many of his peers were resisting the needed change.

I recall how a diverse group of university deans learned over the course of several years how to have consistently great conversations about the performance of their people, when in the past these conversations had been political and mundane. And I remember an early morning focus group with the night shift of chemical plant operators who were all chewing tobacco and who would not say a single word because, as I later found out, one of the operators was viewed as a corporate spy by the others (it was a very short meeting). With particular fondness, I recall a chief executive of a retail company, who was the epitome of calmness and grace, but would suddenly—in the middle of a meeting—grab his two-iron and attack the turkey buzzards that would periodically land on the veranda attached to his tenth-story office. And I can recall hundreds more characters that in aggregate represent the entire continuum of conscious and unconscious participation inside their organizations.

Reflecting on the Times

It is impossible to adequately describe the degree of change we have experienced as participants on planet earth over the last two decades. To even begin to describe the nature and magnitude of change along social, economic, geographic, political, or commercial dimensions would be to immediately, and I think irresponsibly, introduce my own subjective thought and reality into our collective experience. Yet, after walking the hallways of many different enterprises, I cannot ignore the common themes, patterns, and phenomena that exist throughout the world of organizations. In a sense, my experiences have accumulated year-after-year to construct a story that reflects my personal reality, my personal view of how organizations work, how they survive, how they succeed, and how they fail, and what it all means for the future of the enterprise.

Now in the second decade of the new millennium there is no question that people are more connected than ever before, that communication is even more important, that new ways of organizing people are emerging, that new values and belief systems are taking root and spreading, that webs of activity are more complex and more global, and that we are increasingly interdependent in the day-to-day activities of our lives. The world is getting smaller and flatter; time seems to be speeding up; traditional boundaries are breaking down; complexity is ever-increasing; and the laws of cause-and-effect are ever more complicated.

Within this seemingly chaotic landscape the vast majority of us spend most of our awake-time *participating in organizations* to get our work done, accomplish specific goals, and enhance our individual and collective life-situation in some way. We are social beings and organizations are social systems intended to fulfill our social and economic needs. And yet, despite an extraordinary amount of attention over the past several decades to the arena of organizational theory, dynamics, and effectiveness, the truth is that most organizations simply do not work very well in meeting the needs of their members and constituencies. Or perhaps put another way, there remains an almost unlimited opportunity for organizations to perform better than they do today, if they could just *awaken* from their slumber and walk a new, more conscious path.

The story of my experience in working with organizations is without question my personal, subjective reality. Given this, it is my hope that the reality of my experience resonates with the reality of others in meaningful and constructive ways. In walking the countless hallways and participating in the endless meetings that pervade organizational life, several themes seem very clear to me. In my experience, enterprise *owners* still over-emphasize short-term financial results at the expense of longer-term value creation. And they still measure enterprise performance as if the organization is an isolated island, showing little insight into how the needs of one organization might be best served while meeting the needs of the broader community. Enterprise *leaders* still exhibit siloed, territorial, and hyper-controlling behavior. They often engage in political gamesmanship and self-serving schemes rather than demonstrate the wisdom and courage required to build and support a healthy, inclusive, and collaborative environment. In my experience, organizational *members* and *employees* continue to feel disconnected from the purpose and strategy of the enterprise. They are less engaged in the critical work activities of the organization than they could be, would like to be, or are allowed to be.

Moreover, throughout the organization, at all levels, *people in general* still spend too much time and energy on activities that do not create value for their customers or constituents, and feel confined and uninspired, limited by artificial rules and constraints that have little to do with what really matters. And finally, with respect to the *enterprise as a whole*, there continues to be a bewildering absence of meaningful recognition, acknowledgment, constructive feedback and other forms of positive reinforcement that inspire, motivate, and reward the efforts and contributions that people make—or have the potential to make—on a daily basis.

Exploring Our Shared Reality

Moving from personal experience into the realm of perhaps a more objective reality, there is clear, overwhelming evidence that many organizations, large and small, commercial and non-commercial, continue to struggle to survive and thrive in our demanding and challenging global, socio-economic ecosystem, often doing the exact *opposite* of what they could and should be doing to ensure long-term success. Consider the number of organizations that reduce headcount during challenging economic times, when study after study after study has shown that downsizing is very expensive, drains institutional knowledge, substantially damages employee morale, and does not achieve *any* improvements in productivity or value creation in the long term. And yet, organizations still cut headcount when times get tough to achieve minor efficiencies for maybe a few months, one or two financial reporting quarters at the most, when instead they should be doing the opposite: intelligently *investing* in the future of the enterprise to avoid being at the blind mercy of inevitable environmental forces in the first place.

Also consider how many organizations achieve some measure of market power and/or societal influence and that, as a result, actually begin to reduce their value creation activities because of this power and influence, rather than increase it. As an example, in the previous decade, many airline carriers retrenched to build greater regional market power around their hubs, which led to staff reductions, fewer choices for customers, increased fares, and an erosion in both the quantity and quality of services provided. It is not surprising, then, that most airlines consistently perform (and will continue to perform) poorly relative to most financial yardsticks. They still do not understand the linkages between workforce satisfaction, customer satisfaction, financial health, and value creation.

In my consulting experience, I have worked with many organizations that were considered highly successful, perhaps were even leaders in their industry or sector. Early on I learned that in our dualistic culture of worshipping the winners and castigating the losers, these "star" organizations are often placed on pedestals and emulated for their strategies and practices. Yet, too often—*much too often in my view*—these organizations are not as effective as they might seem, their success often due to singular phenomena with short shelf-lives and serendipitous origins, which the organization itself had little influence in creating. The real capability demonstrated by many of these organizations involves their ability to leverage and exploit singular phenomena to achieve short-term success, an important capability to be sure, but not sufficient in the long-term. Examples of singular phenomena that can lead to temporary competitive advantage include regulatory change, hard-to-duplicate product innovation, patent acquisition, a new macroeconomic trend, or new technology.

For example, early in the new millennium significant legislation was passed that placed tighter controls, along with greater executive accountability, on the accuracy and clarity of corporate financial reporting. This regulatory change led to a huge windfall for public audit and accounting firms. Similarly, and more frequently, pharmaceutical companies enjoy windfalls when they "accidentally" stumble upon second or even third indications for drugs that are already on the market, substantially broadening the use of the drug and increasing their revenues, dramatically in some cases, even while their research and development pipelines are floundering.

Even more disconcerting are those organizations that achieve some measure of success *in spite of themselves!* I have encountered organizations that succeed in the short-term while at the same time engage in activity that does not contribute much of anything to the sources of their success nor establish the conditions for future success. In fact, some of this activity is actually harmful to long-term sustainability. It is truly remarkable how some organizations continue to survive based on what seems to simply be critical mass and general inertia. This is not a good business model for long-term success. Inertia is the insidious enemy of evolution and change.

As an example, a major insurance company enjoyed healthy profits for a number of years due entirely to its treasury function's ability to invest premium dollars in high-return investment vehicles while the rest of the organization operated at huge losses due to bureaucracy, inefficiency, and a long-standing lack of competitiveness. Not surprisingly, the poor performance of this organization was clearly revealed when the markets collapsed and investment income dried up. In another example, a professional sports league has allowed the quality of its sport to slowly devolve while making up for its decline through global marketing and expansion efforts. However, the success of this strategy will be short-lived as the integrity of the game dissolves and permanently alienates fans for good.

Summarizing the Challenge

So what is really going on out there among the vast majority of our organizations? *Why is it that some organizations are much more successful than others over the long-term?* What differentiates those organizations that contribute significantly more value to our world, relative to their size, scope and purpose, from the others? Why do so many organizations under-perform relative to their goals? Why are people who participate in organizations so often dissatisfied and resentful of their organization and its actions and behaviors? Why is it that with decades of available research and empirical information linked to improving enterprise performance, many organizations still grind-away, seemingly "in the dark," and stubbornly and blindly fight for survival?

The primary problem is that most organizations act and behave as *unconscious* entities that develop strategies and implement operating models based on the harmful patterns of their collective, ego-based "mind," and the old mechanistic, dualistic, and cause-and-effect view of the universe that has guided our socio-economic activities for centuries. The great anthropologist, Gregory Bateson, once said that "In modern society, those variables that require flexibility are too controlled and those that require control are too flexible." Organizations have always been microcosms of the broader cultures and societies within which they participate. And as reflections of our most recent century, which on a global scale was the most devastating in all of human history, our institutions are still in significant trouble. They spend too much time and energy on the things they cannot control and too little on the things they can. Most remain imprisoned in the fortress of the unconscious, a prison of their own making.

Organizations still believe that if they simply communicate a new program or policy change from the top down, it will be fully embraced by the workforce. They still believe that if they can copy a best practice from some other company, they too will improve. They still believe they can control their external environments and defeat their challengers through separation, opposition, and conflict. They still believe that having the lowest price, the most shelf-space, or the coolest packaging will drive real profitability. They still believe that having the most charismatic executive at the helm is the fast-track to prosperity. They still believe that marketing and advertising is the key, even when their products and services are not aligned with customer needs and wants. They still believe that they know what is best for their members and other constituents despite heaps of data that suggest otherwise.

And they still believe that their individual interests are superior to the broader interests of their external world. These are only a few examples among many. This common unconsciousness at the organizational level has helped create what has been termed by Patricia Auberdene and others as *unconscious capitalism*, and the harmful consequences of this reality have become very clear over the past several years.

In reflecting on this state of affairs, consider the following questions that both commercial and social sector organizations are more seriously exploring these days:

- To what extent is there an emerging view among leadership that the enterprise is significantly underperforming relative to its potential?
- To what extent is there a belief throughout the enterprise that it is not well-prepared for the new realities of our world's social, economic, and environmental challenges?
- To what extent is there an emanating desire to move beyond short-term financial metrics and explore a broader definition of success, one that includes how the enterprise contributes to the social good of our world?
- To what extent is there a sense that the enterprise is not effectively evolving with the needs and wants of the communities within which it operates and serves its constituents?
- To what extent are there indicators that the workforce of the enterprise is not as productive and effective as it could and should be?
- To what extent are the values of people in the organization changing to include a much greater desire for meaning and personal fulfillment in the workplace?

There is no doubt that some organizations have made good progress in establishing elevated and enduring strategies, operating models, and cultures that enable them to achieve greater harmony with the changing environment and their evolving constituencies. These organizations are at the forefront of a change in direction and momentum toward a wholly different way of creating value through more conscious organizational activity and increased social responsibility. Unfortunately, however, most organizations have *not* fundamentally changed their beliefs or assumptions about how the universe actually works, how success should be defined in our highly interdependent world, or what it takes to be sustainably successful and create value in the long-run. This in part is why we continue to experience destructive bubbles in various industries, market swings and crashes, corporate scandals, and brutal and extended recessions. As worsening climate change creates more and more severe weather systems, so too does ongoing unconsciousness within our organizations create more and more severe socio-economic shocks. In this way, not only are unhealthy organizations a reflection of an unhealthy society, they are also a primary cause.

In summary, the performance of most organizations, as *unconscious* entities, remains dramatically sub-optimized due to the following fundamental challenges:

- **Organizations do not define success and value creation broadly enough in the context of the social and business ecosystems in which they participate.** Rather, they define success as if they are independent and isolated entities that simply need to generate cash, make money, and/or achieve specific operating results over some narrowly defined period of time, without enough consideration for the broader community and environment in which they exist.
- **Organizations continue to attempt to predict, coerce, direct, and control their internal and external environments.** They do this through misguided actions—plans, policies, programs, processes, and practices—that constrain enterprise creativity and agility, diminish the ability to adapt and evolve, and de-motivate people to do their best work. They do not understand that the more they try to control, the less control they have. They do not understand that "winning" control over the environment in the short-run means "losing" in the long-run and not surviving the inevitable environmental corrections that come. These organizations create too much negative energy in their crusade to *confront and bully* reality, and too little positive energy in the pursuit to *create and flow* with it.
- **Organizations spend too much time on things such as structure, hierarchy, and senior leadership and spend too little time on key processes, value networks, and the workforce as a whole.** Organizations focus too much on structural and programmatic solutions such as re-organizing functions and departments, installing store-bought technologies, and conducting leadership "training," and do not effectively build the qualities and create conditions that optimize the effectiveness of the whole workforce. Because of this narrow focus they do not come remotely close to unleashing the true potential energy, creativity, and productivity of their people.
- **Organizations continue to talk about people as their most important assets, but often treat them like capital, rather than as human beings with physical, emotional, mental, and spiritual challenges and needs.** Organizations do not invest enough in the conditions that create a meaningful, fulfilling, and inspiring workplace. Moreover, they do not pay enough attention, or assign sufficient time and resources, to the health and wellness of people and the health and

effectiveness of their interactions and relationships, which are the foundation for almost all organizational activity and the generation of superior value creation.

Introducing the Book Chapters

In chapter one, I explore the true nature of the enterprise as "its values-in-action," and challenge the traditional ways in which organizations and their members define and leverage their identity, and how this identity shapes perceptions of reality and guides the activity of the organization. This chapter introduces critical concepts that relate to enlightenment and consciousness that are further explored in subsequent chapters. It provides several in-depth examples of how organizations can and should have a vision and mission that transcends the typical ways enterprise leaders think about value creation.

In the second chapter, I discuss the basic elements of the enterprise, and suggest that the most important objective of an enterprise is creating and delivering value, emphasizing the critical role that values-in-action play in the value creation process. The chapter provides a broader and more compelling definition of value and the sources and drivers of creating and delivering value. This includes the need to think about enterprise success relative to a broader set of stakeholders and explores the relationship between value creation and the organization's capabilities, processes, and networks.

In chapters three and four, I introduce the concepts of energy exchange, co-evolution, and organizational sustainability. These concepts are central to the discussion of why and how organizations tend to fight the natural flow of the universe, rather than flow with it, and the need to embrace and realize the potentiality that exists everywhere and at all times even in dynamic and chaotic environments. It provides a strategic framework for how an organization can co-evolve with its socio-economic ecosystem to achieve enduring success.

In chapters five, six, and seven, I explore the specific conditions and qualities that are required to drive enterprise innovation, productivity, and value creation. These chapters provide highly applicable and practical tools, models, and frameworks for creating a highly meaningful and productive workplace. Their central themes pertain to the importance of and applications for meaningful work, effective collaboration, and healthy relationships as fundamental ingredients for superior, long-term value creation and delivery.

In the eighth chapter, I explore in detail the concepts of consciousness and the conditions for improved organizational performance *from the perspective of the enterprise participant.* It discusses in-depth how the individual within an organization can achieve lasting fulfillment and meaningful value contribution through self-empowerment, the development of new competencies, and the demonstration of greater awareness, attention, and courage to change unproductive and restrictive organizational practices.

In the final chapters, I review many of the concepts already introduced in previous chapters and explore more deeply the concept of organizational enlightenment and consciousness. The chapters delve into the importance of a deeper and broader awareness of what makes organizations truly effective over the long term, given the dynamics, complexities, dangers, and opportunities of our world in the new millennium. These closing chapters integrate many of the tools and frameworks from previous chapters into a conceptual blueprint that serves to help an organization walk a new path toward greater consciousness and superior performance.

Regarding This Material

I wrote this book for *anyone* who works in or is involved with almost any type of organization, and who cares about how well the organization functions and performs. This book is therefore not just for executives or people in formal leadership roles. The intent of the book is to integrate important principles and concepts from a diverse set of domains, including the physical sciences, behavioral psychology, human consciousness and spirituality, and organization effectiveness, with the goal of providing some fresh insight into creating a more *enlightened and better performing enterprise* of the future. It is intended to share a wide array of thought-provoking ideas and suggestions that, if embraced, can dramatically influence and shape the way in which organizations operate and perform in the current and future turbulent, demanding environment. Almost all of the concepts found here are based on my own direct personal experience in working with many different types of organizations across a wide variety of industries, and from the findings of many and diverse organizational research studies that are mostly available in the public domain.

What is this book not? This is *not* a book of programmatic best practices since I do not believe in the strict emulation of other organizations as a viable strategy for improving the effectiveness of any single organization. It is *not* a how-to guide since I believe that every organization should walk its own path of lasting success. It does *not* provide extensive case studies since these often reflect dangerously narrow perspectives, leading us right back to the problem with best practices. And it does *not* represent any single major research study but certainly leverages many of the major studies and research projects conducted in the arena of social systems and organizational dynamics over the past several decades.

Concurrent with the increasing attention devoted to organizations, there has been a substantial increase in the energy and attention devoted to the human experience within organizations, and the worthiness of a more conscious and spiritual approach to our daily activities and lives in general. There are a number of teachers, writers, and philosophers, such as Ernest Holmes and more recently, M. Scott Peck, Dan Millman, Eckhart Tolle, and others, who have written extensively to share their thoughts on the nature of the human soul and spirit and the social and economic benefits of living a more spiritual life. These important concepts originate from *both* Eastern and Western traditions and philosophy.

Recently I have personally experienced an "awakening" and now live a more conscious and fulfilling life. I will share more on this subject later in the book. My strong personal belief is that many of these secular, spiritual concepts can be applied to organizations, if we subscribe to the idea that organizations are not all that different from other intelligent, self-regulating organisms. There is an incredible consistency among the various schools of spirituality and philosophical thought concerning consciousness and the nature of our active participation in the collective energy and intelligence of the universe. There is a lot of agreement that *how we see reality is highly influenced by our own subjective thought patterns*, and that if we reframe, re-focus, and ultimately transcend our minds, individually and collectively, we can achieve greater levels of consciousness and shape the actual reality we experience for our own benefit. In other words, what is real is basically just a point of view, and if we can clear our minds together and mutually *unlearn* many of the destructive patterns that influence our current thinking and actions, we will not only see our world from a more common viewpoint, but we will be more successful in collectively creating the world we want. Think about the power of this premise in the context of an enterprise! This is the path of the conscious and high performing organization.

As a very basic definition, organizations are simply collections of individuals drawn together to carry out purposeful activity. With this in mind, I firmly believe that there is such a thing as organizational consciousness, an enlightened awareness that involves all of us, as members of organizations as well as participants in this universe, creating something far greater than our sum through our unified thoughts and actions. Perhaps the central premise of this book is that the more conscious an organization is, the greater the probability is that it will succeed and survive in an enduring way.

To help you in your journey through this material I utilize throughout the book some concepts from Eastern philosophy to highlight specific terms, ideas, and knowledge. These include:

- **Dharma:** a higher truth, law, or principle. Throughout the chapters I have recorded a dharma log that represents specific findings from my personal experience regarding good organizational practice.
- **Koan:** a mind expanding story, question, or dialog. Throughout the book I have provided definitions of key terms and concepts that are critical to understanding the material.
- **Samadhi:** a higher degree of concentrated meditation. Throughout the book I have shared personal experiences that reflect deeper insight into my own personal learning over the past twenty years.
- **Satori:** a sudden flash of awareness, understanding, or insight. At the beginning of each chapter I tell a story that introduces an important insight to be gained from the main body of the chapter's text.
- **Sutra:** an important scripture, a record of oral teaching. I have provided excerpts from other resources that enhance and help to validate the main concepts of the chapters.
- **Tao:** the true nature of the world: the way, the path. At the end of each chapter is a series of questions and considerations that will help the reader process the material and begin to think about how it may apply to your own organization.

My Samadhi *A Personal Memo*

This book is *not* written for a particular group of people (there are already an ample amount of good books focused on leadership, or written for managers and leaders). **It is my hope that this book will appeal to a highly diverse group of people who bring different skills and knowledge to the different roles they play in their organizations.** However, I feel it is important to include the following letter, recreated from memory, that I wrote to a general manager of a "big-box" retail outlet not too long ago, as a way to introduce many of the concepts that are explored here.

Dear General Manager:

I am writing you as a frequent and loyal customer who also has some experience as a consultant in helping organizations become more effective. As you know, I spend a great deal of time in your store (and spend a great deal of money too!) and have had the pleasure of getting to know you and several of your managers and associates. I have certainly appreciated the brief conversations you and I have had, and I always feel very welcome. That said, over the past several weeks I could not help observing some patterns of behavior and activity that may be getting in the way of your organization performing even better than it already is. Moreover, I have had several impromptu conversations with your people that confirm these observations.

In a nutshell, a work environment has evolved at your location that is not enabling your people to do their best work. Store results are below target in the majority of your departments. At times there is confusion, conflict, and apathy among associates and general morale is low. Furthermore, my observation is that as the leader of the organization, you are spending too much time on administrative tasks and activities and too little time on helping to create and support a more positive and productive workplace.

Currently there is too much focus on carrying out top-down corporate-driven programs and too much emphasis on trying to control employee behavior through rules and policies that have little or nothing to do with providing high quality service to the customer. Recently, for example, employees were told that their top priority was to sell store memberships to customers, which was received poorly since most of them feel (and have historically been told) their top priority is to serve customers and sell products. In another example, one of your best and most professional employees, whose department is the *only* one above target in revenue, was reprimanded for being several minutes over her allotted break time, causing her great frustration. (Note to the reader: This person left the organization soon after this letter was written.)

In working with many different types of organizations over the years I have learned a few things about the conditions that need to be present to increase workplace engagement, productivity, and overall performance. What I've learned was nicely supported by a research study conducted several years ago in the retail and hospitality industries that focused on the *service-profit chain*. This study showed very strong, data-based correlations between employee satisfaction, the quality of customer service, the loyalty of customers, and the financial health of the organization.

Very simply, the more satisfied employees are with their work and their work environment, the better they perform, and the better employees perform, the more satisfied customers are, all of which leads to improved profitability. Consistent with these findings, I have summarized below what I have personally learned about high performance work environments (these are true regardless of industry, by the way):

People at all levels should have a good understanding of how their role directly contributes to store performance, and they should have a good sense of how well they are doing relative to expectations. People want to do meaningful work, not necessarily always complex or cutting edge work, but they want to have an impact. People place great value on a strong sense of dignity, meaning, and community in the workplace. People are more likely to change their own behavior when they can participate in the actual problem solving, and are more likely to carry out decisions that they have helped to make. In general, people like some degree of variety, challenge, flexibility, feedback, and customer contact in carrying out the daily responsibilities of their work. The vast majority of people care about their jobs, care about their organization, want to grow and develop in their role, and want to do good work, as long as the organization pays them a living wage, provides support when they need it, and treats them with respect.

I hope that this does not seem overwhelming to you, because it is not. I suspect that you would agree after some internalization, that these universal principles are quite simple and straightforward. Improving the work environment at your store does not require fancy new programs or processes, and certainly not new policies. Rather, as the leader, you can make significant progress through your own behaviors and actions as a role-model of more conscious thinking and doing.

Forgive me if I am being too direct, but if I were in your shoes I would first begin to build stronger personal relationships with your people. Invest some time in getting to know them, who they are, what they like to do, and how they like to do their work. Second,

I would quietly and reasonably loosen up on policing strict adherence to the policies that most irritate people, like getting "written up" if they are a few minutes late from lunch. Third, I would have discussions with department managers to brainstorm with them on what is going well and not so well in their areas and what they think the business should do about it. Then, give them the flexibility and time to take the lead on making needed improvements.

Next, I would begin to take a more active, but still somewhat subtle, approach in informally coaching people, not on administrative tasks, but on the some of the specific activities that drive revenue growth and customer satisfaction. Finally, I would enlist the help of people on the floor in making important real-time decisions as needed. No formal process is required, just informal, unscheduled conversations that give people the opportunity to give input and influence decisions that affect them.

There is no question that your role is hugely important to the success of the enterprise. Studies in the restaurant and retail industries consistently show a strong relationship between the performance of the general manager and the performance of the store. You clearly have an exciting opportunity to change the way things are done using some of the principles and strategies that I've outlined. And keep in mind there are a few fundamental values that are essential to your personal success in pursuing these things. Always tell the truth. Treat people with respect and dignity. Avoid being a "manager" and instead become a "role model." And in leading the charge, stay humble, be a great listener, and have some fun. Your people will appreciate keeping things light and in the right perspective, since there are many things in their lives that are more important and more serious than working for you. Always stay mindful that your "power" does not come from control or hierarchy; rather it comes from the energy you radiate outward through your complete attention to, caring for, and collaboration with the people in your workplace.

I would be more than happy to discuss these thoughts further with you if you are interested. And thanks again for the nice welcome I always get when I walk through your doors. Talk to you soon.

Sincerely,
Chris Ellis

ONE

The True Spirit of the Enterprise

Imagine that you are in large dining room. The mid-day sun is shining through the many windows of this beautiful, airy room with high ceilings and plants of all kinds, as if a vast greenhouse. Every single employee is there, enjoying a delicious, catered lunch to celebrate several of your company's largest and most loyal customers. The positive energy in the room is powerful and palpable. At your table, you are talking about the local baseball team that continues to play inspired ball every day for its fans, even though it is having a miserable season. A stranger sits at the table, an employee whom you have not met before. So far he has mostly listened, but at a break in the conversation, he suddenly poses a question to the table: "Since we seem to be talking about spirit, how would you describe the spirit of our own organization?" After a few moments of consideration, the table bursts into conversation, which goes in many directions with many diverse and creative ideas. You feel a sense of pride as you listen to your tablemates talk, share their experiences, tell war stories, and have some fun with the question, while also taking it seriously. The theme that emerges seems to be that while spirit is hard to define, it is elevating, reflects passion, and represents a being's true nature. During this lively debate you lean over to the stranger, introduce yourself, and offer to refill his coffee. He smiles, thanks you graciously, and then respectfully interrupts the table dialog and thanks the others as well. There is a brief, pregnant pause until someone speaks up and says: "But we have not answered your question yet!" The stranger then looks around the room, looks at those around the table, and looks at you, and says: "You actually have, in your own way." **This is satori.**

IN THIS CHAPTER WE WILL EXPLORE IMPORTANT CONCEPTS regarding the true nature of the enterprise, as summarized by the following principles:

- **An enterprise is a purpose-based social system that exists to achieve specific goals for its participants through interdependent and collaborative activity.**
- **There is recent convergence occurring where the domains of science, psychology, and consciousness overlap to give us new insight into organization effectiveness.**
- **The true nature of the enterprise is represented by a conscious, elevating, and enduring sense of spirit, as demonstrated by its values-in-action: how it creates value through products and services.**

We are all participants in a dynamic universe. We are all members of a global community. We are all contributors to a collective consciousness. We are all co-creators of a shared reality. And we are all spiritual beings in human form. Within this active and sublime realm of existence, full of disruptions, disturbances, chaos, and constant change, we evolve and continuously create new arrangements, structures, and systems of varying and increasing diversity and complexity. Individually and collectively, we exchange energy and create order through our relationships with each other and everything else in our world.

The societies, cultures, and communities of our world are uniquely human constructs intended to make our existence easier, safer, less lonely, and more fulfilling. They help us live in meaningful and productive ways through the comforts of tradition, the safety of family, the stability of law, the division of labor, the specialization of knowledge, the sharing of resources, the economies of scale, and the efficiencies of cooperation. Within our society and its organizations, we see the laws of nature at work every day. We see extraordinary beauty, elegance, and simplicity emerge even as our world becomes more intricate and complex. We learn new paradigms of scientific thinking and inspiring spirituality even as our world suffers from the pains and sorrows caused by pervasive ignorance, intolerance, and greed. We sense the importance of preserving and sustaining the natural resources and ecosystems of our world even as we continue to pollute and destroy our natural environment.

Through these trials we learn more and more about the nature of our role in the universe, and we believe more strongly than ever that we have the capability to apply our increasing understanding of nature's laws to actually collaborate with nature, to *co-create*—to collaboratively create—our future, releasing the power of our emerging awareness and the interconnectedness of all things.

SUTRA LESSON ***Awakening from Unconsciousness***[1]

In her revolutionary book, *Conscious Evolution: Awakening Our Social Potential*, Barbara Marx Hubbard discusses our responsibility to create sustainable, evolving social systems. She writes with elegant clarity:

"Through conscious evolution we realize, for the first time as a species, that it is our responsibility to proactively design social systems that are in alignment with the tendency to higher consciousness, greater freedom, and more synergistic order."

Our emerging belief in the collective power that we have to create our future is of critical importance to how we perceive the role of the enterprise in walking a more conscious and meaningful path. Organizations are everywhere and do almost everything; they are perhaps the single most important construct that we as humans have in our journey to a higher level of meaning, a new plane of existence full of prosperity and abundance for all.

Defining the Enterprise

The human enterprise, or organization, is a network of relationships with the shared intent of creating value for its environment, such as the broader community, society, or even the world. Every organization is inherently temporary since it will cease to exist when it stops its activities; there is no infinite source of energy at its core. Every organization is a web of activities, interactions, and relationships ranging from the very simple enterprise that involves only a few people, perhaps in close proximity, to the enormous and complex enterprise that involves thousands of people worldwide.

The enterprise is a purpose-based social system. It exists to achieve a goal or set of goals for its participants. Some organizations are *commercial* in nature and seek to maximize their profitability, while other organizations are *social* in nature and seek to serve their constituencies without seeking a financial return above what is required to exist. In the most general sense, the successful human enterprise is a source of positive energy in our world that enhances our individual and collective existence.

The enterprise is also an open system, with highly permeable boundaries, that exchanges energy with the environment in the process of value creation, using coordinating and guiding mechanisms such as values, processes, networks, and operating procedures to guide the behaviors and actions of people as they do work and interact within the organization and across its "borders" with other organizations.

KOAN: WHAT IS A *PARTICIPANT*?

A participant is an individual who actively participates in the enterprise as a member and/or employee.

There are many types of human enterprise with an extraordinary range of scale, complexity, and purpose. Multi-national corporations, professional and trade associations, universities and colleges, government agencies, family-owned businesses, medical systems and hospitals, social cause foundations, sports leagues, labor unions, military units, state prison systems, farming cooperatives, public school systems, social service agencies, research centers, think tanks, retail stores, transition living homes, gated housing developments, and youth soccer programs are among the many and diverse forms of organizations, or enterprise. A full typology would most likely include hundreds of organizations. Traditionally, the term *enterprise* has often meant a *for-profit* organization. This material uses an expanded definition where an enterprise *is any organization* that intends to create value for its internal participants and/or its external environment.

Organizations are comprised of several fundamental elements that are responsible for carrying out the activity of the enterprise *(from low to high complexity)*:

- **Individuals:** The individual participants in an organization also referred to as employees or members.
- **Groups:** Collections of individuals that interact in a single location, or in multiple locations, to exchange information and ideas, create new ideas, carry out activities, accomplish tasks, and/or achieve specific goals. Groups can be small or large, formal or informal, temporary or permanent.

- **Networks (internal):** Broad associations of groups and/or individuals that interact together across multiple locations to exchange information and ideas, create new ideas, accomplish tasks, and achieve specific goals. Internal networks are similar to groups but typically do not gather in one location and often utilize technologies such as email and the internet to carry out their activities.
- **Networks (internal/external):** Broad associations of groups and/or individuals both *internal and external* to the organization that interact together to exchange information and ideas, create new ideas, accomplish tasks, and achieve specific goals. External networks are similar to internal networks but include participants in the external environment that are not members of the organization.
- **Communities:** A network of individuals that includes participants who are typically in close proximity, commonly involved in face-to-face interactions, have strong personal relationships, and share common ideals, beliefs, interests, or goals. Communities are typically more diverse than groups, and are often comprised of groups as well as networks. The participants within the community are bound by a more rich and complex set of factors than those of working groups or networks.

Unfortunately, there is human enterprise that intends to create negative energy and acts as an energy sink, an enterprise that by intent exists to create disharmony, discrimination, and destruction. Organizations of this type are typically represented by extremist groups and radical associations that are so lost in the artificial construct of the mind that they can only *extract* energy from our world and fuel entropy through their obsessions of fear, anger, and hate. This type of enterprise represents the absence of consciousness and enlightenment, and will not be explored in this book.

Revealing the Great Convergence

In our efforts to better understand and influence our societies, communities, and organizations, we are beginning to see a hugely important convergence of thought with respect to the science and complexity of social systems, the important role of interrelationships and the interpersonal dynamics that represent their foundation, and the central tenet of the need for a greater collective consciousness, a more enlightened path. We understand more and more that how people behave, act, and relate to one another in the thousands of interactions that take place every second within a social system, such as a large organization, shape the overall quality of the system. Timeless as well as newly emerging principle in the areas of science, behavioral psychology, human consciousness, and organizational effectiveness are converging in exciting and inspiring ways. They help us conceive new ways of thinking about how our world works and, more specifically, how organizations work and how they can reframe and renew their visions of success going forward.

This amazing confluence focuses on the nature of energy, reality, relationships, awareness, and consciousness, and how we can break down old patterns and transcend old, destructive ways of thinking to achieve greater coherence and harmony in our daily organizational activities. We are learning how an expanded awareness, or consciousness, can create and channel energy to build stronger relationships and influence more directly a reality of success and prosperity that can emerge from those relationships.

More specifically, through discoveries in the *physical sciences*, the first domain, we understand more and more that our view of the world is not reality, but our fabrication of reality, and that our seemingly "objective" views of our environment are deeply enmeshed in creating the very reality it is observing. This has been shown to be true in the world of atoms and energy where the location of certain sub-atomic particles can only be determined by where the observer actually looks. In this way, the concept of matter exists *only* in a state of *potential* locations until someone actually looks for it. In other words, by observing something, we are actually participating in the event itself, and to some degree affecting its outcome.

In the world of organizations, as a parallel concept, consider how often our interpretation of enterprise phenomena influences their perceived outcomes. Take for example the observation of customer shopping patterns by a merchandising professional in a department store. Imagine that this individual created a new floor design that was shaped by her assumptions of previous customer patterns and buying decision-making processes. The merchandiser would definitely use her understanding of old patterns as well as her own belief in the efficacy of new floor design as she observed the new patterns of customers, to determine the degree to which behaviors had changed favorably, contributing to increased revenue per square foot. The involvement of this participant in the observation process would in fact affect its perceived reality.

In the physical world we are also learning more about the laws and forces that govern energy and matter from the smallest sub-atomic "particles" to the largest galaxies. For decades scientists have had to apply principles of relativity to the macro-world of outer space, quantum mechanics to the micro-world of "inner" space, and classical Newtonian mechanics to the space in-between—almost everything we can reach out and touch, such as apples falling from trees! But recent breakthroughs in the study of complex systems, on *any* scale, are showing us that there are fundamental geometric patterns, shapes, forces, and relationships that underlie all of energy, matter, space, and time. In fact, it appears that only three types of geometric patterns, termed point, periodic, and strange attractors, are enough to characterize almost all phenomena throughout the universe. We are finding that within the mysterious sub-atomic world, beyond our solar system and our outer arm of our galaxy, and across the parsecs of galactic clusters—*in all that we term our physical reality*—there is a consistent, coherent, and harmonic order.

Perhaps the most important breakthrough, however, is the new understanding regarding the energy field of the universe. As we go from the macroscopic to the microscopic, traveling through the quantum mechanical realm where energy and matter begin to converge, the universe becomes even more alive and dynamic, and the forces that affect everything also converge into a single, unified field of energy, what some scientists describe as the universal field of intelligence and consciousness.

Within our traditional definitions of space-time, nothing can travel faster than the speed of light, not even information. In the newly emerging, and experimentally supported, view of the universe information can be transmitted and received instantaneously within the unified field. The complex systems of our universe are therefore networked systems. Everything is connected to everything else through this field in ways that go beyond our historically perceived limitations of energy, space, and time. Some call this *entanglement*, and while it might seem to some of us that untangling our lives might bring a little peace, the reality is that we are closely linked through the energy vibrations, currents, and fields of the universe. These fundamental frequencies of the unified field are the same frequencies of human consciousness.

Moving on to our second domain, through our knowledge of *behavioral psychology*, we are learning that as individuals, when we rely on our minds, we look at the world through a collection of filters and screens that represent, as well as contribute to, our biases, beliefs, and opinions that can easily distort reality. Furthermore, there is a shared recognition that most of us are behaving, working, and living as unconscious beings, caught in the maelstrom of always *doing*, rather than simply *being*, and with a pathological guide leading the way, generally called the ego. The ego of the mind is the great deceiver, the cause of most of the problems we create or encounter. The ego of the mind is totally enthralled with "I," "me," or "mine," and does not understand that the more an individual includes and involves others collaboratively, the more effective he will be. Moreover, with respect to the organization as simply a larger platform for individuals, when we rely on the collective mind—the collective ego—a similar result occurs, where we have a tendency to perceive and modify the objective world to fit into a single enterprise perspective. This phenomenon can work in our favor and against it.

For example, as participants in an organization, and as the organization as a whole, it is quite common to believe that the enterprise is superior and unique compared to its competitors. This is the egoic mind, or *org-ego*, of the enterprise. This can instill a sense of pride and support a commitment to excellence while also setting the stage for unrealistic assumptions and expectations about the needs and performance of the enterprise relative to other organizations. In one case, a mid-sized professional services firm had traditionally viewed itself as the "premiere" firm in its arena, and this belief was a central underpinning to its culture and its commitment to only the highest standards for its clients; however, this belief was just that, a belief, and the firm had little data or insight into how it actually performed relative to its competitors (in fact, it did not perform financially as well as it thought). Interestingly, when leaders in the firm developed a robust method for measuring client impact, it was met with apathy, fear, and open resistance, demonstrating how powerful of a force the org-ego can be.

Even more harmful, the org-ego can prevent the enterprise from effectively operating in a way that is consistent with the fundamental laws of nature. And, our understanding of these laws is changing. Through ever-greater scientific rigor, research, and experimentation, we are learning that the activities of our minds and bodies, with their associated energy frequencies, are connected through the universal energy field, where cooperation has been proven to be more effective than competition time and time again. Each of us, in a way, is a coherent energy-information field. As we move beyond our ego-based mind and attune ourselves to higher levels of consciousness, we are able to transcend egoic constraints, more freely share valuable information, and more easily unleash our collaborative energies. Through this transcendence, the potential for our societies and our organizations are limitless.

Through our evolving beliefs and understanding about *human consciousness and spirituality*, the third domain, we are learning more about how the reality we have constructed for ourselves takes us further away from, rather than closer to, the inherent openness, curiosity, creativity, and awareness we are naturally born with. We have a greater understanding today that we cannot find our true nature through the perceived logic of our learned thought processes, and certainly not through the clever distortions and misperceptions of our ego; rather, we must return to our true nature through not-thinking, a return to our beginner's mind, our spirit-consciousness. One of the greatest ironies of our evolution is that the ever-evolving brain, an entity of unimaginable complexity, actually obscures consciousness with its endless and chaotic electrical activity.

And yet, it is through our intelligence that we are beginning to understand this dynamic and transcend it through the practice of stillness, awareness, meditation, yoga, empathy, and other harmonizing actions. Through these practices we can create more order, or rather, strip away the veils of disorder and, from a place of equanimity, become stronger together. This is the path we must walk, and will walk together, but we have a long way to go

Our true nature has never left us, but we have created a subjective thought atmosphere around ourselves—a toxic cloud for many—that acts as a barrier to the demonstration of our authentic self, or spirit. What we have learned and observed from others, and what we have inherited from our ancestors, has created thought patterns that block this inherent energy. In this way we should not seek the light, but break down the walls that prevent our light from shining through.

In the world of organizations, the world of form, we create rules and structures that prevent our collective spirit from emerging in its full potency. We constantly confuse linear reasoning, analytical rigor, and critical, logical thinking with simple insight and wisdom. We confuse the *need to prove results*, and their cause-and-effect, with simply *doing the right thing*. We confuse the all-consuming priority of *making money* with the more fulfilling goal of *value creation*. And we confuse this shared purpose of *creating value* for our world with the *need to survive* in our world at any cost.

In this domain of spirituality, our exploration is helping us understand how to dissolve these confusing and veiled barriers, and envision a more enlightened way of being. We understand that often less is more, that we can recognize our world as essentially a realm of illusion, and that we can unlearn those things that slow down the energy transmission of our spirit and prevent our inner light from shining through. More practically speaking, we are beginning to realize that we can move beyond the ever-growing employee handbooks, the over-stuffed binders of data, the omnipresent executive committees, and the endless PowerPoint decks to actually see the world more clearly and more holistically, make better decisions, and express ourselves in our natural authenticity.

The conditioned view of our world is therefore based on a combination of what our senses, memories, belief systems, and emotions allow us to see. In a way, the "real" world is not all that different from the world portrayed in the extraordinary film, *The Matrix*, where the world is actually an artificial construct of an intelligent computer, an infinitely elaborate illusion created to make people think they are living in the real world, when in actuality they are essentially batteries that supply energy for the computers. The inhabitants of this holographic world believe with all certainty that they live in reality, and because of this certainty, one could argue that it *is* reality for them, and yet the viewer knows otherwise.

Similarly, our "real" world is an artificial construct as well, a type of organic holographic world representing our subjective perceptions and ideas where we behave and act almost as if we are unconscious actors in the play of our lives. What we experience in our day-to-day is of course *real* to us, but it is not necessarily *reality*. There is increasing agreement from diverse disciplines of knowledge that the old cause-and-effect, identity-driven, and control-oriented models of organizational behavior are less effective than the more organic, fluid, and natural models in understanding how we can relate to each other and to our environment in a more enlightened, meaningful, and productive way. Referring back to a scene in the film, we are now prepared to decide whether to take the red pill, and create the real world in its true potential, or take the blue pill and continue to suffer from the delusions of our egoic-mind.

To illustrate the power of the convergence of these domains and concepts in the world of organizations, consider the experience of a leading healthcare management system with respect to a recent initiative. The organization decided to measure and publicly recognize care coordinators (care providers who visit clients in their homes) who had achieved low levels of patient hospitalizations, based on the beliefs that having fewer hospitalizations is always better and the perception of a (negative) link between hospitalization and overall health. However, this view of reality did not factor in important variations in the complexity of caseloads across care coordinators, and was perceived to be confusing since there were often situations where hospitalization was considered as a strategy for *improving* health—in the case of preventive procedures—rather than an indication of declining health. Moreover, this approach assumed a significant degree of influence on the part of care coordinators in the hospitalization process, ignored the broader web of roles and activities that were typically involved, and reflected an oversimplified view of the causation between the performance of the coordinators and the health and hospitalization rate of their clients/patients.

After receiving a lot of feedback and concern regarding this initiative, the organization realized a more systemic view was required, one that included greater understanding of the complexity of the issues and a more objective sense of reality. Today, it continues to monitor hospitalization rates, but pays close attention to the interrelationships involved, and the decision-making processes that include outpatient managers, inpatient managers, care coordinators, and discharge planners. The enterprise invests less in the actual data and more in the understanding of how the organizational web of activity helps people maintain or improve their health while also managing the overall cost of care. The original initiative that involved a measure of control and biased assumptions about cause-and-effect has been replaced with a more fluid process for assessing the overall flow of information and interactions among its members when providing critical services to patients.

Exploring the Nature of True Nature

An enterprise can be viewed as an organism that is born, lives, evolves, and dies. Its birth and death are nothing special since that is the natural way of things in our universe. Organizations are born each day and die each day. Commercial organizations file for bankruptcy or go out of business. Similarly, social organizations close down or simply dissipate and cease to function. As an open system—a social system that interacts and exchanges energy with its environment—an organization is highly dynamic in how it goes about its business. The organization as we know it dies every second. In some small way each organization is different right now than it was one second ago. In fact, the organization of one second ago no longer exists in reality; rather, it exists only in our subjective memory with all of its biases, filters, and influencing beliefs.

Each organization is constantly transforming, and when sources of energy expire or go away, the enterprise may expire or go away as well. Again, this is nothing special. It is the natural way of things. What *is* special is *how* the enterprise lives and evolves to sustain itself as a positive energy source, create value, and benefit our world along the way.

Most organizations do not understand their true nature and carry out their daily activities at an unconscious level. They typically define their identity based on their products and services, their bricks and mortar, their leaders, their followers, and their image, the perceptions of the world-at-large. They seek permanence and stability through command and control behavior, wasting valuable energy and precious resources on such things as public relations programs, hierarchical decision-making protocols, internal controls and processes that add no value, and over-engineered, compliance-oriented policies. They seek an artificial separation from their environment by reinforcing how unique and different they are from other organizations.

Even organizations known for being innovative and flexible in their practices are still plagued by unconscious and ego-driven activities from within that drain energy and produce less-than desirable results. For example, a prominent on-line retailer known as a leader and pioneer in its industry recently decided to "control" customer behavior by eliminating the option of contacting customer service by telephone, creating significant dissatisfaction with an important segment of its customers. Unbelievably, this massive company has no phone number for its customers. How did this decision get made? How could such a lack of wisdom survive the layers of "intelligent" decision-makers? How does this practice reflect or not reflect the organization's true nature?

KOAN: WHAT IS *TRUE NATURE*?

True nature is defined as spirit of the enterprise, its energy field that vibrates in sync with, and contributes to, the energy field of the universe. The frequency of this energy is directly related to the purity of the enterprise mission, its reason for being. An organization in touch with true nature understands that the intangible sense of *who it is* transcends the tangible sense of *what it does*.

Enlightened organizations that understand and leverage their true nature carry out their activities with transparency, passion, clarity, and confidence in the face of constant and challenging uncertainty. They possess something of a sense of serenity about who they are and what they do. There is a certain degree of stillness, alertness, and awareness in how people carry out their work inside the organization, and in how people inside the organization interact with others in the external world. These characteristics are vitally important to an awakening to one's true nature, either as an individual or as an enterprise. These are the fundamental ingredients for consciousness that enable an organization to see itself and the world without judgment, anxiety, or superiority, but through clear discernment, and make better decisions and take more enlightened action.

The organization that is aware of its own true nature is very comfortable explaining who it is to the outside world (even though its actions demonstrate its true nature every day and should be very apparent), and perhaps more importantly, who it is not. In one example, a food production and distribution enterprise described itself as a marketing business with the primary objective of building and sustaining its brands, regardless of how it actually processed and packaged the food and distributed it to customers, which was often through multiple third-party partnerships. In this way the organization understood that *who it is* becomes the intangible value of its brands in the eyes of consumers, and it recognized that *what it does, where, and by whom,* was unimportant—even though more tangible—as long as predefined quality and cost standards were met. The organization defined its true nature as that of a brand and not as a producer or distributor.

In another example, a prominent southern university with a deeply religious foundation, transcended prevailing ideology and invested substantial resources in a new science building to attract high quality faculty and students. The principles of evolution are taught there, reflecting the university's true nature as an important place for scientific education and enlightened learning, rather than as a vessel that spreads rigid religious doctrine.

DHARMA LOG

The **unenlightened** organization is more disconnected from its spirit, limiting its perception of its own being through narrow beliefs, principles, or structures. The **enlightened** organization is more connected to its spirit, appreciating the passion and beauty of simple existence while also broadening and elevating its purpose beyond standard definitions of being and doing.

The practices of the enlightened organization reflect a higher level of consciousness and purity. With respect to the concept of its *true nature*, then, the enlightened enterprise understands its spirit as its only source of permanence. Other less enlightened organizations suffer from identity through form and structure, under the illusion that these tangible things are stable and solid. But they are not stable; rather, they offer the illusion of stability and provide a false sense of identity.

The enlightened organization understands that form and structure may shape its perceived identity, but is aware that structures such as products, buildings, organization designs, technologies, and equipment do not define its true nature. Products become outmoded. Buildings no longer serve their purpose. Technology becomes obsolete. People leave the organization. Chains of command dissolve or become irrelevant. With its greater understanding, the enlightened enterprise understands that stability and sustainability come from its values and culture: the intrinsic patterns of behavior and action that reflect how the organization carries out its activities on a daily basis. It takes a long-term approach and effectively leverages its self-awareness to pursue advantages, differentiate itself from competitors or imitators, and succeed in the constant turbulence of its environment. This is especially important in today's world of shortening life-cycles, instantaneous access to and dissemination of information, major geographic and demographic shifts in consumer demand, and eroding barriers to the flow of talent in the global labor market. In this crazy world, nothing stays the same, except for the spirit with which the enterprise undertakes and enjoys its journey.

(Re)Discovering True Nature

In the complex and cluttered world in which we live, it is easy for both individuals and organizations to "lose" their sense of their true nature. True nature is actually never lost, but the sense of it can be, and the connection with it often is. Defining its true nature is therefore essentially a discovery process, or in the case of some organizations, a re-discovery process of those characteristics and values that reflect the energizing spirit of the enterprise. Successful organizations that have a strong sense of their true nature, and leverage this to their advantage, typically do not need to undertake a "process" of discovery, as they sustain and strengthen their true nature each day through their behaviors and actions. For some, though, a discovery process may be the right approach to remember who they are, not unlike an individual going through a discovery process, perhaps on a personal level with the help of a therapist or life coach.

A number of years ago, a renowned professional football franchise with a strong tradition and history of success had fallen on hard times. The team had experienced more than a decade of mostly losing seasons and had become frustrated with its inability to turn the franchise around. It decided to undertake a major study to identify the ingredients that make-up a sports dynasty. It asked the question of what separates the great, enduring teams from the good and mediocre teams. After much information gathering, analysis, synthesis, and discussion, the organization essentially learned what it already knew: that it needed to attract the best possible talent and pay them well but not extravagantly, return to the same demanding work ethic it once had, demonstrate a total commitment to excellence, and reinforce a high level of quality in *all* of its operations—on the field, in the front office, and in the back-conference rooms—that had characterized its true nature during the glory days.

Few new programs were implemented and few policies were changed. Instead, the organization re-dedicated itself, through the talent it acquired, the aspirations it communicated, and the environment it created, to living its true nature and acting *as if* it were already a dynasty. For the next ten years, the franchise had the best record in the National Football League. The spirit of this enterprise remains healthy and strong today.

MY SAMADHI *A Personal Discovery*

For the first twenty years of my career, I had the extraordinary experience of having worked at the same firm, advancing from an entry-level associate to a senior executive and managing partner over that period. Quite often colleagues, clients, and even candidates would ask me why I had stayed at the firm for so long, since the level of tenure I had relative to my age was perceived as so unusual (in a world where young professionals seem to change jobs or organizations every two to three years).

It did not take me long to come up with a concise response that I then used for many years. Their standard question: **What has kept you for so long at one organization?** My standard answer: **The challenging mix of work, the diversity of clients and projects, and the quality orientation and professionalism of the firm.** Later in my career I shortened this on occasion, responding with: **Great work, great clients, great colleagues.**

There is no doubt that all of those things were true throughout my career. Moreover, my compensation and benefits were fine. My work/life balance was not always great, but was within my control when I wanted or needed it to be. The weekly travel was a real killer of course, yet I rationalized that it was better than sitting in the same cube all day. But again, most important to me was the nature of the work and the nature of the people I worked with, including both clients and colleagues, and I was almost always very satisfied with my work experience.

As I pause and look back at that chapter in my life, it is clear to me that I stayed and thrived at the firm for other reasons as well, the most important of which had to do with the alignment between my personal value system and value system of the enterprise. This process of reflection revealed to me an important discovery: that the most satisfying periods for me occurred when the firm clearly demonstrated its good values as its true nature, and when those values were most aligned with my own.

Every firm has its ups and downs, its ebbs and flows, and my firm was no different over those years. The organization had several different ownership situations. There were significant swings in the size of the firm and the number of people employed. There were high growth periods and no growth periods. There were acquisitions of other firms and there were sales of internal units. And there were quite a few different leaders/management teams that at times demonstrated different value systems.

The period of time that sticks out in my mind as one of the most satisfying was when the firm explicitly stated a set of values that were very consistent with my own, and lived those values as true nature. The values were consistently communicated as well as demonstrated both internally in how we worked with one another and externally in how we served our clients. These values included: Integrity, Impact, Collaboration, Experience, and Long-term Relationships. Interestingly, the core group of consultants at the time was highly diverse with respect to personalities and backgrounds.

Perhaps even more interesting is that these consultants were extremely independent and had very different views on how the firm should go to market and what types of consulting work the firm should focus on. But for whatever reason, despite these differences, there was extraordinary alignment and consistency among our people regarding the culture we were creating and supporting, and the standards we were applying in serving our clients. It should come as no surprise that the enterprise was growing and nicely profitable during that period as well.

I think my experience may not be that different from the experiences of others who are fortunate enough to work in an environment where the organization demonstrates its values as true nature and where this demonstration is very natural—almost organic—and not forced or contrived. During this period, I was not consciously aware that the powerful positive energy we were creating at the time had a lot to do with the power and alignment of our value system.

It is my hope that more and more, organizations and their people can become more aware in real-time of the importance of this alignment and the energy that comes from values-in-action. This awareness will help them further support, increase, and sustain their positive energy fields.

Demonstrating Values as True Nature

A substantial amount of energy has been invested over the years on the concept of values as critical to long-term organizational success. Values are clearly foundational to the mission, vision, strategy, and culture of an organization. How the organization pursues its mission and vision, executes its strategy, and builds its culture over time is based on values as its true nature. These intangible, yet critical elements of true nature transcend the physical nature of the entity itself. They act as energy fields, the unseen forces that influence the decisions, behaviors, and actions of participants and the organization as a whole. Values offer people a foundation for their engagement in the enterprise, a sense of belonging and membership, and stable mooring in the chaos of constant change. In a recent study that focused on leading organizations around the world, a strong and stable value system along with consistent standards of (high) performance were found to be the key ingredients to the longevity of the enterprise and its enduring success.

The most powerful values remain the simplest ones: integrity, quality, courage, creativity, innovation, responsibility, collaboration, inclusion, freedom, openness, sustainability, and impact, among others. Many organizations spend a lot of time and effort in identifying and defining their values, often iterating them for months and years, and then revisit this exercise periodically to reiterate again. At the end of the day, it is not the terminology used to label the value, or the extreme care that is applied to the word choice used in its definition, but how the value is continuously talked about, demonstrated, and leveraged in weaving the cultural fabric of the enterprise. The values-based organization does not need to say to its employees, customers, or investors that it lives its values: the enterprise *is* its values, and this is evident to any observer paying attention.

As an illustration, it is sensible for a metropolitan symphony orchestra to understand its true nature as being "a source of beautiful and entertaining music for a community." In this sense, the purpose, identity, and nature of the enterprise are all captured by this simple and clear intent. *But what might be more elevating? What might be more enduring? What might be more real in the sense that it transcends time and space and form?* A more enlightened symphony orchestra might define its true nature as "bringing serenity and harmony to its community through the gift of music, inspiring the next generation of musicians from all walks of life, and evolving with each generation to ensure that music is an important part of the community experience." The organization may not necessarily communicate this formally to the public; instead, it demonstrates its true nature through the consistent quality of its performances, the activities that it sponsors and participates in to promote music education and support aspiring musicians, and the choice of music it performs as it balances tradition with the evolving musical tastes of the members of the community.

In another example, it would be logical for a regional hospital to understand its true nature as being "a place where people come to get healthy and lead more satisfying lives." *Again, what might be more elevating, enduring, and transcendental?* A more enlightened hospital might define its true nature as "creating a healthier and more prosperous community that builds stronger, more flourishing future generations." In this scenario, the organization demonstrates its true nature through the quality of healthcare that it provides, its activities in sponsoring and participating in preventive healthcare and wellness programs for all people in the community (as well as targeted segments with specialized needs), and its ongoing involvement in the education of younger generations on good health practices. In both examples, a statement of values is helpful, but true nature is shown only through the consistent demonstration of desired behaviors and actions over time.

Dharma Log

The **unenlightened** organization spends too much time talking about *what* its values are. The **enlightened** organization demonstrates its values in everything it does and spends more time talking about *how* these values translate into value creation.

The more enlightened organization defines its purpose more broadly than other organizations, applying a heightened awareness of how it helps to shape and influence its environment as a whole today, and in the future. Its spirit—its true nature—transcends what it does to who it is and how it creates a shared reality with its constituencies. The spirit of a food producer is more than making and distributing food products. It involves activity that transcends the product and builds an image, a brand, an experience that adds to the lives of consumers who believe that good quality food is a critical part of creating and sustaining a healthy family. The spirit of a symphony orchestra is more than playing beautiful music. It involves activity that transcends the music itself, where the musicians not only bring harmony to the lives of the community through how they play music, but also through creating awareness of the healing magic of music and promoting and teaching music to young people. And the spirit of a hospital is more than treating patients. It involves activity that transcends the required daily care, creating a sense of holistic health and wellness through the interactions and services the hospital provides to the region it serves.

More and more, organizations are awakening to their higher purpose, and describing the elevating values of their true nature, often involving the intersection of what is good for both the enterprise and society. Consider, for example, a retailing enterprise that publicly embraces the values of beauty, simplicity, and joy, and defines its purpose as to inspire simplicity, creativity, and delight. In another example, a graphics design company espouses the values of truth and love and openly describes its culture as more of a community than a traditional business. At the same time, both organizations connect the importance of these principles in creating value and making money.

In a final example, and perhaps the most inspiring as well as representative illustration of what may emerge in our age of expanding consciousness, and the courage that comes with it, consider the vision, mission, and values of a start-up company in the media industry, as stated in its overview for potential investors:

- The mission of the enterprise is to ensure a culture of artistic endeavor that enhances the public good and nurtures the creativity, freedom of expression, and diversity of imagination that is essential to the survival and evolution of a free and strong society.
- The enterprise will contribute the highest quality, most productive, and most creative expression in the media world and will share its creative voices worldwide. The enterprise will finance, develop, and

nurture creative talent on a global basis so that great works of art and culture reach millions of people.

- The enterprise, in achieving its vision and mission, will become a leading, global, multi-media corporation that will fundamentally change the nature of the media landscape and re-energize the value that media brings to humanity.
- The enterprise will grow profitably each year through its innovation and synergistic operation in the publishing, film, television, music, social networking, and software industries in concert with developer, user, and consumer communities.

The purpose and spirit of the enlightened enterprise rises above the day-to-day, energizes values-based behavior and action, and inspires a more elevated and enduring belief in the goodness of the organization's contribution to the world. The enterprise aligns its inner purpose of being with its outer purpose of acting in a socio-economically valuable way. Without this alignment, there is suffering for internal participants and external constituents. The enlightened enterprise seeks to become a powerful energy source for the universe as a conscious and evolving entity. Its fundamental goal is to create value through positive energy for its customers and/or constituents, create meaningfulness for its members, and support the community and environment as a whole.

THE TAO: Walking a New Path

In getting started on the path toward understanding, enhancing, protecting, and leveraging your organization's true nature, consider the following diagnostic questions:

- ***How would you characterize the true nature of your organization?*** Consider the characteristics of the organization that stay relatively consistent over time through changes in the internal and/or external environment. Consider the extent to which the true nature, or spirit, of the organization is elevating, enduring, and transcending in its qualities. Consider how one would describe the mission of the organization in a sixty second "elevator" speech.
- ***How does this true nature manifest itself?*** Consider how the true nature of the enterprise is reflected, or not reflected, in the values of the organization. Consider how the characteristics of the orga-

nization's true nature, and the associated values, are translated into behaviors and actions on a daily basis. Consider how the performance and achievement of the organization may or may not be consistent with what its true nature suggests.

- ***To what extent is your organization aware of its true nature?*** Consider how the organization distinguishes and reinforces *who it is* from *what it does* as the source of its true nature. Consider how the organization communicates and facilitates dialog regarding who it is from what it does.

- ***How does the organization form its perceptions of reality and translate this knowledge into action?*** Consider the extent to which the organization leverages its true nature—its sense and confidence of self—in perceiving, interpreting, and acting on internal and external environmental stimuli and dynamics. Consider the degree to which the organization views its external environment objectively, without filters and screens. Consider how it uses this information to maintain a purity of purpose and reinforce its values-in-action.

- ***To what degree is the organization a positive source of energy in the universe?*** Consider the extent to which the organization leverages its true nature—its only permanent source of power—in generating constructive and productive energy that leads to value creation. Consider how the enterprise makes important decisions and the extent to which it can easily take action that is aligned with its values and simply "the right thing to do."

- ***How connected are people to the purpose and true nature of the enterprise?*** Consider how widespread understanding is within the workforce of who the organization is and what it truly stands for. Consider how engaged people are in actively contributing to the purpose and desired results of the organization. Consider how the decisions, behaviors, and actions of people are consistent with organizational values and related aspects of the organization's true nature.

TWO

The Virtue of Value Creation

Imagine you are at an off-site workshop with several hundred other colleagues to learn about some of the trends taking place in the external environment. During the afternoon break, you run into your manager who is also attending the workshop. At the coffee-bar, you and he strike up a conversation about how the consolidation of customer organizations is shifting the balance of "power" in your industry, and the strategic implications for the company, a topic explored in the session after lunch. After both of you share your views on this topic, your manager says, "By the way, how are things going for you?" You respond with a few thoughts about your progress on key projects and suggest that one or two of your performance goals need to be updated. He agrees and also gives you some specific feedback on one of your key areas of responsibility. He then asks, "Are you clear on the things you need to accomplish over the next several weeks?" You mention your desire to get more involved in one of the company's key strategic imperatives focused on improving the performance of key partner alliances, because you believe you can contribute more to the initiative. Your manager agrees and pledges to support your increased involvement. In turn, you affirm that your other responsibilities will not suffer. As you and your manager walk back to the meeting room, you feel good about the openness and quality of the discussion. Then you mention it is time for your quarterly performance review. With a twinkle in his eye, your manager says, "What do you mean? We just did it." **This is satori.**

IN THIS CHAPTER WE WILL EXPLORE IMPORTANT CONCEPTS regarding the virtue of value creation, as summarized by the following principles:

- **The enlightened enterprise has a strong sense of how it can best create and deliver value in its environment.**
- **The enterprise should have a compelling and distinctive value creation strategy and proposition for its internal members and external constituents.**
- **The sources of value creation within an enterprise reflect the mix and integration of organizational networks, processes, practices, relationships, and people.**
- **Organizations that develop strategic and operational capabilities aligned with their mission and value proposition have a greater chance of success and survival.**
- **Values and culture, reflecting the organization's true nature, are its only lasting elements in a dynamic world.**

The long-term viability of an enterprise comes from a values-based commitment to value creation. Effective organizations create value for both their internal participants and external constituents: customers, partners, and other stakeholders—those that have a stake in the organization, perhaps as an owner, investor, or advisor. Furthermore, they create value today in a way that enables them to create even greater value in the future. The foundation of value creation is a strong value system in action that is sustained over the course of the organization's evolution and life-cycle.

The primary purpose of the enlightened enterprise is *not* survival in the world of form through structure, but value creation in the real world of energy through being and doing. The enterprise creates value and therefore ensures its own survival. Similarly, the enlightened organization does not just belong to its environment—society at large or some segment thereof—it helps create its environment through the positive energy generated from creating and delivering value to both its internal and external participants. Enduring value creation requires creating and maintaining productive coherence within the enterprise and within the networks outside in the environment. The goal is not to live per se, but to allow the life spirit to flow through and out of the enterprise into the world. Value creation therefore equals energy creation, the foundation of prosperity and abundance.

Unfortunately, there are many institutions and organizations that either have forgotten the critical difference between survival and value creation, or never understood the distinction in the first place. These organizations are often highly unconscious about how they act and interact with the world, and unaware—or perhaps uncaring—of how this confusion between survival and value creation does more harm than good from a societal standpoint. For instance, the national postal system, in its infinite wisdom, has chosen to virtually ignore the opportunities presented by the Internet over the past decade plus, and instead, has gone into a survival mode by raising delivery prices and cutting costs. The Internet has fundamentally changed the nature of correspondence and communication forever and yet, to-date, rather than exploring whole new ways of creating value by leveraging this wondrous technology, the postal service is still investing energy in horsewhips and wagon wheels in the effort to simply stay on life-support.

Labor organizations represent another example where there is often pervasive and destructive confusion regarding the difference between survival and value creation. While the concept of organized labor was critical in the development of our industrial society, and in some cases, still serves a purpose today, the history of these institutions is rife with examples where organizational leaders have made choices to pursue adversarial relationships with companies, further reinforcing the need for the union *as an entity* and ensuring its survival, as opposed to placing the needs of its members and the broader community first. These organizations have lost sight of their original mission: the union *as a source of energy* for positive change. They have forgotten their true nature and in their unconsciousness are asleep in the world of form rather than awake in the world of the spirit; they seek win-lose agreements and attempt to *control* through negotiation rather than *enable* through partnership.

There is at least one whole industry, or perhaps sub-industry, that has lost sight almost entirely of the virtue of value creation, and that is our financial markets and the firms that "play" in those markets, including investment banks, some units of commercial banks, trading companies, and investment management companies. Recall that the origin of the stock market, along with the firms that grew up around it, was to create an efficient market for sellers and buyers so that the general public could have the opportunity to grow their own wealth while also helping companies grow and create value for society. *How far we have strayed from that original mission!*

We all know how the degeneration of this industry has affected the global economy, but few understand how simple the cause of this obscene disaster is: the replacement of a *value creation* philosophy with that of a *value alienation* philosophy, a gambling mentality, an obsession with getting rich quick and often at the expense of someone else. The overall health of our financial markets has been and continues to be at the mercy of mathematicians who are more interested in such things as currency arbitrage or short-selling than in honest public offerings. They care little to nothing about our financial markets as an engine for value creation and economic growth.

KOAN: WHAT IS *VALUE CREATION?*
Value creation represents the act of creating, and often delivering, a product or service that provides a *net* social and/or economic benefit to a specific group of constituents.

The enlightened organization demonstrates a passion about its purpose and value contribution to its environment. It has a strong sense of how it is distinctive in delivering value and understands what it is best in the world at. The organization demonstrates humility at the same time that it continuously builds on and leverages its strengths to be a dominant source of energy in the communities and marketplaces in which it participates. Within the organization, participants demonstrate this passion in their daily activity through genuine belief in the mission, positive attitudes, and disciplined action in engaging in productive interactions and carrying out their responsibilities with excellence.

Over the last several years, a movement within the world of organizations has focused on increasing corporate social responsibility, involving policies, programs, and practices that support the achievement of financial success while also honoring ethical values and respect for people, their communities, and the environment. It is interesting to note that at the same time this movement has gained momentum we have witnessed levels of corporate wrong-doing and unethical behavior that we have not seen since perhaps the days of the robber-barons.

Moreover, like many initiatives that begin with good intentions, corporate social responsibility has been watered-down in many ways when put into application, and often falls far short of its aims when treated as a program to be complied with than as a culture to be created and sustained. The good news is that over the past twenty years, organizations in both the commercial and social sectors have made extraordinary progress in creating *safer work environments*. For many firms, the safety of people has been and remains the number one baseline condition in achieving enterprise goals. The bad news is that in this era of arrogance and avarice, we are still witness to shocking irresponsibility when it comes to safety in the workplace. Recently, a well-known national newspaper on its famous (and infamous) editorial page reminded us of how unconscious supposedly smart people can be. In a piece about the coal mining industry, the editor wrote that *a balance has to be struck between zero accidents and letting the industry function*. Really? One wonders how the families of the twenty-five miners who had died that week felt about the journal's unconscionable claptrap.

Enterprise social responsibility goes well beyond safety, however. And more and more organizations are evolving from a "mitigating harm" strategy to a "creating social good" strategy. They are becoming more intelligent in understanding the social issues that play a role in the key drivers of enterprise competitiveness and success. And they are investing in the identification, development, and implementation of focused initiatives that serve to achieve mutual benefits for the organization *and* society. As an example, a leading technology services organization gave brand new technology to research scientists *outside the enterprise* who were working on curing deadly diseases *before* the company rolled out the new product to its commercial customers.

With all this in mind, what *is known for sure*, based on several studies conducted over the last two decades, is that organizations that create a culture of social responsibility and that are serious about social aspects of value creation consistently achieve top-tier financial success and often outperform peer organizations in their industry or sector. Several of these studies and meta-studies show a positive correlation between social responsibility, environmental responsibility, financial performance, and value creation. All of this of course begs the question about the nature of value in the first place. *What do we actually mean by value creation?*

In a nutshell, the enlightened organization takes an expanded view of value creation to include most or typically all of the following elements:

- The social and economic impact that enterprise products and services have on its customers, customer organizations, and other constituents.
- The financial impact that the enterprise achieves in terms of its profitability and associated return on assets and/or invested capital.
- The financial gain from invested capital for owners in the form of stock and equity appreciation, or increased ownership valuation.
- The social and economic impact the enterprise has on its participants, their families, and their communities, with respect to the quality of

opportunities, their health and well-being, and overall standard of living.

- The environmental impact the enterprise has on its communities and anywhere else it has operations, as well as on society as a whole.

Developing the Value-Creation Strategy

In the highly entertaining film, *Duplicity*, two arch-rival companies attempt to kill each other in the marketplace through competitive counter-intelligence and corporate espionage. The sophistication of the spying technologies and tactics used is a fascinating juxtaposition with the entirely mundane nature of their products: toothpastes, skin creams, body lotions, and shampoos. While highly amusing and clever, the film is also a very sad example of how far some organizations will go when they are *unconscious* and lose complete sight of what really creates value for the enterprise and its constituents.

On the plane of greater consciousness, the enlightened enterprise views success more broadly (as we have already explored) as a function of inspiring values-in-action and enduring value creation. It understands that the end and means are one, that how the organization creates value and achieves success is integral to the definition of success itself. The successful organization infuses a standard of quality into everything it does. It cares about people. It is aware of the consequences of its actions and decisions. It pays little to no attention to "discovering" competitor secrets. It creates, not exploits. And it seeks unity and sustainability within the environment in which it participates. Enduring success is how the enlightened enterprise walks its path each moment, each day.

Every organization has a set of implicit and explicit beliefs and principles about how and why it creates and delivers value. Enlightened organizations view every key decision, and pursue every key imperative, from this value creation perspective. Will the action/imperative help serve its customers? Will it help make money and/or strengthen its financial health? Will it enhance or disrupt the broader socio-economic ecosystem? Is it consistent with organizational values? These organizations have a clear and enduring value creation strategy that is characterized by broadly shared, well-understood, and inspiring strategic intentionality. More specifically, based on personal experience, and drawing in part on the work of Michael Porter, Gary Hamel, C.K. Prahalad, and others, the characteristics of a potent enterprise value creation strategy include the following:

- **A stable, focused, and differentiating value proposition** that describes what value the organization intends to create and deliver relative to what already exists in the competitive environment and its constituent's expectations and requirements. Typically, the value proposition is defined primarily from an economic perspective that is compelling to the interests of both its owners and customers or members, and in some cases, secondarily from a social perspective that is compelling to the interests of its communities. As an example, an oil-drilling firm created a differentiated value proposition through its promise of minimizing environmental damage, and subsequently was very competitive in attracting major energy companies as customers.
- **A clear set of performance requirements with established metrics and performance targets or performance ranges** that specifically define what good performance looks like from several vantage points, including those of the community, the customer, the owner, and the enterprise (sometimes broken down into organizational, operational, and financial perspectives). These metrics can represent both process-based and results-based indicators, as well as lead and lag indicators. They are intended to reflect a clear picture of the overall health of the enterprise as a value creating entity. As an example, a small insurance company goes through an efficient process each year of either confirming or enhancing a balanced set of 5-7 metrics and performance targets that reflect the most important drivers of value creation for the coming year.
- **A clear set of strategic imperatives that are closely aligned with the organization's value proposition,** updated periodically as appropriate, and that lucidly describe the priority actions and initiatives the enterprise is investing in to best achieve its value creation goals. Strategic imperatives are not simply objectives nor are they highly complex project plans. They represent the major initiatives that will increase value creation and directly impact the organization's ability to realize its value proposition. They often include a set of goals, guiding principles, deliverables, key accountabilities, key boundaries, and timeline. As an example, each year a large grocery chain develops and communicates a one-page set of one-year and three-year strategic imperatives to its workforce, organized by each principle in its value proposition/mission statement.

- **An openness about the threats and challenges of the environmental and competitive landscape,** and formal and informal opportunities for organization participants to understand, internalize, and discuss potential action regarding these threats and challenges. This ongoing openness creates and sustains a degree of "business" literacy within the workforce that enables it to better recognize the things that can affect value creation and create new ideas and approaches for addressing the threats and challenges from a "bottom up" perspective. As an example, a large township periodically conducts town-hall meetings to share information with members of the community regarding environmental, commercial, economic, and demographic trends and issues, and provides an open, but facilitated, forum to discuss these issues and generate potential ideas and actions that will maintain the high quality of life in the area.
- **An understanding and cultivation of the internal conditions and activities that enable actual focused strategies to develop** gradually from within the organization and evolve with high levels of ownership and commitment from the workforce. These conditions are critical to the organization's ability to build and sustain a culture that generates high levels of engagement, productivity, and innovation. As an example, the finance organization of a professional sports league decided that it needed to eliminate, automate, or outsource certain administrative activities. This would enable its financial analysts to develop a more strategic relationship with their internal business partners and develop customer-based strategies from the ground-up.
- **An understanding of the organization's strengths and capabilities that are critical to realizing its value proposition,** along with a clear sense for how these strengths and capabilities will evolve with the environment to ensure that strategic intent stays fresh and relevant over time. This entails a clear understanding of what the organization is good/great at, and what it must be good/great at to be successful in the long-term. As an example, at one of the world's largest snack cake and cookie bakeries, the organization continuously preserves and strengthens its capability in the area of designing and installing custom process technologies that help it produce baked goods at levels of quality and cost (while minimizing waste) that are superior to its competitors.
- **A simple, but clear framework for how the organization will co-evolve with its environment to survive and thrive over the**

long-term, including how organizational networks, operational processes, and people systems (such as reward systems) will stay aligned and evolve with enterprise strategies. This framework entails the specific capabilities and activities that the enterprise demonstrates to effectively flow with and influence its environment. As an example, a consumer products division of a global pharmaceutical undertaking a major transformation over a long period of time developed and updated a "roadmap for change" that it co-developed with its workforce in semi-annual, highly interactive community meetings.

DHARMA LOG

The **unenlightened** organization spends too much time and energy on developing formal, detailed, and precise strategies that are intended to *direct* actions and behaviors, that are often too complex to be understood, and that are frequently obsolete by the time they are "implemented." The **enlightened** organization believes in the power of strategic intent that establishes the conditions for simple, focused, and flexible strategy development and execution.

Creating Compelling Value Propositions

Enlightened organizations create differentiating, enduring, and compelling value propositions. For *external* participants, these organizations create an *external value proposition* that defines the full *value exchange* between the enterprise and its customers and other external constituents, reflecting the distinctive and meaningful value delivered through products and services in exchange for financial payment or other form of economic and/or social returns. For *internal* participants, successful organizations create an *internal value proposition* that defines the full value exchange between the enterprise and its members, involving the whole continuum of meaningful rewards and benefits (using these terms in their broadest sense) that come with employment or membership. In this context, value exchange reflects the value of the work performed by employees and delivered to the enterprise, in exchange for the compensation, benefits, recognition, as well as other highly valued non-financial rewards, such as training and development, provided by the organization.

Koan: What is a Value Proposition?

A value proposition is represented by what the organization offers its internal constituents (e.g. employees) in return for their commitment and contribution, and what the organization offers its external participants (e.g., customers) in return for social and/or economic gain.

The external value proposition is the cornerstone of an organization's economic model, strategy, and value creation strategy representing *how* the enterprise interacts with its environment to exchange energy and *what* it delivers to external, or in some cases internal, constituents in the process (such as with professional organizations where members are also customers). The external value proposition often has dominating elements that are critical to its true nature, and often involves unique combinations of key capabilities like operational excellence and efficiency, customer intimacy and experience, innovation and creativity, or superior quality and service. An organization's external value proposition can be described in a robust way using three elements (which are not mutually exclusive): impact, experience, and advantage. They are defined as follows:

- **Impact:** The distinctive impact that the organization's products and services has on its external customers and/or customer organizations. Impact reflects the degree to which the products and services have a positive social and/or economic effect on the consumer or customer's organization and its own value creation process. This impact is most compelling when it is measurable, and effective organizations invest significant resources in the measurement of impact and its associated value. An example of *impact* for a financial consulting firm would involve helping its clients better manage cost, reduce financial risk, and improve the return on capital investments.
- **Experience:** The experience involved in exchanging energy between the organization and its external customers and/or customer organizations. Experience reflects the degree to which the energy exchange is positive with respect to both entities, involving positive interactions and relationships, where the *experience* is in and of itself, valuable. Extending the example of a financial consulting firm, the experience would entail the co-creation of financial management solutions that build client capability to develop cash flow scenarios that enable the client entity to prepare more effectively for, and even influence future challenges.

- **Advantage:** The advantage that the organization's products, services, and interactions brings to its customers and/or customer organizations. Advantage reflects the degree to which the organization's relationship to the customer entity brings that entity competitive advantage in its environment, positioning it best for the future and enduring success. As a final example using the financial consulting firm, *advantage* involves the application of deep industry expertise to develop customized, practical, and enduring processes that the client organization can manage on its own and apply to help create its preferred future.

In assessing the degree to which an organization's external value proposition is clear, distinctive, and compelling, consider the following diagnostic questions:

- To what extent are enterprise participants able to clearly and consistently communicate the external value proposition?
- To what extent does the value proposition clearly distinguish the enterprise from other similar types of organizations?
- To what extent does the value proposition clearly define the social and economic value creation that the enterprise delivers?
- To what extent does this value creation clearly reflect something that would be extremely difficult, or even impossible, to replace if the enterprise no longer existed?

Like the organizational mission of creating value, each of us as individuals who participate in organizations has a similar mission of creating value. Through our personal free will, creative expression, and contribution ethic, we participate in organizations to add value that contributes to the overall value creation of the enterprise. And each of us possesses our own personal value proposition and preferred value exchange with the enterprise as a whole. This is easily revealed through several fundamental questions. *Why do I participate in this organization? Why do I work here?* Why do I stay? What do I like about this organization? What do I not like? How important on a relative basis are these things that I like and dislike? Why do I not work somewhere else? What would it take for me to leave and work elsewhere?

From the enterprise standpoint, every organization has an internal value proposition that is implicit and explicit, and that has both strengths and weaknesses. An organization cannot afford—and would find it impossible—to be all things to all people. An organization's value proposition for its participants often reflects a specific theme that is reflective of the true nature of the enterprise. For example, some organizations provide a value proposition for their members that is dominated by the opportunity for financial gain and wealth creation, such as investment banks. Others establish a value proposition that is dominated by the opportunity to help specific segments of society and make a difference in the lives of people, such as universities and healthcare systems. Others establish a value proposition that provides stable, secure, long-term employment and a relatively low-stress workplace, such as companies and family-owned businesses that are patriarchic in nature.

None of these value propositions have an inherent quality that is better or worse than another. The important point is that successful organizations establish and sustain internal value propositions for their people that are aligned with their true nature and balanced with respect to the overall value exchange with their participants. In other words, the internal value proposition fits well with the mission of the enterprise and the expectations of its people. An internal value proposition includes five elements: association, relationships, development, activity, and rewards. They are defined as follows:

- **Association:** Association reflects the fulfillment and self-actualization that comes from being a member of the enterprise, typically linked to the nature of the organization's internal values, character, and culture, as well as its role and stature in the broader community. *Association* reflects the market position of the organization, the degree to which it is a "winning" enterprise, the strength of its customer or constituent orientation, the quality of organization communications, and the binding nature of its closely held traditions. *Association* also reflects the physical work environment, the location of its workplaces, and the degree to which it creates healthy working conditions, supports participant needs, and promotes healthy work practices. An example of *association* for a community college would involve the degree to which the organization serves the region in ways that enables highly diverse students to find skilled and good-paying jobs. In this way, participants take pride in the value of the service the organization provides and can see how their work has a positive effect on the community. The stronger *association* is in the enterprise, the more important it is to the overall internal value proposition (relative to other elements), and the more it will influence the attraction, engagement, performance, and retention of people over time.

- **Relationships:** Relationships reflect the nature of interactions and connections within the organization and the extent to which they are of high quality, productive, healthy, and fulfilling, especially between an individual and his manager and colleagues/coworkers. *Relationships* reflect the degree to which people listen to one another, trust one another, care about one another, respect one another's opinions regardless of hierarchy, and invest in building a productive connection that can grow in meaning and value over time. The quality and nature of *relationships* also greatly influences the prevalence, meaning, and impact of recognition and feedback. In the case of the community college, *relationships* entail the collaboration and camaraderie among and between faculty and staff, and the degree to which there is mutual respect in serving the community in different but important capacities. The stronger *relationships* are in the enterprise, the more important the element as a whole is to the overall internal value proposition (relative to other elements), and the more it will influence the attraction, engagement, performance, and retention of people over time.
- **Development:** Development reflects the opportunities for ongoing personal growth and professional development that enable the individual to acquire new capabilities and knowledge that support her personal and professional goals, advancement aspirations, and ability to begin and/or augment a career. *Development* reflects the degree to which the work environment in the enterprise emphasizes formal and informal learning opportunities that include mentoring, coaching, and training activities. It involves the degree to which organizational learning conditions, processes, and experiences are aligned with individual needs and goals. Extending the community college example further, *development* includes the career opportunities that exist for administrative staff in terms of gaining greater depth of skills and knowledge through advancement within a department and/or greater breadth of skills and knowledge through lateral movement into other departments. The stronger *development* is in the enterprise, the more important it is to the overall internal value proposition (relative to other elements), and the more it will influence the attraction, engagement, performance, and retention of people over time.

- **Activity:** Activity reflects the nature of work—the tasks, actions, projects, procedures —that are carried out in fulfilling one's responsibilities of her role, and the degree to which the overall work experience reflects variety, challenge, feedback, flexibility, learning, and meaning. *Activity* reflects the degree to which the design of work—that is, the design of jobs and roles—involves a manageable workload, customer and colleague interactions, and a measure of wholeness and significance (i.e., a complete sets of tasks and activities) that can be easily linked to the value creation processes of the enterprise. The quality of *activity* within an enterprise is essentially the quality of the overall work experience, and the extent to which the work itself is a strong source of positive energy. In the case of the community college once again, *activity* and work experience would entail the degree to which jobs across the variety of staff departments are designed in such a way that they involve meaningful tasks that directly enhance either the quality of education or the experience of students. The stronger *activity* is in the enterprise, the more important it is to the overall internal value proposition (relative to other elements), and the more it will influence the attraction, engagement, performance, and retention of people over time.
- **Rewards:** Rewards reflect those things that have a specific monetary value and directly affect the financial well-being of the participant. *Rewards* reflect all forms of compensation, such as salary, incentives, financial recognition and long-term wealth creation, and all forms of benefits, such as health, wellness, medical, and retirement. Rewards also include financial recognition such as one-time cash awards, gift certificates, and other items that have monetary value. As a final example: At a community college, *rewards* include the process used to determine annual merit (salary) increases based on the merit budget of the institution, the value of the job in the marketplace, and the performance of the individual performing the job. (Research studies have indicated that the adequacy of the *process* for determining financial rewards is as important to people as the actual *amount* of financial rewards delivered). The stronger the element of *rewards* is in the enterprise, the more important it is to the overall internal value proposition (relative to other elements), and the more it will influence the attraction, engagement, performance, and retention of people over time.

The internal value proposition can be viewed as the mix of foundational (cultural) conditions and ongoing investments used in the attraction, engagement, inspiration, and retention of participants in the organization. Different people often have different *personal* value propositions based on factors such as ethnic heritage, personality type, performance-orientation, and life-stage. For instance, a highly motivated, single, young person just starting his career, with a large amount of college debt may look for an organization that pays high salaries, offers lower benefits, and promises fast-track advancement opportunities. An older, successful person with a large family, and who has already advanced to a desired level of responsibility, may look for an organization that has excellent medical benefits, perhaps fewer promotional opportunities, but substantial wealth creation potential. In the case of a leading software development company that is consistently profiled in the press regarding the strength of its internal value proposition, the enterprise has achieved outstanding levels of loyalty and retention not through high salaries (even during the tech bubble of the last decade) but through the attraction of family-oriented employees who greatly value the flexible work hours, on-site schooling (for children of employees), and other amenities and services the organization provides.

Successful organizations often create an overall value proposition for the enterprise as a whole along with the flexibility to invest in one or more of the five elements disproportionately for specific segments and specific needs of the workforce or membership. They design programs and processes that clearly link development, new work activity and rewards to participant behaviors (that are consistent with the organization's values) and participant contributions (that add to overall value creation). These organizations view reward programs as an investment in people rather than a necessary cost of doing business, and furthermore, expect a good return on their investment. As perhaps the most critical set of investments an organization can make in itself, the internal value proposition can be a source of competitive advantage in attracting a desired and specific type, quantity, and quality of talent to the enterprise.

Enlightened organizations make strategic and smart investments in their internal value proposition. Consider the example of a leading consumer products company that dominates its marketplace through the delivery of unassailable value (in this case, price relative to quality). Through formal employee sensing the organization assessed the strength of each of the five elements of the value proposition as well as their relative importance to specific segments of the workforce. As a result, it was able to prioritize and make targeted investments in specific employee groups, including improving communication to all participants regarding industry forces and threats, improving the quality of on-the-job feedback for professional staff, increasing the competitiveness of salaries for specific engineering roles, and redesigning the paid-time-off program for production workers.

DHARMA LOG

The **unenlightened** organization overemphasizes and over-engineers its financial rewards programs—and often without the necessary degree of alignment between employee groups—under the assumption that compensation can be used with precision. The **enlightened** organization ensures that financial rewards generally reinforce the values and value drivers of the enterprise and invests more in the non-financial elements (i.e., development, relationships, and work activities) of its internal value proposition.

With every new generation of talent that emerges in both the commercial and social sectors, there are important forces and trends that influence value systems and shape value propositions. Increasingly, studies show that the most capable and talented people are more attracted to organizations that help fulfill a personal need for *meaning* in the workplace and are serious about making contributions to society beyond simply making money.

One trend that is of great importance to the emerging consciousness of people and organizations is the increasing desire among Americans to live a more spiritual life. One study showed that over a five-year period of time there was an increase of over fifty percent in the number of Americans wanting to experience spiritual growth and live a more spiritual life. Because of this, more organizations are weaving spirituality into the fabric of their internal value propositions and cultures. In one example, among many emerging examples, a technology company introduced the practice of meditation to its workforce and subsequently reported improvements in absenteeism, safety, and productivity.

In assessing the degree to which an organization's internal value proposition is clear, distinctive, and compelling, consider the following diagnostic questions:

- To what extent are enterprise participants able to clearly and consistently communicate the internal value proposition?
- To what extent does the value proposition serve the enterprise well in attracting the preferred profile of participants (and meets their needs and wants)?
- To what extent is the value proposition coherent and consistent across the whole organization, but also differentiated in specific ways to align with specific segments of its people?
- To what extent are investments in the value proposition clearly linked to the attraction, retention, and productivity of talent?

Moving Beyond Value Drivers to Value Capabilities

A clear value creation strategy and value proposition sets the stage for determining and reinforcing the actual work activities within the enterprise that directly create value. For every organization, there is typically a set of critical few "drivers"—critical value creating activities, or the highest impact activities of an enterprise —that play a significant role in achieving competitive advantage and desired results. For a consumer products enterprise, the cycle time of new product development may be a critical driver. For a restaurant chain, it may be demand creation through re-branding. For a hospital, it may be the ongoing balancing of in-patient and out-patient treatment and services. For a trade association, it may be the translation of member needs into a coherent lobbying strategy. For a municipal water works enterprise it may be quality control and regulatory compliance.

Value drivers in organizations are often viewed as key *business processes*, but this is too simplistic. A more robust view of value drivers is represented by the concept of organizational *capability*. Organizational capabilities reflect a specific mix of processes, individual, group, and network interactions, technologies, work practices, and individual competencies that when combined and synchronized often create a unique proficiency that drives competitive advantage. Value drivers are also often viewed as *financial indicators*, but this is also too simplistic, and not even correct, since financial metrics typically reflect either activities or outcomes that are at the end of the value chain, far downstream in the value creation process. Financial indicators and metrics, and the financial statements that are generated from them, are also *lag* indicators that drive nothing except for a lot of unnecessary accounting activity in most organizations.

SUTRA LESSON ***Our Common Enemy***[2]

In his provocative book, *Less Is More*, Jason Jennings writes about financial indicators and statements as the "real enemy" of productivity-driven value creation:

"A highly productive company does not use a financial statement for leading and managing the business. It uses carefully selected drivers to keep moving forward and constantly becoming more productive."

In the case of a joint venture between two large chemical companies, significant work was done to identify the specific value drivers that were clearly linked to the economic value creation engine of the enterprise. *Operational excellence* reflected the key business processes and resources that drive superior performance globally. *Corporate stewardship* reflected the safety, regulatory compliance, and environmental responsibility committments demonstrated through behaviors, operations, and products. *Customer and market focus* reflected the development and delivery of a differentiated advantage to customers. And *value growth* reflected the generation of revenue through selling high margin (high positive economic profit) products and services.

It is helpful to think of organizational capabilities in terms of their strategic and operational qualities. Strategic capabilities reflect a blend of things that enable the organization to effectively carry out its strategic intent and *directly* create value for its constituents through the development and delivery of products and services. Strategic capabilities make the difference. Operational capabilities, on the other hand, reflect a blend of things that enable the organization to operate, evolve, and survive over the long-term and *directly or indirectly* create value for organizational constituents. Operational capabilities run the enterprise. Both strategic and operational capabilities are critical to the long-term success of the enterprise. Moreover, these capabilities can and should evolve with the changing environment under the right conditions. Those organizations that develop and apply capabilities that are fully aligned with organizational purpose and true nature, supportive of strategic intent, unique to the entity, hard to imitate, difficult to replicate, invisible to outside entities, and impossible to transfer will have a far greater chance of success and survival over time.

There are a wide variety and potentially infinite number of strategic capabilities that are specific to an organization's purpose and strategy. A *few* examples include (more on capabilities will be covered in later chapters):

- **Achieving rapid growth through the efficient and effective acquisition and assimilation of other organizations.** This capability involves a wide variety of focused activities that need to be integrated and well-executed to ensure that the acquired entity efficiently merges with the enterprise, quickly adopts new processes and utilizes shared resources, minimizes redundancies in work activities, blends culture with minimal disruption to the combined workforce, and attains expected levels of productivity and growth that justify the acquisition.
- **Creating new kinds of demand through innovative approaches to customer intimacy.** This capability involves a wide variety of focused activities that need to be integrated and well-executed to build much more personal relationships with customers, exchange information between the enterprise and the customer, and utilize customer insight into new ways of creating demand across the broader customer base.
- **Capturing and synthesizing consumer-based intelligence to quickly enter and dominate (in the short run) emerging markets with a distinctive and compelling market value proposition.** This capability involves a wide variety of focused activities that need to be integrated and well-executed to collect accurate consumer and competitive data, draw insights from the information, develop new go-to-market strategies, and quickly mobilize to actually enter the market with current or new differentiating products and/or services.
- **Managing logistics and supply chains—or supply webs—to enhance collaboration across diverse organizations, reducing variances that contribute to inefficiencies and waste.** This capability involves a wide variety of focused activities that need to be integrated and well-executed to keep track of a vast number of interactions inside and outside of the organization to ensure the whole front end of the fulfillment system is well synchronized and efficient.
- **Outsourcing the coordination and management of product testing, clinical trials, and/or research studies to reduce cost while maintaining quality.** This capability involves a wide variety of focused

activities that need to be integrated and well-executed to ensure that the priority level, sequencing, and quality of outsourced activities are aligned with the constantly-changing priorities and requirements of a high number of products, materials, and/or other compounds and concepts that are at different stages of development.

- **Acquiring, enhancing as needed, and rapidly disseminating regulatory and legislative information to organization members through a variety of media and channels.** This capability involves a wide variety of focused activities that need to be integrated and well-executed to quickly identify and digest relevant information, determine potential implications, develop potential responses, and effectively communicate a clear story-line to members that enables them to best respond to or take advantage of the changing regulatory climate.

In identifying, developing, preserving, and strengthening strategic and operational capabilities, the enterprise should be aware of their common, critical characteristics. To summarize from the examples above, each organizational capability involves the effective integration of a unique mix of activities that require synchronized and coordinated execution to carry out important work that has a significant impact on the value creation efforts of the enterprise.

DHARMA LOG

The **unenlightened** organization invests too much in organizational structure, often using organization redesign as the first and most important strategy for addressing challenges and solving problems. The **enlightened** organization invests less in structure—and in fact, minimizes the amount of structure necessary—and invests more in the effectiveness of key capabilities, processes, and networks.

Moving Beyond Value Chains to Value Networks

Traditionally, organizations have focused on optimizing *value chains*, linear processes where value is created through the transformation of inputs into outputs. A value chain typically represents a set of segmented and sequenced activities (the key activities being drivers) that add or create value along the way to ultimately create the product or service of the organization. Common value chains include the merchandising supply chain of a retail organization, production lines of a consumer products manufacturer, the service delivery processes in a hospitality business (such as a hotel chain), the knowledge generation process within a research university, and the exploration and development process of an energy company.

As our world becomes increasingly complex and interconnected, where mutual dependencies, distributed capabilities, diverse (and perhaps even competing) distribution channels, and new technologies that span across traditional boundaries are commonplace, organizations must go beyond an understanding of "value chains" and apply a broader concept of "value networks," or "value webs." In other words, organizations should shift their focus from a process orientation to that of a network orientation. A value web, or network, represents a more comprehensive construct of how activities inside and outside of the organization align, interact and synchronize to execute strategy and achieve results in an optimal manner.

KOAN: WHAT IS A *VALUE* NETWORK?

A value network is a web of relationships that generates value through dynamic exchanges between individuals, groups, organizations, and other networks.

More enlightened organizations today are embracing the network concept as the new way of thinking about organizational structure, a dramatic improvement over the traditional hierarchical and matrix models of the past, since the emphasis is no longer on boxes and reporting lines but on the nature of interactions and how work actually gets done. In a sense, then, the enterprise itself can be viewed as a value network. Consider the following principles associated with the enterprise as a value network:

- In our new era of interconnectedness, work and the coordination of work occurs in formal and informal networks.
- Nodes in the network reflect places where key work activities are completed, information is exchanged, or decisions are made.
- Specific roles, individuals, or groups are often associated with specific network nodes.
- Network nodes are connected to each other through a vast web of interactions and communication channels ranging from email to face-to-face meetings and everything in-between.

- Cultural norms, organizational capabilities, and workforce competencies are distributed across the network (but not uniformly).
- The quality of interactions and the efficiency of connectivity in large part determine network, and therefore enterprise, performance.
- Related, network performance is also driven by the degree to which structures, processes, and practices support and energize productive network activity.

The enlightened enterprise takes a sophisticated view of value creation involving the interconnected network of activities that are often non-linear and more complex in terms of their relational dynamics. Moving beyond the enterprise, complex value networks typically involve internal and external participants. They often distribute operations over many different types of organizations, leverage capabilities across separate supply chains, integrate know-how and technologies across loosely-defined alliances, involve multiple channel partners, and utilize complementary services from diverse service providers.

Specifically, internal/external value networks often involve the synchronized and harmonized interactions of:

- Financial and legal resources and institutions that provide critical capital and risk management value.
- Customer, supplier, vendor, and distribution organizations that reflect the whole supply web of products or services.
- Intellectual capital domains and database/information resources that provide critical inputs into organizational activity.
- Support, advisory, and consulting organizations that help to transform information into knowledge and build internal capability.
- Regulatory and other government agencies and resources that establish policies and require internal enterprise oversight.
- Media and communications resources and organizations that translate enterprise activity into information in the public domain.
- Professional, trade, and other special interest groups that support, challenge, and influence enterprise activity.
- Multiple communities and diverse talent markets that reflect the pools of enterprise participants and their extended networks.

In this realm, organizations treat their networks, and their value webs within them, more like ecosystems than traditional supply chains. The breadth, flexibility, cohesion, ease of information exchange, and fluidity of transactions in the network all determine overall effectiveness.

There are a *wide variety* of types and potentially *infinite number* of value networks. A *few* examples of highly networked value creation activity include (some of these are internal while others internal/external):

- **The research and development of a new chemical compound** in a pharmaceutical organization, which involves the integration and sequencing of many internal and external processes such as clinical trials coordination, database management, regulatory communications, and pre-production planning.
- **The annual planning and execution of a professional association's national conference**—often the cornerstone of an association's value proposition to its members—which is comprised of complex, and often concurrent, activities that involve designing and developing the program theme and topics, acquiring the site and working out all logistics, selecting and scheduling speakers, communicating and marketing the event to members, inviting and confirming participants, and executing overall conference management services.
- **The local, regional, and national marketing of a professional sports league** where different teams require different marketing messages in different geographic markets to different market segments, requiring synchronized and consistent marketing messaging and activities among teams and between the teams and the parent league.
- **The loan "process" of a global, not-for-profit financial institution** that provides financial capital to organizations in developing countries, requiring the coordination of activities with multiple departments of the lending institution, with multiple agencies of the country, and with multiple constituents representing the country's enterprise that is responsible for the loan it receives.
- **The building of a new nuclear power plant** where the energy company's project/development team must interface concurrently (as well as at key milestones) with company management, partnering design, technology, and engineering consulting firms, local community leaders and planners, state government officials, Federal EPA and DOE representatives, general contractors, and a variety of different builders and materials suppliers.

My Samadhi *A Personal Perspective*

There has been an extraordinary amount of material generated over the past few decades focusing on organization theory, design, and effectiveness. And there are numerous research-based frameworks and models developed over the years to help organizations examine their inner workings and improve overall effectiveness.

Many of these helpful frameworks and models tend to focus on specific elements of an organization and its operations. These elements include: mission, vision, values, goals, strategies, structures, capabilities, systems, technologies, processes, practices, roles, people (the new term is *talent*), and metrics. Under the common banners of "business process redesign," "best practices" and "high-performing organizations" organizational interventions typically involve the improvement of one or more of these enterprise elements, and often make the case for greater integration, linkage, alignment, and synergy among the elements as well.

Unfortunately, too often the models and frameworks that drive these improvement efforts tend to reinforce a linear and over-simplified view of the organization, with the belief that focusing on one or a few elements can bring them into "control" and enhance the overall system. While organization improvement initiatives often pay lip service to the concepts of integration and alignment, my experience suggests that many of these initiatives are sub-optimized due to a lack of emphasis on the whole organization as a networked system, the key interdependencies among system elements, and intangible and foundational types of interfaces, transactions, and exchanges found within. Frequently organizations focus too much attention on the parts and not enough on the whole.

The most egregious example of this phenomenon occurred during the late 90s and continued into the new millennium, and involved the installation of enterprise resource planning (ERP) systems. Pervasive throughout industry for over a decade, ERP installations falsely represented the holy grail of alignment, integration, and efficiency. Time and time again I witnessed organizations investing unimaginable amounts of capital and time and energy into ERP technologies that, in turn, drove organizational restructuring and business process redesign efforts that were almost always based on assumptions about interdependencies that were over-simplified, too linear in terms of cause-and-effect, or just flat wrong. Repeatedly I questioned the wisdom of technology determining organization structure and process, when it should be the other way around. And after going over budget by 2x or 3x as well as extending timelines by 2x or 3x, and after massive disruptions to the workforce and the operations of the organization, every ERP system I encountered did not remotely deliver on its promise.

Many enterprise initiatives often fail due to a lack of understanding of how organizational networks work and within those networks, the true drivers of value creation and their interdependencies with other parts of the whole system. These initiatives do not focus enough on the fundamentals of what makes an organization successful in the long term: the value orientation and effectiveness of the webs of activity, interactions, and relationships within the enterprise and with its broader external environment.

The ability of the enterprise to create value is directly related to the strength of its strategic and operational capabilities and the effectiveness of its processes and networks. All of these organizational phenomena are based on the effectiveness of interactions between people and the productive nature of the activities they carry out in doing their work. Many of the concepts explored by thought-leaders such as Michael Hammer, Geary Rummler, and Alan Brache that have traditionally been applied to improving process performance, can also be applied to improving network performance. In thinking about the things that make up process and network effectiveness, an organization can consider and explore the following questions (that have been used over the years by many organizations in examining value generating processes, but are also just as relevant to value webs):

- To what extent are processes and networks defined and prioritized relative to their contribution to value creation?
- To what extent do process or network activities take too much time, require too much energy, result in too many defects, or cause too much waste?
- To what extent do process or network activities and nodes include bottlenecks, overload points, obstacles, mini-silos, or gates that constrain or disturb other important activities?

- To what extent do process or network activities reflect too little value relative to their complexity and the amount of value they add to the overall process?
- To what extent are process or network activities adequately resourced, supported, monitored, guided, and measured?

In answering the above questions and collecting diagnostic information regarding the effectiveness of network activities, an organization can begin exploring potential directional solutions through these additional questions:

- To what extent can processes and networks be better defined in terms of their criticality to value creation?
- To what extent can process or network activities be simplified, streamlined, synchronized, or standardized?
- To what extent can process or network activities be redesigned, automated, or eliminated?
- To what extent can process or network activities be re-assigned, off-loaded, or outsourced?
- To what extent can process or network activities be regulated through the refocus or redesign of individual roles, teams, and groups?

Inculcating a Value Creation Culture

Value creation begins with a compelling value proposition and value creation strategy—the strategic intent—for the enterprise. The foundation of the supporting value creation *culture* is essentially the *performance orientation* of the enterprise in executing strategy, achieving its goals, and thus creating value. An organization's performance orientation reflects the degree to which its culture and internal workings is characterized by an emphasis on superior results, a broad understanding within the workforce of how to achieve those results, the capability and engagement of people in contributing to those results, and a widespread focus on continuously improving work activities, processes, and networks to exceed desired results in the future.

Almost every commercial enterprise as well as larger non-profit and social sector organization has some form of "performance management" process where individuals, and in some cases, groups, are assessed on their performance relative to specific responsibilities, expectations, and goals. The common elements of these processes include goal setting, periodic opportunities for written feedback, formal assessment, development and improvement planning, and the linkage to reward systems where compensation decisions are theoretically tied to the overall contribution of the participant. Unfortunately, most of these processes are laden with misguided, dysfunctional, and non-value adding behaviors, activities, and tools. It could be argued that many of these "programs" actually destroy value rather than create value for the organization.

Moreover, for too long too many organizations have attempted to use technology to improve performance management effectiveness, and have failed miserably. For example, after implementing an on-line assessment system to reduce the perceived administrative burden of the old pencil-and-paper process, a mid-sized hospital found that its people were still spending a lot of time inputting data and checking boxes and that the amount of meaningful activity, such as quality performance conversations and shared goal-setting, had actually *decreased* and not increased. Moreover, the change had *further reinforced* the overall perception that performance assessment was simply an exercise in compliance rather than in real performance improvement.

KOAN: WHAT IS *CULTURE*?

The culture of an organization can be defined as the influencing beliefs, behaviors, and attitudes that characterize the social fabric and functioning of the entity.

There are many reasons why performance management systems fail, the most important of which is clearly identified within the term itself: the performance of individuals, groups, and networks cannot be "managed" or controlled. Rather, human performance, and the creation of a high performance culture—or a *value creation culture*—is enabled, nurtured, and unleashed over time only when the right conditions are present. Some organizations have attempted to address this superficially through enhanced processes with fancy new terminology, perhaps through a greater emphasis on development rather than assessment, calling their process/program *performance development*, an improvement to be sure. But even still, these organizations continue to demonstrate many of the same ineffective practices. *So why do performance management processes fail?* What does it take to fix them? Can something that is, in fact, not a thing at all actually be fixed? And what are the implications for reframing a tangible performance management process into an intangible value creation culture?

There are a number of reasons why performance management processes fail, or fall short of expectations, in most organizations:

- There is an unclear purpose for the process in the first place—is the purpose to drive results, build capability, or make reward decisions?
- The process itself is treated as an event-driven, top-down program that is forced onto people to "complete" by a specific deadline.
- The process is perceived as time-consuming, tedious, and administratively burdensome, resulting in perceived high effort with low return.
- The process is designed and maintained so that the worst managers can execute it, rather than being designed for the best managers that can role model great performance improvement behaviors.
- The process involves measurement that is often too broadly or too narrowly focused, highly subjective in nature, and not very relevant to how work actually gets done and how results are achieved.
- Performance objectives are not clearly tied to the actual key responsibilities of the role or well-aligned with the objectives and value drivers of the organization.
- The process has been automated using slick technology that actually reduces the need for, rather than facilitates the use of, candid and constructive conversations about performance.
- The process is treated as a way to weed out poor performers rather than as a way to help good and excellent performers improve.
- The process does not effectively create the conditions for, or even support and reinforce, ongoing and real-time feedback.
- Performance management is treated like an operating process as something that should be consistently executed, rather than as a set of flexible, good practices that are demonstrated by people throughout the organization in different ways, based on the nature of work activity and outcomes.

There is no question that the more performance management is treated like an important business process within an organization, the more effective it can be. But the enlightened enterprise moves beyond a program or process orientation and inculcates a value creation culture through the conditions it creates to reinforce high levels of performance expectations, standards, and accountability. It does not apply a specific and singular process to do this; rather, it creates and sustains certain elements that foster a strong continuous improvement orientation over time. There *are* specific conditions that can be created in place of traditional performance management processes and programs (often, organizations simply dress these things up in new clothes using web-based tools, and they remain ineffective) that strengthen enterprise performance orientation. These conditions for inculcating a value creation culture include:

- **A results-based orientation where organizational activity is guided by simple and clear enterprise goals rather than by rules, policies, and complicated plans.** As an example, a manufacturing facility developed a process where it communicated its key goals and metrics using a highly visual and engaging set of images on display in the entryway of the facility to provide all employees with an updated set of priorities each morning.
- **Constant and diverse learning opportunities that are hard-wired into how work gets done and support the development and application of new skills, knowledge, and abilities.** As an example, the project consulting unit of a petroleum company included an inventory of learning strategies and opportunities for on-the-job developing of consultant competencies.
- **Accessible and relevant performance information that participants can use to do their work and make real-time adjustments to meet and exceed high standards and expectations.** As an example, in another manufacturing facility, each production team utilized and kept current a whiteboard showing real-time performance on key indicators and metrics of the production line.
- **Continuous training on how to have good quality, real-time conversations about performance, where individuals have the needed competencies to openly give, seek, and receive constructive feedback.** As an example, a mutual insurance organization conducted periodic practice sessions where diverse groups of participants learned, practiced, and role-modeled the activities of seeking, giving, and receiving performance feedback in both informal as well as formal and planned settings.
- **A straightforward, well-defined, and clearly-understood linkage between skill development, results achievement, and rewards.** As an example, an Internet start-up made it very clear to all participants

that annual incentive compensation would be directly tied to individual and group achievements, paying one-time cash awards for *past* performance, while annual salary increases would be directly tied to the development of individual competencies that in part determine *future* performance.

The most effective organizations are fully conscious of the paramount importance of values-in-action and value creation as the key to long-term success and survival. Rather than investing vast amounts of energy and resources in the development of detailed strategies and plans that are then cascaded "downstream" to the rest of the organization, these enlightened organizations conceive a compelling intent to invent distinctive value creation strategies. They establish these conditions over time to build and sustain a culture that unleashes powerful energies in the organization to achieve extraordinary results. In the next chapter we will explore in more detail the nature of energy as the foundation for value creation and all other organizational activity.

THE TAO: Walking a New Path

In getting started on the path toward the development of a robust values-based culture and value creation strategy, consider the following diagnostic questions:

- ***What are the strengths and weaknesses of the organization's internal value proposition?*** Consider the nature of the value exchange between the organization and its members: what the organization offers its people in exchange for their contribution and commitment. Consider the degree of alignment between the needs of top contributors and what the organization provides them for consistent excellent performance.

- ***Given these strengths and weaknesses, to what extent does the internal value proposition drive the attraction, engagement, and retention of desired talent?*** Consider the extent to which the organization attracts the type and quality of talent it needs. Consider the extent to which it attracts and retains top contributing talent in critical jobs.

- ***How does the organization create value today?*** Consider how the organization determines, understands, and preserves and/or strengthens specific bundles of activities and capabilities that have the greatest impact on value creation. Consider the elements of the external value proposition, and from a customer perspective, how the organization is fulfilling this proposition.

- ***How will the organization evolve to create value in new ways?*** Consider what the organization is doing on a daily basis to develop new ways of creating and delivering value. Consider what investments are being made and who is involved. Consider the extent to which the organization is able to translate information about its external environment into potential new strategies for enhancing its external value proposition.
- ***How does the organization build value creation capability?*** Consider what investments the organization is making in the drivers of value creation. Consider how concentrated or distributed activities and capabilities are that directly impact value creation. Consider the mix of investments in short-term versus long-term value creation capability.
- ***What conditions are present today that build, support, and reinforce a value creation culture?*** Consider the degree to which performance management activities are carried out as an administrative program, an important business process, or as an imbedded way of working in the organization. Consider what indicators exist that show the organization is helping people to continuously improve their performance and increase their overall contribution.
- ***How does the organization talk about, measure, and reward value creation?*** Consider what kinds of value creation related communications and discussions take place in the organization on a formal and informal basis. Consider how value creation is measured and the degree to which this information is shared broadly within the organization. Consider the degree to which financial reward systems motivate, support, and reinforce value creation behaviors, skills/competencies, actions, and results.

THREE

The Flowing Fields of Energy

Imagine that you are sitting in a conference room with a few colleagues to participate in an important webinar, facilitated by a project team who is presenting their recommendations for how the organization can improve key processes to be more efficient and productive. Other organization members around the world are sitting in similar rooms participating as well. The team's findings are surprisingly creative and innovative, and challenge some of the fundamental operating principles of the enterprise. After a while the project leader suggests it is a good time to get feedback, and asks that the groups in each location discuss what they have heard so far and send in their reactions to the webinar facilitator, who will post the information in real-time. Soon after the ten minutes are over, a stream of feedback begins to show up on the video screen. Hundreds of ideas appear almost all of which focus on how impractical the recommendations are and how difficult they will be to implement. You can see on the split-screen the project team reviewing the input, and can sense their disappointment. This is not what they had expected. You can feel the energy dissipating from the initiative. Then you see the project leader take the team's conference phone off "mute" and hear him say, "Well, we appreciate all the feedback from around the organization. We have concluded it is in the best interest of the organization to replace all of our recommendations with a single, simple mandate." You can feel the curiosity and tension in your conference room and suspect it is the same everywhere else. The project leader then says, "We recommend that if nothing else, we as an organization stop being so negative and simply start being positive. Let's start now." ***This is satori.***

IN THIS CHAPTER WE WILL EXPLORE IMPORTANT CONCEPTS regarding the organization as a powerful source of energy, as summarized by the following principles:

- **Organizations influence their own reality through the generation of positive energy fields.**
- The quality **of interactions and relationships in the enterprise is the main determinant of the frequency and strength of its overall energy field.**
- **The overall energy field is largely determined by relational energy that is generated from the healthy, creative, and collaborative thoughts, actions, and interactions of people.**
- **The more conscious an organization is the more likely it will create positive energy that contributes to greater value creation**

Everything in the universe is connected to everything else. Within an organization, everything is connected to everything else as well. Energy is the fundamental ingredient of all that exists, its vibrational patterns and frequencies are the connecting medium of all that there is. For millennia, the Chinese have believed this to be true. They believe in Qi (pronounced chi), the universal force. In their philosophy, culture, science, and medicine, Qi is the universal energy that comprises as well as flows through all things. It is the pulse of our universe. Interestingly, the concept of Qi is hard to define in Western terms because the Chinese do not easily distinguish matter from energy.

At the subatomic, or quantum, level of existence, where we once thought particles such as protons and electrons and their sub-components were the foundational stuff of the universe, we now know that there is a more fundamental level to all that exists, that in fact the stuff of life is not a particle or a wave or even a "wavicle," but the vibration of pure energy, currently characterized by quantum physicists as superstrings, infinitesimally small vibrating chords, that comprise the universal field of energy.

At the sub-quantum level of our universe, science has shown us that matter does not really exist, only energy does; matter is in fact energy that is constantly flowing in magnificent, harmonic resonance. Nothing exists as a separate entity; everything exists in relationship to everything else within this universal, pulsating energy field. This universal "intelligence" is fueled by the invisible and unified forces of energy, the power train of our being and doing and everything else in our world.

SUTRA LESSON *The Cosmic Dance of Energy*[3]

In his groundbreaking book, *The Tao of Physics: An Exploration of the Parallels Between Modern Physics and Eastern Mysticism*, Fritjof Capra elegantly describes the nature of energy at the quantum level:

"The particle interactions give rise to the stable structures which build up the material world, which again do not remain static, but oscillate in rhythmic movements. The whole universe is thus engaged in endless motion and activity; in a continual cosmic dance of energy."

Swimming in the Fields of Energy

All that exists is fundamentally energy that is in a certain frequency of vibration. Drawing from the ground-breaking teachings of theoretical physicists/philosophers, such as John Hagelin and William Tiller, we believe there is a specific vibration associated with every thought, action, and thing. This vibrating energy that comes from all things reflects the universal field of energy. In this way, the energy field of an organization is the sum of its vibrating thoughts and actions. The true nature and culture—in a way, the *beingness*—of an organization is a reflection of the frequency and density of its energy field, and the degree to which this field is in harmonic resonance. Subcultures within organizations are like localized energy fields with their own energy frequencies and densities. Further yet, each participant in an organization has his or her own local and subjective energy field. These individual energy fields create regional energy fields, forming subcultures, and regional energy fields create the organization's energy field, forming the invisible fabric of the whole of the enterprise.

We are fish swimming in a sea of many different forms of energy. As we have learned over the past two-hundred years, these major sea-currents reflect the far-reaching electromagnetic energy fields. We cannot see or feel most of these waves of energy, but we know they exist in the form of radio waves, microwaves, x-rays, and gamma rays, and of course, light waves (the ones we can see). Each type of electromagnetic wave is characterized by its velocity, wavelength, and frequency. As humans, we are aware only of the visible spectrum of electromagnetic waves, which essentially consists of light waves which oscillate at a specific wavelength and frequency that our senses are programmed to detect. At most wavelengths, however, the information carried by electromagnetic radiation is not directly detected by our human brain. While we cannot touch, see, hear, or smell these flowing waves of energy, they affect the quality of our life-situation every moment of every day (how could we survive without our cell phones?).

There are many sources and forms of energy that create electromagnetic radiation, including electrical, solar, chemical, nuclear, and geothermal. But with respect to the nature of energy *within organizations*, another realm of energy exists, three types of energy that are important and practical to consider: kinetic, potential, and relational energy. Any object in motion is demonstrating *kinetic*, or active, energy. A production line that makes polymer-based products through injection-molding is almost always in a kinetic state of energy. Any object at rest has a certain amount of *potential* energy, energy stored due to the object's position or condition. An x-ray machine in a hospital that is not being used has significant potential energy. At all times, all objects demonstrate *relational* energy, which is also known as the unified, zero-point, or ground-state energy that connects everything in the universe to everything else. Relational energy is in fact the medium of the universal energy field.

The power of this relational energy field is extraordinary. For many years we have viewed space as mostly empty—essentially a vacuum—whereas today scientists believe that this "emptiness" is actually full of energy that we cannot yet measure or detect, but hypothesize that this energy field is more powerful than what we can comprehend. The currently accepted theory of the nature of the universe accounts for about only 4% of the matter and energy that is implied by observing the universe and the effects of gravitation and relativity; the other 96% seems to be missing. There is growing evidence that the universal, ground-state field represents the missing energy, and reflects the resonant field of connectivity, the universal field of energy that connects our minds in ways that transcend the limitations of space, time, and the speed of light.

In an experiment that has been replicated many times, scientists create a pair of twin particles and then separate them. Regardless of how far apart the particles travel in space, they behave as a *single entity*. If the attributes of one changes, its twin instantaneously changes as well. As more of these experiments are conducted, we will learn about their implications for the activity of the mind and of consciousness, where our thoughts can be connected, transmitting information in similar, "nonlocal" and immediate ways. Through this omnipresent relational energy field, everything in the universe is connected and we as humans are all connected, with each of us affected to some degree by what everyone else is thinking, feeling, and experiencing. The ramifications of this are both clear and extraordinary: the more harmonic and aligned our shared energy field is, our power to create is amplified and our ability to make manifest our intentions is strengthened. This startling axiom raises many questions and leads many of us to require more proof, but that would be no different than those who questioned the existence of electromagnetic energy less than two centuries ago.

SUTRA LESSON *The Sea of Energy*[4]

In her fascinating book, *The Field: The Quest for the Secret Force of the Universe*, Lynne McTaggart nicely summarizes the nature of energy and writes:

> **"All living things are a coalescence of energy in a field of energy connected to every other thing in the world. This pulsating energy field is the central engine of our being and our consciousness."**

We therefore are also fish swimming in a sea of relational energy fields. We are immersed in the relational energy field of our own making which is the direct result of all we have ever said, thought, or done. In this sense we influence and create our own reality through the energy fields that we generate. We exist in a participatory universe, where our energy fields interact to create our perceived reality. Our relational energy fields can have a positive charge or a negative charge. They can be strong or weak, more dense or less dense. They exist at different wavelengths and frequencies, transmitting information at different levels of consciousness.

What gives energy its overall frequency and density is the health of participants, their conscious receptivity to higher frequencies, and the nature of their interactions and relationships. As humans that are born conscious and become more unconscious with time, due to the accumulating influences of our daily life, our range of frequencies that we can tune into becomes more and more limited. In a sense, this is like the ability at birth to see and feel all forms of electromagnetic radiation including radio waves, microwaves, and so on, but upon adulthood, we lose this ability and can only see certain waves of light, a phenomenon not at all to be confused with *seeing the light*. On the contrary, as adults, it is perhaps more appropriate to suggest we are trying to see in the dark.

However, altering our state of mind through healthy endeavor such as meditation, learning, unlearning, exercise, mind-expanding activity, and creative self-expression can loosen these self-imposed constraints and expand our ability to tune into the full spectrum of relational energy, enabling us to more fully resonate with our world. In our sea of energy we swim among the invisible and interconnected currents that interact to create relationships that in turn create our reality. We cannot see these fields but we can feel their effects, and the more we are conscious, the more we are open and receptive to broader fields of frequencies, the more we can realize a more robust field of possibilities for ourselves and for our organizations. Understanding and embracing this reality is part of the awakening process that some individuals and organizations are experiencing today.

And increasingly, individuals and organizations believe that spiritual exploration is of critical importance in achieving this greater resonance and expanding the field of possibility. They believe in the power of the spirit—our most fundamental connection to the energy of the universe—as a portal into a new realm of consciousness. At a regional health center, for example, weekly department meetings include thirty minutes of reflection and thirty minutes of dialog about spiritual issues in management. In another example, a leading telecommunications firm provides ongoing workshops that are highly spiritual in nature, and which help to create more positive energy, build better decision-making capability, and improve overall health and well-being.

Understanding Energy Sources and Sinks

The enlightened organization generates powerful and strong positive energy that results in a resonant, harmonic field. This energy is generated from robust interactions, healthy relationships, and productive activities that create value. The organization, as an open system, exchanges energy with its environment: it draws energy from its environment through its external relationships, information capture, and resource attraction and acquisition, and in exchange transfers energy through value delivery from its products and services.

Within an organization there are energy *sources* and energy *sinks* that create the overall energy field of the enterprise. These fields are created through the internal beliefs, thoughts, behaviors, actions, interactions, and relationships of its participants. For example, positive energy is generated through healthy, collaborative, harmonious, and unifying interactions while negative energy is generated from unhealthy, dissonant, ego-driven, and fear-based interactions. From the strictest scientific standpoint, drawing from the first law of thermodynamics, energy is not actually created out of thin air, nor is it destroyed into nothingness. However, the second law tells us that without generating energy to sustain an open system, it will naturally break-down due to the universal villain, entropy. Therefore, for the purposes of this book, we will use the concept of energy creation as something akin to the harnessing of the universal energy field, where we can influence the state of energy, creating a more positive charge and higher vibrational frequency.

Positive (and negative) energy flows are like currents in the organization that create, reinforce, and also reflect the culture and overall quality of the organizational experience. The sensation of these flows is palpable and unmistakable, and a direct result of how we charge the relational energy field through meaningful and productive activity. There are important and pervasive *positive* energy sources, or localized energy fields, within the organization that have varying degrees of power. From *low to high power* these include:

- **Individual thoughts, behaviors, and actions:** the degree to which the vibrational density and frequency of individual participant thought generates and transmits positive energy to the organization. The positive thinking that individuals generate leads to constructive behaviors and actions that create a positive, localized energy field within the enterprise.
- **Group ideas, behaviors, and actions:** the degree to which the collective vibrational density and frequency of group activity generates and transmits positive energy to the organization. Positive and constructive group behaviors and actions create a positive, localized energy field within the enterprise.
- **Organizational processes:** the degree to which key organizational processes—workflows that transform inputs into outputs to carry out the work of the organization—create positive energy for the enterprise through the individual, group, and network activities and interactions that are involved.
- **Network ideas, behaviors, and actions:** the degree to which the collective vibrational density and frequency of network activity generates and transmits positive energy to the organization. Positive and constructive network interactions create a positive, regional energy field within the enterprise, or in the case of internal/external networks, an energy field that extends into the external environment.

- **Organizational initiatives:** the degree to which key organizational initiatives, such as technology installations, new process improvement implementations, and employee wellness programs, create positive energy for the enterprise through the nature of the individual, group, and/or network activities and interactions that are involved.

SUTRA LESSON *The Resonance of Being*[5]

In their visionary book, *CosMos: A Co-creator's Guide to the Whole World*, Ervin Laszlo and Jude Currivan write about the principle of resonance:

> **"We both affect and are affected by the energetic tenor of our surroundings. Higher frequency feelings, such as the expression of love, joy, and hope, inspire and energize us; lower frequencies, such as chronic fear, anger, or despair, drain us."**

There are also important, highly damaging, and pervasive *energy sinks* within the organization that generate negative energy and/or drain energy from the entity, feeding on the natural forces of entropy. Unfortunately, too many organizations create the conditions that facilitate and reinforce these negative energy patterns. Borrowing a phrase from the classic film, *Star Wars*, the manifestations of these patterns are like "disturbances in the force," the force being the energy field of the enterprise. In unconscious organizations, these energy sinks are often widespread and terribly destructive, substantially reducing the ability of the enterprise to create value and survive in the long-term.

Drawing from the works of Dr. David Hawkins, Eckhart Tolle, and other contemporary thought leaders in the areas of psychology, consciousness, and human behavior, the primary cause of negative energy is the ego, the portion of a person's psyche that is experienced as the "self," and its propensity to act in unconscious and self-centered ways. The ego is the part of the mind that is responsive to the surrounding physical and social world. It creates the defense mechanisms that theoretically protect the mind and the individual from external dangers. In our complex and highly social world, these defense mechanisms often do more harm than good, especially in the context of the greater good of the community or the organization. These ego-driven behaviors at the individual level translate into negative energy at the organization level, which then manifest as energy sinks with their associated destructive forces. Some of the most pervasive and harmful organizational energy sinks include:

- **The separation of self:** The ego of the individual mind, and similarly, the collective ego of the organization, thrives on fear and insecurity. The ego wishes to be separate, to prove itself special and stable in an unstable world. Due to the separation of the self, people often behave in ways that are intended to call attention to themselves and make them stand-out from their community. These behaviors manifest themselves in actions that are neither good for the individual or for the collective. Simlarly, the organization as a whole invests great amounts of energy in proving to the outside world that it is unique and separate rather than fully integrated into broader networks and other social systems in its environment. For an example, one entertainment company has invested substantial resources in its internal training and development function given its belief that there is little to learn from its environment and that all processes and programs must be "home-grown." This practice limits the amount of knowledge that the organization has access to and therefore limits the reality that it can create. Anathema to the ego, an awareness of not knowing usually leads to greater understanding, not less. An enterprise can move beyond the separation of self through the belief that as an entity it is nothing special, but what it does is something special. Some of the most successful and admired organizations are those that dominate their space through superior value creation with grace and humility; some are even practically "invisible" in their use of market power.
- **The absence of accountability:** The ego of the individual mind, and the collective ego of the organization, thrives on a sense of security and separation from perceived conflict. While many people indicate they would like more accountability for what they do, the collective ego can actually create environments and systems where, by design, or not, actual accountability is either too highly concentrated or too broadly distributed. Moreover, people often, and misguidedly, perceive accountability as the consequence of making a mistake or achieving something less than expected, giving accountability a bad name. Some organizations that undertake initiatives to increase accountability within their operations actually end up doing the opposite by creating overly complex and over-engineered processes for making important decisions. For these reasons, an organization as a

whole can unconsciously create an absence of accountability. In most airports across the country, for example, there is virtually no structure of accountability within the carrier organizations for travelers to address issues or resolve problems: there is no authority designed into the jobs and there is no one "behind the curtain" to elevate the situation to solve the problem. In another example, there are some government agencies, such as the state department of motor vehicles, that have designed a system where there is accountability, but constituents have absolutely no access to those who are accountable. It is essentially an organization that is *by design* (perhaps unconscious design) intended to frustrate and confuse those that should benefit from it. In a much smaller and less significant example, but appropriate nonetheless, a large regional youth soccer program established no system of accountability during its tournaments with respect to officiating, and so when concerns and complaints arose, there was nowhere for parents to go for review or answers. An enterprise can move beyond the abdication of accountability through job/role design that clearly places accountability where it should be: in the hands of those participants who interact with customers and other constituents in the process of delivering value for the organization.

- **The tyranny of time:** The ego of the individual mind, and the collective ego of the organization, feeds on a preoccupation with time. The only real time is right now, and yet, the ego constantly wants to focus on the past or on the future. The ego loves to dwell on the past or worry about the future in order to avoid the reality of the now. When individuals and groups can be fully present in the now, there is essentially no need for the ego. Time-based thinking is obsessively pervasive within organizations, where almost every type of interaction—conference calls, meetings, conversations, presentations, brainstorming sessions, and so forth—is governed and bound by time: start times and end times. And often the organization as a whole creates artificial time-based constraints under the guise of speed-to-market and first-to-entry, at times sacrificing long-term health for short-term results and allowing the tyranny of time to overshadow important and creative activities. A major health system, for instance, developed an unrealistic and unnecessary timeline for developing and implementing a new performance review process that resulted in the constant revising of project plans and re-allocation of resources, reducing productivity levels and frustrating leaders and initiative team members along the way. Almost every timeline was overly optimistic and unneeded, and did more harm than good. An enterprise can move beyond the tyranny of time by re-evaluating and/or eliminating all unnecessary time-based constraints that are attached to plans, programs, processes, initiatives, and so on, and can give more autonomy to individuals and groups to determine in real-time how necessary time-based milestones and time-driven activities are going forward.

- **The delusion of duality:** The ego of the individual mind, and the collective ego of the organization, thrives on the seductive quality of absolutes. Once again, the ego wishes for stability, and pushes away the natural ambiguity of its environment, avoiding shades of grey. Most people think and behave with the misconception that every situation or problem has two discrete and opposing characteristics such as right or wrong, good or bad, leader or follower. And often the organization as a whole feeds this phenomenon using the rigid, false logic of trade-offs in making decisions and investments: short-term or long-term, strategy or operations, consistency or flexibility, cost or quality, management or employee. One Native American organization struggled with its Board's requirement that it meet unrealistic hiring quotas of its native shareholders (many of whom were undereducated or under-skilled) versus non-shareholders with the belief that this was the most effective way for the organization to best benefit its shareholder base. In reality, organization leadership knew that focusing on hiring quotas was not the "answer" to maximizing value creation, even in the short-term, given the quality of available talent; rather, hiring the right balance of shareholders and non-shareholders was the best strategy at the time for driving the long-term growth trajectory of the company. An enterprise can move beyond the delusion of duality by reframing the prevalent concepts of either-or trade-offs and choosing only the best alternative. Individuals and groups can begin to practice the art of using continuums, building multiple scenarios, and exploring the possibilities of implementing multiple alternatives/solutions instead of only searching for the "best" or "right" one.
- **The hubris of hierarchy:** The ego of the individual mind, and the collective ego of the organization, wants to stand-out and be in control. Under the guise of efficiency and execution, people in organizations build chains-of-command. They believe they can control situations and activities by concentrating accountability and decision-making among a few participants based on status,

seniority, and level in the enterprise. And often the organization as a whole creates policies, programs, and structures that reinforce hierarchy (through things like decision approval, budget responsibility, benefits eligibility criteria, pay grades, and job classification systems), further reinforcing separation and establishing artificial barriers to communication and collaboration. For example, one major university had nine separate pay structures with close to 100 pay grades for about 2000 staff members resulting in confusion regarding the value of specific jobs, their associated compensation opportunities, and the career paths within job families, all of which contributed to a hierarchical orientation and siloed behavior among staff members. An enterprise can move beyond the hubris of hierarchy by dramatically reducing the number of things in the organization that are attached to level. Moreover, hierarchical chains of command and approval processes should in most cases be eliminated and replaced with a more collaborative and network-based operating model.

- **The stranglehold of structure:** The ego of the individual mind, and the collective ego of the organization, thrives on the illusive permanence of structure. Through the building of structure, people perceive a greater sense of stability. Structure reflects something that is seemingly real and tangible; participants can touch it, and yet by the time structure is formed and functional, the environment has already changed. And often the organization as a whole falls into this trap as well, constantly investing in structure-based solutions, such as new or reorganized departments and functions—as opposed to network-based or relational-based solutions—to meet environmental challenges and improve enterprise performance. One organization in the restaurant industry chose to create a project management organization *structure* in an attempt to more centrally *manage* the portfolio of project-based work, rather than build project management skills among natural leaders in the workforce that would have resulted in a more distributed, effective, and lasting organizational *capability*. An enterprise can move beyond the stranglehold of structure by simply eliminating it as a potential solution or focus area for performance improvement activities and initiatives, and replacing it with an emphasis on critical capabilities, processes, and networks.
- **The paradox of policies:** The ego of the individual mind, and the collective ego of the organization, wishes to be empowered but also in control. This dynamic creates competing tensions, a constant pull-and-

push in the conflicting desire for strict rules versus flexibility, defined boundaries versus elbow-room, compliance versus creativity, and guiding constraints versus limitless possibility. And often the organization as a whole uses rules and regulations to control participant behavior and direct how people interact and carry out their work, while at the same time sending messages to the workforce that it values flexibility and personal initiative. One retail chain that had achieved major growth in part through its focus on customer service, implemented a new policy that required its employees to push selling memberships rather than selling books or serving customer needs. This contributed to confusion and dissatisfaction among employees regarding their own responsibilities and the overall values of the enterprise. In another example, a leading financial institution that openly touted its engaging culture had a policy that employees could not "surf the net" at work. Unbelievably, an employee who had to use a non-approved internet site to complete an important proposal was monitored and reprimanded for her non-compliance and "waste of time." An enterprise can move beyond the paradox of policies by simply eliminating most of them or by minimizing the number of policies used in the first place. Policies should be replaced with reinforcing communications on values-in-action and clear, simple principles that represent the strategic intent and desired value creation culture of the organization. The enlightened enterprise creates discipline through freedom, while most other organizations tend to create confinement through policies.

- **The mania of measurement:** The ego of the individual mind, and the collective ego of the organization, thrives on the illusion of objectivity in metrics and measurement. People want to believe that measurement gives a clear and unbiased view of reality so that they can simplify their world and more easily make decisions. And the organization as a whole typically ends up measuring too much, too little, or the wrong things. Moreover, it often wrongly believes that developing complicated scorecards that essentially measure everything equates to having a clearer picture of reality, when in fact, the nature of measurement itself is inherently a subjective exercise. By making assumptions about what to measure, making choices about how to define the measure, and creating imperfect processes to actually do the measurement, the organization may actually measure the wrong things or measure the right things in the wrong way, *reducing* its knowledge base rather than *expanding* it. One organization in the automotive industry used an incentive program that had over ten measures of performance, and these measures could change from year-to-year. Due to its complexity, lack of focus, and perceived instability, the plan did little to motivate employees or provide clear information that was needed for continuous improvement activities. In fact, the plan was viewed as a "moving target" subject to the whims of management and created significant distrust within the workforce. In another example, a health management organization implemented an initiative to collect data on the overall health of its patients. Due to the highly inconsistent ways in which health-care providers assessed patient health, and the highly subjective nature in which patients responded to assessment questions regarding their health (basically, how they felt the day of the measurement), the organization ended up with a useless database that raised more concerns and questions than it helped to answer in the first place. An enterprise can move beyond the mania of measurement by establishing a few simple and critical metrics that evolve with the strategic intent of the enterprise. All other measurement can be done at the local level within groups and networks based on their specific work activities and information needs.

- **The pathology of patterns:** The ego of the individual mind, and the collective ego of the organization, feeds on imprinted memory patterns from the past. People are more comfortable repeating old patterns—whether positive *or negative* in nature—than they are in creating new ones. Individuals rarely behave and act for the reasons they think. They constantly suffer from the phenomena of transference and displacement. Transference reflects the application of negative patterns from bad experiences and/or wrong thinking to situations in the workplace and the decisions and activities involved in doing work. They bring the wrong thinking used in their personal lives to the organization and apply this wrong thinking while carrying out their work. In one manufacturing organization that had just built a state-of-the-art facility to promote flexible work systems and encourage employee self-direction, the new general manager called an all-employee meeting where he claimed that since he could manage four adolescent children at home, it would be easy for him to manage the people at the facility. One can imagine the groans coming from the workforce. The second phenomenon, displacement, reflects the application of negative patterns from one situation into another situation, where negative energy that is created has nothing to do with the current situation. An individual may react poorly in a situation, not because of the nature of that situation, but because of a separate, recent experience. At a retreat for field consultants of a major franchisor, a senior leader paralyzed by a dysfunctional relationship with the chief executive (who was not even in attendance), and his palpable fear and lack of confidence, failed to build trust among attendees or guide them effectively in the work that needed to be done. In a similar way to individuals, the organization as a whole tends to repeat old patterns of behavior *regardless* of how unsuccessful or sub-optimal they were in the past. As a final example, one professional association with several thousand members continues each year to schedule up to twenty concurrent presentations every hour at its annual conference, despite continuous feedback from its members that this practice causes significant dissatisfaction and frustration. This organization unconsciously makes a poor strategic decision each year on its path of perceived least resistance. Transference and displacement are only two examples among many pattern-based behaviors. An enterprise can move beyond the pathology of patterns by first being aware of their insidious nature. At the organizational level, it can let go of past practices. This does not mean re-inventing the wheel all of the time, but it does mean the constant questioning of why things are done in certain ways and how they might be done better. At the individual level, the enterprise can educate participants on how to become aware of and break down the power of patterns. Through simple and disciplined acts of *unlearning* and *undoing* this energy sink will dissipate and go away.

MY SAMADHI *A Personal Challenge*

One thing I have learned time and time again while working with many organizations is that not only is it misguided for them to try to control their environments, it is impossible in our complex world. I challenge any organization of virtually any size to think and do otherwise.

Right now, your organization is an active ocean of energy ebbs and flows. It is 11:00am on a Wednesday morning. Consider the range of *localized* energy sources and sinks that are occurring simultaneously in this scenario of the common workplace:

A single mother of four just found out that she did not get the promotion she desperately needed to support her family. A high-performing and relatively young person received a call from his doctor to learn that he has diabetes. A marketing team just had a major breakthrough on a re-branding initiative. A new trainee accidentally sent pornographic material via email to a large network of participants.

At an off-site meeting, several hundred mid-level managers are learning important skills for giving and receiving performance feedback. A global video-conference just ended with exciting results regarding potential new product offerings and revenue streams. A long-standing and respected executive is drinking vodka in his office. A six-sigma initiative team is starting a meeting to discuss analyzing one of the organization's key value networks. An executive committee just decided on a new policy regarding headcount forecasting that is not aligned with the new strategic planning process used in most departments. And so on.

Now consider the potential *non-localized* energy sources and sinks that are occurring simultaneously in your organization's external environment:

A former executive has filed a law-suit against the company regarding his recent termination. On Capitol Hill, new federal legislation has just passed that may have positive implications for one or more lines of business. A political demonstration in a country overseas has shut-down a key production facility. A competing firm has just significantly reduced prices on several products that are substitutes for yours. An important supplier to a direct and critical supplier has filed for bankruptcy protection. A consumer advocacy group has just posted a blog on the net recognizing your organization as environmentally friendly. Your financial partners just sent the organization a letter with some concerns about your financial covenants along with new guidelines that could significantly affect cash flow. And so on.

Clearly, it is impossible to even remotely control these single, chaotic moments in real-time. Enlightened organizations understand that these scenarios reflect the nature of reality of every complex enterprise every single moment. Unfortunately most organizations do too little to *prevent* their negative energy sinks from occurring in the first place, and don't do enough to *facilitate* and *recognize* the potential and active positive energy sources. Rather, they attempt to control and "manage" the current state through unhelpful, unrealistic, and after-the-fact policies and practices.

I recall a customer service center I worked with that had invested a fair amount of energy (which was itself a frustrating energy sink for those involved) into changing its shift eligibility policies because too many high performing, highly tenured service reps were moving to lower volume shifts. After exploring the issues a little further we determined there were a variety of reasons for this phenomena, including family- and health-related reasons. Rather than change the shift policies, which would have undoubtedly caused unintended consequences, we engaged some of the reps themselves in a problem solving exercise that resulted in a better solution, including a change to a more strategic staffing model (rather than the traditional personnel policy-driven model) to re-balance call volume while meeting the personal needs of those involved.

It is my experience that through a strong and pervasive set of values in action that focus on collaboration, community, and caring for people, organizations can best survive the inevitable chaos of organizational life, prevent or minimize much of the associated negative energy, and more effectively harness the inherent goodness that is always present in the human spirit.

Increasing the Strength of the Energy Field

New ways of thinking and doing come from detaching from, unlearning, and de-programming the old ways of thinking and doing. New ways of thinking and doing take root from loosening control over and unleashing the creative spirit of individuals, groups, and networks. These sources of positive activity represent new or strengthened energy fields that act as a sort of *magnetic attraction* that further attract positive behaviors, actions, interactions, and situations. The more positive energy an organization generates the more it can exchange energy with its environment, and the more it can create and deliver value to its participants, customers, and other constituents.

The enlightened enterprise understands the power of positive energy comes from increasing the overall consciousness of the organization. It understands that energy fields increase in density and frequency, and flow through the strength of positive interactions among individuals, groups, and networks throughout the organization. It understands that its overall energy field is an accumulation of the thinking, communicating, learning, and creating that occurs over time. It creates the conditions that catalyze and enable these activities to exist everywhere inside the organization and with its external partners. It neutralizes common habits and patterns of thinking and acting that are low in energy or even energy sinks, and diligently nurtures a culture where new ways of thinking and acting are established. It explores diverse approaches to learning and observes internal patterns of thought and behavior to adopt new and innovative methods that build more unifying and productive energy flows. It searches to find meaningful ideas and practices that create positive energy in a local area of the system and utilizes networks to adopt these new ideas and apply these new practices throughout the system as a whole. It understands that the energy from a continuous commitment to innovation and quality generates more power than the energy from short-term forays into efficiencies and cost-reduction.

In this spirit, the *true* role of organizational *leaders* is to create and support the conditions for the generation of a positive energy field throughout the enterprise. In *We Were Soldiers*, the heroic film based on a true story, the theatre of activity is *far* from the comfortable environs of the enterprise, but its lessons about authentic leadership are compelling and timeless. The main character of the film, a lieutenant colonel in charge of the air cavalry, is a role model for his men in terms of integrity, commitment, courage, and honor, both on and off the battlefield. He genuinely cares about each man and his family. He creates the conditions that foster unity and loyalty. He is always fully present with his men, fights next to them, and supports them under extreme pressure. He promises that *no man will be left behind* and promises that *they will all come home together*. His men defeat the enemy against all odds and he keeps his promise: he is the last soldier to leave the battlefield, after every single man, dead or alive, has been air-lifted out. Thirty years later he would walk that same "valley of death" side-by-side with the commander of the enemy force whom he fought against with the grace, dignity, and empathy of a true leader.

Back in the world of organizations, the enlightened leader similarly communicates with passion, focus, and clarity, and demonstrates a deep level of integrity through words and actions. She ensures the organization invests energy in the practical reality of the present as opposed to the folly of past or the obscurity of the future, with the awareness that organizational performance is dependent on flawless execution in the now. She helps unify individuals, groups, and networks through clear goals and the leveraging of value drivers and networks. She makes decisions and takes action when needed and does so in alignment with values of the organization, its true nature. She understands that embracing constant change and disruption—chaos if you will—are essential to long-term survival.

At the same time she understands that the priorities around which people order their psychic energy is constantly in flux as well, and she helps to improve the quality of interactions and productive activity in a way that enables people to reprioritize sensibly and efficiently. She places less importance on structure and hierarchy and more importance on the processes and networks that carry out the work. She is open to new ideas, aware of the biases of her own belief system, and always seeks win-win solutions.

So who is an organizational leader in the enlightened enterprise? Potentially, everyone. Leadership can be demonstrated by all participants at all levels in various capacities and in various ways. There is no other path to walk.

DHARMA LOG:
The **unenlightened** organization invests too much in leadership capability based on hierarchy, level, and authority. The **enlightened** organization invests more in the development of distributed leadership capability at all levels throughout the enterprise.

Energizing the Organization through Positive Action

All individuals, groups, and networks within an organization are potential and powerful sources of positive energy. It is not just the role of traditional "leaders" to generate positive energy through standard motivational speeches, open-door policies, brown bag lunch discussions, problem solving workshops, recognition banquets, and the many other superficial ways in which managers/leaders attempt to engage the workforce. In fact, these are neutral at best in energizing the organization. It is the responsibility of all enterprise participants to constantly engage in activity that generates positive energy, creating the overall energy field. In this way, enlightened organizations are disciplined in staying in constant and broad-based positive *action-schemas*. Several powerful schemas include:

- **Trust people to do their best:** Enlightened organizations trust the value that comes from creating conditions and situations that empower people to do their best work and to have the freedom to make good decisions. They have faith that quality experiences lead to productive behaviors and actions within loosely defined boundaries and constraints. They emphasize values and principles rather than policies and protocols, cultivating a strong sense of mutual respect and accountability among their diverse participants.

- **Live and work with passion:** Enlightened organizations continuously imbed and connect their purpose, values, and principles to elevating things that people are passionate about and truly care about, including the quality of human life, the preservation of the environment, the impact on customers and their families, the financial success of their own enterprise and their customers' organizations, and the overall prosperity of the communities in which they participate.
- **Seek opportunity out of the ashes:** Enlightened organizations treat major obstacles, barriers, perceived "failures," and unplanned and unfortunate events as challenges that provide the organization with the opportunity to learn, grow, evolve, and develop new ways of value creation. Certainly, perceived failure or the achievement of less than optimal results needs to be taken seriously and addressed, but at the highest levels of consciousness, failure is an illusion. There is no such thing as failure, only situations that present further opportunity to improve and become even more successful.
- **Take risks and be experimental:** Enlightened organizations create the conditions, balanced expectations, and safety nets that enable, facilitate, and support individuals and groups to explore new ideas, experiment with new methodologies, and take calculated risks to constantly improve results. The organization that spends a lot of time determining how much risk is acceptable and within what boundaries for many of its work activities is still in its traditional control-mode. The more conscious organization understands that people who are well-informed, skilled, and engaged in the operations of the organization will sufficiently self-monitor and work within appropriate, practical boundaries and sensible levels of risk.
- **Be of service inside and outside:** Enlightened organizations believe in and support the practice of serving others both inside and outside the organization. They believe in caretaking and not controlling. They care about people and understand that true power comes from giving, not taking. They give to receive. They believe in the wisdom of "pay it forward." They provide the necessary flexibility, seek out and provide real opportunities, and make available reasonable resources that enable enterprise participants to serve others within the organization that have special needs, and serve others outside of the organization in the community who have special needs or who may have shared interests in specific social causes and initiatives.

- **Embrace the laws of nature:** Enlightened organizations embrace, rather than fear or fight, the laws of nature. They flow with the dynamic energy currents of the universe rather than swim against them. These organizations understand that the competitive forces of natural selection reveal important weaknesses and dangerous threats to organizational survival, and they welcome this as the foundation for continuous learning and improvement. They do not look at environmental challenges as problems as much as they are opportunities to evolve, improve, and become stronger.
- **Commit to quality in everything you do:** Enlightened organizations infuse excellence into everything they do. They believe that superior quality in organizational processes, programs, and practices is essential to building and sustaining a distinctive culture, and positively differentiates them from competitors and imitators. They role-model the standards *internally* that are expected *externally* in serving customers. The quality of how the organizations operate determines the quality of what they achieve. The means and the ends are one and the same. These organizations understand and embrace the simple precept that the quality of today—the quality of thoughts, behaviors, and actions right now—determines the quality of tomorrow.
- **Blame the process and not the person:** Enlightened organizations rarely personalize or blame unmet goals and less than optimal performance on specific people; instead they continuously apply diagnostic problem solving and critical thinking in the examination and improvement of activities, interactions, and processes, engaging the help of those involved at all levels to participate in the improvement efforts. Moreover, there is a strong emphasis on reducing and eliminating waste of all kinds, but this is balanced with an acceptance that curiosity and creativity are not always "efficient" by traditional standards and that not all processes must *always* perform within tight and rigid tolerances, or with minimal variances.
- **Stay present in the moment:** Enlightened organizations create cultures where people are consistently engaged in the present moment, performing their work with a sense of purpose, focus, concentration, and alertness. They are very strategic and targeted in the time they invest in the *past*, reviewing past practices in the context of improvement, and very careful about the time they invest in the *future*, developing scenarios that create a broad field of

opportunity with potential for value creation. These organizations do not dwell on past "mistakes," spend much psychic energy on old war stories, or obsessively worry about future uncertainties.

- **Practice the power of compassion:** Within enlightened organizations, people pay attention to *how* they speak, listen, interact, support, and empathize with their colleagues. These organizations support the development of friendships in the workplace and foster an environment of compassion, where people care about each other and recognize that there is more to life inside the enterprise than just productivity and profit, that there is a need for balance and meaningfulness. These organizations understand that people perform their roles as best they can within their capacity and what they are able to bring at the present moment. Rather than punish limited capacity and capability, enlightened organizations seek to expand the capacities and capabilities of people, reinforcing empathy and compassion in the process.
- **Invest in sound mind, sound body, and sound spirit:** Enlightened organizations strongly believe that productive interactions and the quality of relationships are based on the mental, physical, and spiritual health of individual participants. These organizations make significant investments in the health and wellness of their people by educating and motivating them to maintain good health and by facilitating opportunities to be proactive about health improvement. They are careful not to stigmatize or punish people for physical or mental conditions and do not confuse these conditions with the quality of the human soul and spirit. They inherently care about their people and work with them to improve the quality of their lives for both personal and professional reasons. They understand that at times unhealthy people do unhealthy things, and they have the courage to help those individuals who show a willingness to change.

In the quantum world, nature is pure energy. In the world that we can see and touch, nature is a complex web of organisms, actions, events, relationships, and relational networks. An organization represents a similar—yet smaller scale—system of network interactions participating with other networks within the whole web of life. In this continuous exchange of energy with nature, organizational activity occurs as patterns of interactions that emerge, evolve, and dissipate. How the organization reduces or eliminates negative energy, increases positive energy, and co-evolves with its environment, is based on generating and sustaining a strong energy field that powers its ongoing success and survival.

THE TAO: Walking a New Path

In getting started on the path toward becoming a strong and positive energy source as an organization, consider the following diagnostic questions:

- ***What conditions are present in the organization today that facilitate the generation of positive and negative energy?*** Consider how the elements of the organization are tuned to create positive or negative energy, including policies, protocols, programs, processes, and practices. Consider if there are particularly strong energy sources or sinks that affect the overall energy field. Consider which positive action schemas are strengths (or not) for the enterprise and what contributes to those actions.
- ***What are the sources of positive energy in the organization? What are the sources of negative energy?*** Consider the actions and behaviors that contribute to integration, harmony, quality, and creativity. Consider the actions and behaviors that are consistent with energy sinks and contribute to entropy, discord, waste, and stasis. Consider what energy sources are prevalent and need to be maintained or strengthened. Consider what energy sinks are prevalent and need to be diminished and/or eliminated altogether.
- ***How would you characterize the relational energy field that exists within the organization?*** Consider the nature of interactions and relationships throughout the organization, within departments and across organization units and job/role levels. Consider what data may be available or could be collected to learn more about the quality of communication and information sharing between individuals and/or groups.
- ***What positive action-schemas does the organization embrace in exchanging energy with its environment?*** Consider behavioral norms and implicit and explicit values that reflect and reinforce positive actions. Consider the degree to which the organization demonstrates cynical and defensive behavior instead of opportunistic and proactive behavior when confronting challenges. Consider what positive schemas already exist today that can be maintained or strengthened.

FOUR

The Elegant Chaos of Co-Evolution

Imagine that you are at a two-day mountain retreat with your whole department to discuss performance objectives and strategies for the next year. You have worked hard with the department leader over the past several weeks to develop a robust agenda that follows a logical strategic planning process. Outside the first snow of the season has fallen, covering everything in pristine white. Inside, the fire casts a warm and cozy glow about the meeting room. Up until now you have felt very comfortable and serene in this setting; the group has followed the agenda very well and is right on schedule as the day draws to an end and the sun begins to set. But something has happened. Suddenly, the tranquility of the day has been interrupted by some serious disagreements among the team members regarding the priority and sequencing of specific department activities. The dialog gets heated. There is tension in the room. Too many diverse ideas are invading the space. Passions are rising. The discord is becoming uncomfortable. So you get the department leader's attention and suggest that it is time to get the team "back on track." He agrees and says, "Hey group, we need to re-focus a little; we have moved off-agenda. If we are going to get through our agenda today we need to move forward." And it is at this moment that one of the team members, a highly experienced colleague who is viewed by most as being very wise, and who always seems to perform well under pressure, perks up and says, "How is it that we are not moving forward? We may not know it yet, but by tomorrow morning I think we will realize we have had a breakthrough." **This is satori.**

In this chapter we will explore important concepts regarding the evolutionary process of the enlightened enterprise, as summarized by the following principles:

- **The consciousness, creativity, and innovation of self-organizing systems affect the environment in which they exist.**
- **An organization's ability to co-evolve with its environment is based on its ability to capture, process, interpret, and utilize information from many sources in diverse ways.**
- **Embracing disequilibrium and uncertainty is critical to innovation, growth, and long-term value creation.**
- **Order does not come from environmental control or from traditional change management, but through the continuous and fluid process of co-evolution.**
- **In co-evolving with their environment, organizations must also operate in a sustainable way that preserves and protects nature and its finite resources.**

An enterprise is a self-regulating system, a community of interdependent people, interactions, and relationships responsible for governing its own activities. An enterprise exists within a broader socio-economic *ecosystem* where a large number of interdependent entities—individuals, organizations, and networks—are connected in diverse ways for their mutual interests, effectiveness, and survival. An enterprise is also an energy field within the broader and larger energy field of the world, where the nature of change—*the natural way of things*—is shaped by strong, flowing, and often turbulent energy fields and patterns such as globalization, technological innovation, macroeconomic shocks, demographic trends, geo-political shifts, and environmental climate change. And our world of nations, societies, cultures, and organizations represent an energy field within the broader and larger energy field of the universe, which as we understand it, is not constant or stable either.

The principles of relativity demonstrate to us that space-time is relative and dynamic; its geometry changes in the presence of matter and energy. The principles of quantum physics demonstrate to us that we actually influence what we observe and that in fact matter is energy in its most fundamental state.

True, there is indeed a coherent harmony to our universe, yet each era in the evolution of our world is characterized by its own set of energy fields and patterns. This is why the conscious and high performing enterprise is not focused on any one particular and defining pattern to "overcome" or "control." Rather it is focused on the process of co-evolution itself. Every enterprise, in any era, must navigate through uncharted waters and unsettling undercurrents and consciously evolve with the constantly changing environment to best position itself for long-term value creation and survival. This is not always easy. But it is always certain. Consider the experience of a young, publicly-traded, and global biotechnology firm in the first decade of our new millennium, and the maelstrom of forces it found itself navigating within (based closely on the *actual* experiences of a similar type organization):

- The emergence of several new competitors from the Pacific Rim that were able to maneuver a fast-cycle entry into the Asian marketplace due to less stringent government regulation, thus reducing a large source of revenue for the firm.
- A fast decline in available research talent due to new immigration regulations on foreign student visas at domestic universities and non-citizen work visas that resulted from government over-reaction to the 9/11 disaster.
- An inability to attract experienced talent to the location of the organization because of extremely high housing prices that more than doubled in the first five years of the decade.
- Periodic threats to the supply chain affecting the ability of the organization to meet consumer demand due to instability in foreign places where several small, but critical production facilities are located.
- A rapid and extraordinary decline in stock price and market value of the organization due to baseless rumors about a key product that circulated throughout the investment community and sparked out-of-control short selling of the stock.
- The evaporation of lines of credit that were needed to make monthly payroll expense and finance new drugs in the third stage of development due to the collapse of the financial and credit markets later in the decade.

KOAN: WHAT IS AN OPEN SYSTEM?

An open system is an arrangement of interacting, interrelated, and interdependent elements that form a complex whole, and that freely exchanges energy with the world. An organizational open system is primarily made of people, processes, and networks that are often organized in temporary structures which have some degree of interdependence with the external environment.

Self-regulating, open systems constantly interact with the environment through a continuous exchange of energy. Closed systems do not exchange energy with their environments. Organizations are, therefore, open systems that exchange energy with the environment, and continue to grow, innovate, and create value in new ways, through feedback loops, constant learning and adaptation, and self-improvement activities. Through internal and external interactions organizations continuously maintain and renew/refresh themselves, using energy to form new structures, implement new processes, create new relationships, and demonstrate new patterns of behavior. Evolutionary forces are constantly at work in our dynamic and turbulent world, and all living systems that openly exchange energy within this landscape must continuously evolve to survive. Organizations are no different in this respect from living, biological systems. Change and transformation are therefore continuous processes and not discrete events.

SUTRA LESSON ***Business Ecosystems***[6]

In *The Keystone Advantage: What the New Dynamics of Business Ecosystems Mean for Strategy, Innovation, and Sustainability*, Marco Iansiti and Roy Levien discuss their views on business networks as ecosystems:

"We found that perhaps more than other type of network, a biological ecosystem provides a powerful analog for understanding a business network."

They go on to say:

"Like business networks, biological ecosystems are characterized by a large number of loosely interconnected participants who depend on each other for their mutual effectiveness and survival."

Reviewing the Laws of Evolution

Through the process of evolution, open systems are able to regenerate and reorganize to better meet the challenges of the environment and more effectively create value as a source of energy. The fundamental law of evolution, *natural selection*, demonstrates that the most successful living systems take advantage of environmental disturbances and challenges to evolve, using them as a catalyst for the system to self-organize into a new form of order. Evolution is based on natural selection, which has little or nothing to do with rules, compliance, precision, or symmetry, but rather requires the organization to constantly interact, adapt, and transform, often in new and creative ways, in order to survive within the ecosystem in which it operates. From a systems theory standpoint, in an environment of strong competition and turbulent change, the entity that can accept the chaotic dynamics of its surroundings most easily, acquire information most broadly, learn from its environment most effectively, discern real opportunities for advantage most strategically, and respond to these opportunities most creatively, will have a greater chance to adapt and survive.

KOAN: WHAT IS *NATURAL SELECTION*?

Natural selection is a process where variations occur in an organism's genetic make-up that may or may not increase its ability to adapt to changing environmental conditions. Variations that increase an organism's chances of survival and ability to procreate are preferred over less advantageous variations.

Not unlike the evolution of biological systems that experience gradual change punctuated by rapid transformation, the evolution of an organization at times involves transformative leaps. This can be caused by significant disruptions or "shocks" to the environment, such as game-changing inventions like the semi-conductor or the Internet, or fundamental changes in the regulatory environment, like a new super-regional trade agreement or the deregulation of the banking system. But more commonly, and more importantly to long-term value creation and survival, the ongoing process of evolution involves momentary advantages, insignificant responses, incremental innovations, and minor interactions that meet immediate challenges, but that accumulate and converge to substantively transform the whole entity over time.

Consider how the convergence of a seemingly disparate assortment of trends and forces has affected *where the work of an organization actually gets done*. These trends and forces include the rise of computers and the Internet, the rise of two-income families, new innovations in telecommunications, overcrowded highways, dramatic increases in the cost of fuel, and the gradual shift in job design from hands-on work to knowledge work. More broadly, who does the work, how they get to work, where they work, and the work itself has fundamentally changed over the past thirty years due to this confluence and many other factors as well. Some more *specific* examples, among an *infinite* number of possibilities, of the types of incremental changes within organizations that can have a profound impact over time when they converge with other variables, include (these are actual examples):

- The development and syndication of a new metrics framework at a telecommunications firm for measuring its impact on customers' business, yielding important data used for future product and service innovation.
- A dinner meeting between a development officer of a major university and a congressperson resulting in the formation of a new relationship to bring to the institution large new funding sources three years down the road.
- The use of a new scanning technology at a hospital that, when adopted by all departments, yields better than expected efficiencies, dramatically reduces the cycle-time of the billing process, and substantially improve overall cash flow, enabling the retention of important services.
- The implementation of a new workforce planning process at a global consumer products company that helps forecast a talent shortage in a key engineering role, resulting in new staffing strategies and preventing major product shortages two years in the future.
- A revised strategy at a social policy institute for gaining current and new member email addresses quickly and cheaply, enabling the organization to build lobbying muscle at the national level and influence a significant piece of legislation.

Dharma Log

The **unenlightened** organization believes that self-regulation equals self-sufficiency, and avoids collaborating with or sub-contracting to partners, alliances, or competitors. The **enlightened** organization understands that further specialization in an increasingly complex and turbulent world requires the ability to coordinate and collaborate as well as compete with other organizations concurrently.

Our understanding of evolution has fallen victim to our self-serving tendency to apply the imprinted patterns in our mind of logical, structured, and orderly change. In this way, we have reinforced an overly-simplistic view of cause-and-effect when it comes to the evolutionary process. In the classical view of evolution, a random mutation within an organism enables greater adaptation to the environment, or conversely, a change in the environment triggers a response, or actualizes an already existing but previously non-helpful mutation in an organism, to increase its chances of survival. The "problem" is there is an emerging view that the complexity we see in the natural world could not have evolved in the time-frame that it has from this purely random type of phenomena.

Stated another way, the creativity of self-organizing systems can actually shape the environment in which they exist due to their own internal forces. For those entities that are especially unconscious, it is truly ironic that the environment the organization worries about was put there in the first place by the organization itself. In this scenario, organisms and their environment *co-evolve* as one ecosystem through a continuous, but uneven and perhaps even somewhat chaotic (although science has shown us that within perceived chaos, there are distinct patterns of order) interplay of proactivity and reactivity, competition and cooperation, and spontaneous creation and mutual adaptation.

In the organizational realm, as previously explored by Erich Jantsch, Margaret Wheatley, and others, the concept of co-evolution suggests that the enterprise, as an open, self-organizing system, can create compelling new capabilities, processes, and practices that are not always in response to external challenges or threats, but that actually shape the external environment itself through energy exchange involving external entities and networks the enterprise can influence.

KOAN: WHAT IS CO-EVOLUTION?

Co-evolution is the phenomena by which living organisms and systems affect the evolutionary process of each other. Each open system in a co-evolutionary relationship can exert specific energies on the other with this interplay affecting the evolutionary path of both systems.

Furthermore, scientific evidence suggests that the *unit* of evolution is *not* the organism, but rather the organism *and* its environment. In other words, there is feedback inherently built into the ecology of a system, another supporting factor for the importance of co-evolution. Based on the work of Gregory Bateson, Julian Steward, and other pioneering anthropologists and social scientists, we know that the mind tends to apply linear and logical thinking, using *selective attention*, to construct cause and effect, without enough consideration for total system dynamics. This lack of holistic awareness can negatively affect the process of adaptation and evolution. An unconscious view of the world utilizes a skewed sample of the total phenomena that are in play, and leads to ad-hoc actions that ultimately hurt the ecosystem as a whole.

A more conscious view utilizes a more complete and systemic set of phenomena and leads to more coherent and comprehensive actions that ultimately support effective co-evolution. In industry today, the number of *self-maximizing* organizations actually threatens the overall ecosystem in which they participate. Their self-serving actions create dissonance within the broader system and the possibility of overcorrection by other organizations, such as suppliers or customers, or ecological forces, such as government regulation or religious extremism. In some cases, such an organism or enterprise, with survival as its only focus, an unconscious view of its socio-economic ecosystem, and a tendency toward *selective adaptation* rather than *strategic adaptation*, can end up destroying its own ecosystem and perish itself in the process.

Consider what has happened to the American automobile industry and its network of labor unions, suppliers and distributors. Decades of poor decision making based on short-sightedness, ignorance, and greed has essentially destroyed this once-thriving network of value creation. In a way, the industry became proficient in survival, not value creation, and this "success" has led it to the precipice of its own destruction. In the arena of healthcare, another industry that has struggled with systemic unconscious behavior, there is better news, at least a glimmer.

Recently, over thirty large medical groups and associations across the country collaborated to develop and announce a new code of ethics that will help to distance them from drug-makers and medical device companies to limit their influence on medical guidelines and patient care. This breakthrough was facilitated by one of the oversight councils in the medical field that felt new and more rigorous principles of activity were needed. These organizations are leveraging broad networks to more consciously and effectively co-evolve in turbulent times.

In the traditional view of organizational dynamics, an enterprise either adapted to its environment or adapted the environment to itself. In our new view of the universe, the successful organizations are able to do both in the harmonious activity of co-evolution. Remember, the enterprise that "wins" against its environment will often destroy itself. Therefore, the key to enterprise survival in the long-run lies in greater consciousness regarding these dynamic relationships, an expanded awareness of organizational ecology and ecological systems, and a commitment to mutual success in the broadest sense.

Demonstrating Enterprise Wisdom

Some organizations are simply smarter and wiser than others primarily due to the level of awareness, with the requisite *discernment* and *detachment,* they exert in their co-evolutionary behavior. The most intelligent organizations—termed by some as *emotionally intelligent* organizations (the concept has been richly explored by Daniel Goleman and others)—are not always those with the deepest or broadest base of knowledge or intellectual capital, but rather those that are able to self-regulate in such a way that they can both adapt to environmental challenges and achieve greater complexity on their own. They are able to do this through strategic learning and creative innovation that in turn affects their networks, influences environmental trends, and shapes their reality going forward. These organizations are more tuned into the interrelationships between organizational ideas and actions and their ramifications on other entities and their ecosystem as a whole. They in essence demonstrate enterprise wisdom.

Consciously intelligent—that is *wise*—organizations are both smart and aware, and bring creative insight to their continuously growing knowledge base. They have a clear understanding of their role within their broader socio-economic ecosystem and the critical points of leverage within their key external value networks (those that span across/outside traditional organizational boundaries). These points of leverage include, but are not limited to, pooling physical assets, sharing customer relationships, using communal tools and technologies, partnering to gain easier access to capital, and creating standardized information sharing platforms.

Consider, for example, a large long- and short-haul transportation company with a leading-edge logistics system and many distribution centers within a specific region of the country. As a smart, "hub" enterprise within a broader network of transportation, warehousing, retailing, and production organizations, the company not only dominated the marketplace for transportation but also led it in the creation of value for the broader network, thereby further increasing its own financial health as a hub entity. Specifically, this involved points of leverage such as: educating retailers on its superior logistics system to create an industry standard, selling extra-capacity in its distribution centers to other firms in the network (including both production and transportation firms), and collaborating with other transportation firms to help ensure they transport at full capacity *while also* ensuring that the hub enterprise remains at capacity, but with the *most profitable* customers and routes.

Wise organizations that co-evolve effectively also have a clear and objective understanding of their internal climates, including an awareness of the degree to which their internal and external value propositions resonate with their participants and constituents. These organizations have formal and informal methodologies for collecting and segmenting information quickly and accurately regarding key climate indicators such as levels of participant commitment/engagement, satisfaction, and desire to stay at or leave the enterprise.

Expanding on the example above, consider how the transportation enterprise periodically surveyed and studied the perspectives and engagement levels of its people, especially those in critical roles and key segments. This entailed understanding the nature of the workforce (the sources of talent, their demographics, and their needs and requirements) and the agents of attraction, engagement, satisfaction, and retention for key roles such as long-haul drivers, short-haul drivers, distribution center managers, and logistics professionals.

In addition to being smart about their internal climates, wise organizations make clear strategic choices, deciding in the short-term whether to "win the war" by going head to head with competitors, or to "see the future" by leapfrogging competitors, or to "change the rules" that obsolesces competitors (or, of course, some combination of the three). In each of these scenarios, wise organizations do not wait to react to their environment, nor do they confront their environment in an inflexible manner, nor do they ignore or over-react to the actions of competitors. They are able to flow with and influence the currents of their environments by recognizing their strengths as well as weaknesses and potential blind-spots. They apply broad environmental scans, invest in the understanding and integration of seemingly disparate patterns, themes, and trends, and syndicate this knowledge within the organization so they can construct scenarios, see around corners, and proactively get ahead of any potential "disturbances in the force."

At the same time, wise organizations do not allow their strategic intent to prevent them from quickly taking advantage of "random" or emergent opportunities. Consider, for example, the political action organization that quickly reprioritized its media strategies and effectively revised its media messages once it learned of a major misstep by one of its rival organizations.

SUTRA LESSON ***Information and the Intelligent Organization***[7]

In her brilliant book, *Leadership and the New Science: Discovering Order in a Chaotic World,* Margaret Wheatley with particular eloquence writes about one organization's view of information:

"Instead of the limiting thought that 'information is power,' they began to think of information as 'nourishment.' This shift keeps their attention on the fact that information is essential to everyone, and that those who have more of it will be more intelligent workers than those who are starving."

Consciously intelligent organizations understand that information is the raw material of evolution. An organization's fundamental ability to meet the challenges of its environment and to evolve is based on its ability to capture, share, and process information. Unfortunately, in most organizations information flow is highly regulated with respect to information storage, access, and sharing. Information management systems often serve to restrict or guard information rather than disseminate it. Gatekeepers often hoard information rather than share it. And managers often "protect" their people by limiting information flow rather than letting it go. In a dynamic and turbulent world, the arrogant and subjective filtering of information—a few minds managing information access and flow for the many—is highly irresponsible and dangerous to the health of the enterprise.

Wise organizations are wide open to new information and possess the capabilities to share and utilize information and transform information into knowledge, increasing the overall intelligence of the workforce and the enterprise. Consider the human resources function of a mid-sized university that wanted to get smarter about the nature of its workforce. After the initial step of working with senior administration to become comfortable with making information more accessible to a broader group of staff members, the team developed a continuum of workforce information. This included staff *statistics* that focused on the cost and composition/demographics of the workforce, staff *analytics* that focused on the descriptive characteristics of the workforce, and staff *metrics* that focused on the overall effectiveness and productivity of the workforce, including leading indicators for future effectiveness.

The purpose of this initiative was to bring greater levels of insight in a simple, user-friendly format to broader groups of people regarding the nature of the workforce and the potential investments for the future that would bring the highest return.

SUTRA LESSON ***Enterprise Intelligence and Change***[8]

In *The Art of the Long View*, Peter Schwartz writes about the timeless conditions for openness to change:

"The flood of complexity... encourages cooperation, productivity, efficiency, and organization learning. People work to achieve, not to control; decentralization and diversity are paramount, but do not block the flow of ideas between regions."

Understanding the True Nature of Change

In exploring the dynamics of co-evolution, the old saying that "the only constant is change," is quite true, however clichéd it might be. And yet, many organizations still perceive change in ways that undermine their ability to co-evolve with their environment. Transformation and change are too often thought of and "managed" as discrete, event-driven activity. Because of this misconception, traditional approaches to change management—and even the term itself—suggest that change is a controlled process based on assumptions of structure and stability as the desired state, and that "leaders" and "managers" in organizations can control change through discrete initiatives that involve unfreezing, changing, and re-freezing (using standard terms from the change management lexicon). This is an illusion and the reason why just about every change management effort fails to live up to expectations, producing results that are often obsolete or irrelevant by the time the effort is completed. Unfortunately, despite a rich and unenviable history of sub-optimal results, many organizations still seek competitive advantage through structural stability, controlled execution, and managed change.

Another related reason for the sub-optimization or failure of change initiatives is the belief on the part of change "agents" that the participants in the organization are fundamentally averse to change. What they do not understand is that this assumption is essentially a self-fulfilling prophecy. Almost any type of change initiative that is event-driven, highly controlled, and top-down in nature will cause resistance, but this is not due to a natural resistance to change within the workforce; it is an understandable reaction to how change typically occurs. Whether by design or not, change leaders and agents often act in *unconscious* ways, *thinking* they are "managing" the change. They censor how much information can be shared. They wait until the last minute to communicate what is changing. They oversell the benefits of the change. They minimize the potential negative aspects of the change. And they request feedback on the change, then do not listen to or take any action on the feedback they receive. All of this creates further distrust than already exists.

Unfortunately, these common behaviors—and there are many more to be sure—actually condition the broader population to resist change, rather than embrace it. People know they will be left to pick up the pieces and "make it stick" whatever the "it" might be. Change is not a thing nor can it be controlled. Change is a natural phenomenon that is fundamental to the organization's process of co-evolving with its environment.

DHARMA LOG

The **unenlightened** organization invests too much energy in new and "cool" programs and initiatives that are meant to radically change things and that are often heavily hyped and rolled-out to people with great fanfare. The **enlightened** organization engages its people in a constant process of often small adjustments and insignificant (at the time) enhancements that enable it to interact/flow with, adapt to, and influence its dynamic environment in small steps on a daily basis.

The enlightened enterprise understands that equilibrium is an *unnatural* state of an open system and the pursuit of stability can actually generate negative energy. Instead, the enlightened organization embraces disequilibrium as a primary *catalyst* for creativity that generates a positive, strong, and flowing energy field. Within open, complex systems that are growing and evolving, such as an organization, or a network of organizations, internal and external forces eventually conspire (due to both gradual and abrupt change) to bring the enterprise to a point of inflection in its life cycle, to what is sometimes called a critical state. Then the system can either break *down* into a chaotic state of disordered and dissipating energy, or it can break *through* into a more coherent state of constructive energy, and emerge at a higher level of complexity and performance.

This is the cycle of living systems: the ongoing journey where disequilibrium can spark increasing complexity that then, in turn, increases the speed of evolutionary development and the possibility of new critical states. And the flywheel of evolutionary success gains momentum. In summary, *embracing* chaos can lead to order and harmony, advances in complexity, and the generation of a strong positive energy field. Confronting chaos can lead to disorder and entropy, the break-down of complex structures, and the generation of a weak or negative energy field.

KOAN: WHAT IS COMPLEXITY?

Complexity, in the context of organization effectiveness, reflects the combination of differentiation and integration. Differentiation reflects the degree to which a system is made-up of parts that are specialized in function and different from one another. Integration reflects the degree to which these different parts interact and align to achieve specific and shared goals.

Evolving, intelligent organizations are most successful when they interact with their environment in ways that leverage their differentiation *and* integration, the keys to complexity and therefore innovation. The effective combination of the two represents the complexity of the organization *and the degree to which this complexity aligns with the changing nature of the environment.*

For example, in a public school system, optimal learning involves engaging the whole community's web of public officials, administrators, educators, parents, and children in an integrative way to best leverage the experiences, competencies, and resources of the various parties, while also filtering and utilizing the extensive input from the outside world. Moreover, to achieve efficiency and ensure that requisite educational standards are consistently met, clear segmentation of departments and other services are established and managed by a well-defined administrative structure. In this way, a public school system can successfully co-evolve with its environment, so that its internal complexity—its differentiation as well as its integration—stays in step with its external world.

DHARMA LOG

The **unenlightened** organization focuses on middle management as its primary "conduit" for the flow of information and the implementation of programs and policies, and blames its middle managers when these activities do not go well. The **enlightened** organization de-emphasizes middle management as a role altogether. Instead of taking a linear, hierarchical approach to information transfer, it applies a non-linear, more network-based approach that involves multiple sources and channels within its web of activity. In this way, the notion of leading from the "middle" is replaced with the broader concept of leading from the "periphery," from key nodes within the network, regardless of hierarchy.

Building Scenarios to Influence Reality

The enlightened enterprise understands there is a relationship between order and chaos. It understands that the act of inviting confusion is actually an expression of wisdom, an openness to and comfort with the complexity of the world around it. In the face of constant uncertainty, the intelligent and *aware* (i.e., wise) enterprise achieves a degree of harmony in its co-evolution with its environment. This is often realized through an *increase* in organizational complexity. In this way, the organization generates new energy through thoughts, behaviors, and actions that *balance* seemingly disparate activities: analysis and synthesis, expansion and conservation, competition and collaboration, quality and quantity, self-assertion and unity, and broad scenario building and focused discernment. These activities can create enhanced energy flows when integrated effectively, a sort of constructive interference among their vibrating frequencies, or they can create diminished energy flows when they are not integrated effectively, a sort of destructive interference. In the chaos of our world, consciousness helps us walk an uncertain path in harmony.

In the case of building and discerning scenarios, organizations that co-evolve with their environments are continuously exploring the field of possibility within the natural world of uncertainty, looking to influence the conditions that result in the most favorable environmental flow of events for the enterprise. The more conscious an organization is, the more it will effectively practice the art of discernment, and the more discernment the organization applies as it envisions and influences its preferred future, the more positioned for success it will be.

Over the past few years, more and more organizations have begun to seriously utilize the strategic process of scenario planning, applying it to both the external strategic landscape as well as to their internal operations and workforce. Rather than attempting to control internal and external forces, these organizations are instead gaining a deeper awareness of the potential challenges and opportunities they might face in the future with the goal of either being best prepared for them or influencing their emergence in the first place.

As an example, a specialty insurance unit of a leading financial services company applied scenario building and planning to specific segments of its workforce and learned that it had to fundamentally change some of its assumptions and processes regarding the retention and internal movement of talent if it were to adequately staff its claims organization going forward. Without a robust scenario planning process, this organization would have been largely understaffed in serving its customers, significantly affecting the results of the unit. In another example, more externally focused, an entertainment organization determined that it needed to re-balance some of its investments in several specific business units due to the emergence of new video and film technologies that were changing the nature of filming on-location, where the location could actually be brought to the film crew rather than the film crew having to travel to the location. Without the scenario planning process, this enterprise would have lost ground in the use of technology to reduce film production costs.

DHARMA LOG

The **unenlightened** organization hates uncertainty and expends significant energy in narrowing the field of possibility. The **enlightened** organization embraces uncertainty and expends significant energy in broadening the field of possibility.

Organizations that effectively use scenario building and planning processes typically walk through the following steps:

- Describe the strategic imperatives and key strategic decisions that need to be achieved and made over the next one to three years.
- Capture internal/external trend data, dynamics, and assumptions, and build a flexible model with the ability to adjust it based on shifts in trends and assumptions going forward.

- Identify specific environmental forces that have/will have the greatest potential impact on the organization, in the form of threats, challenges, or opportunities.
- Identify specific strategy execution and value creation drivers, and determine the leading indicators that affect and/or reflect those drivers.
- Build baseline and alternative scenarios using the model, identifying the leading indicators that may represent *turning point* indicators along with their associated probabilities.
- Analyze the various scenarios with detachment, discern the most critical scenarios to pay attention to, and determine what potential actions the organization can take to become ready for a broad field of possibility.
- Begin taking action based on the scenarios, openly syndicating information within the value networks of the organization as important inputs into decision making processes and actual work activities.

Achieving Balance through Harmony

The ongoing process of balancing diverse capabilities and activities, such as scenario building and discernment, enables the organization to be agile, adaptive, and in-synch with its environment. As an example, manufacturing organizations have known for a long time that they would at some point be required to adopt new and more rigorous, environmentally friendly production standards due to climate change and the depletion of non-renewable resources. But only a few of these organizations saw this inevitability as an opportunity to re-invent their external value proposition and value creation strategy by committing to a more harmonious relationship with the external world, "going green" in their operations and with their products, creating demand for this among consumers in a time of changing attitudes, and thus developing new sources of revenue growth. These organizations will enjoy the abundance that comes from harmony in their business model in the future.

KOAN: WHAT IS *HARMONY*?

Harmony reflects a consistent, orderly, congruous, and unified arrangement of elements of a whole. There is typically a pleasing tranquility, beauty, and elegance associated with a harmonious system.

In the absence of the positive energy of harmony, entropy often exists. Entropy is actuated through an *imbalance* or overall *decrease* in an organization's integration and differentiation (that is, complexity)—and an increase in internal disorder and chaos—with respect to the evolving environment. In this scenario, the organization as a whole becomes an energy sink, draining sources of energy through thoughts, behaviors, and actions that reflect conflicting priorities, mismatched capabilities, ad-hoc initiatives, wasteful processes, and misaligned activities, all types of destructive interference. This ongoing imbalance creates a situation where the organization is out-of-synch with its environment and often in a state of reaction or crisis. Some manufacturing organizations, for example, have chosen to confront and fight reality, rather than create and flow with it, and have therefore streamlined operations and cut costs in response to the increasing prices of non-renewable resources rather than investing in new energy sources. In doing so, they have demonstrated a significant disconnect with environmental trends and consumer preferences that reinforce conservation and the rapid move to new, renewable resources.

Moreover, these organizations do not yet understand that their decisions, often made in isolation, can actually destroy more value than they create, from a broader socio-economic perspective. As an illustration, a leading paper products manufacturer recently decided to log thousands of acres of *first generation* trees in a beautiful and pristine region of North America, causing outrage among consumers and other organizations that will affect this enterprise in unforeseen ways in years to come. The paper products company, and other organizations like it, will continue to suffer from entropy as short-term, self-maximizing decisions conflict with longer-term, societal needs.

SUTRA LESSON *Tendencies in Evolution*[9]

In his exceptional book, *The Evolving Self*, Mihaly Csikszentmihalyi explains the differences between entropy and harmony:

"There are two opposite tendencies in evolution: changes that lead toward harmony (the ability to obtain energy through cooperation, and through the utilization of unused or wasted energy); and those that lead toward entropy (or ways of obtaining energy for one's purposes through exploiting other organisms, thereby causing conflict and disorder)."

Organizations respond to environmental dynamics in a variety of ways, including (from *low to high evolutionary effectiveness)*:

- **Ignore, resist and maintain:** These organizations resist the laws of nature and natural selection through either ignorance of what is happening in their environment or a control orientation of just "plowing" through it. They believe that their strategy, organization model, and processes for value creation are effective enough for the "static" world that they perceive.
- **Acknowledge, improve, and stabilize:** These organizations pay attention to macro trends and obvious changes in the landscape, acknowledge their importance, and take a "change management" approach to change. They treat change as a project or initiative with the goal of reaching a new equilibrium, and a more stable state of functioning.
- **Understand, renew, and adapt:** These organizations have a broader understanding of environmental and evolutionary forces and seek, and often achieve, advantages that enable continuous adaptation. Their change processes are more fluid and ongoing with greater tolerance for disequilibrium. They emphasize the importance of process over structure in driving value creation.
- **Embrace, innovate, and transform:** These organizations are in a continuous and fluid process of evolution, where disequilibrium is embraced and understood as critical to the process of co-creation. Transformation is not a process, but rather a state of being, a value and capability that is inherent within the culture of the enterprise and applied to a "networked" view of the world. Innovation is not an activity that is centralized within a department or function but is an expected activity throughout the organization.

DHARMA LOG

The **unenlightened** organization invests too much attention to what competitors are doing and the trends in the competitive landscape. The **enlightened** organization invests more in deeply understanding the nature of its customer or constituent base to enhance its value propositions, develop new and unique internal capabilities, and actually shape, rather than respond to, forces in the external environment.

Exploring the Power of Memes

The enlightened enterprise does not create order through control-oriented policies and practices or through discrete change management programs. Rather, it creates an open environment and culture in which participants can freely communicate, interact, learn, generate ideas, make decisions, and create. This certainly sounds good on paper but also sounds like it is difficult to do. It is not. *So what is involved in building and sustaining a culture with these characteristics?* This journey begins with understanding the fundamental nature of communication in our participatory universe, how cultures evolve within open social systems, and how participants are influenced within an organization.

Consider first how biological organisms are created. The genetic code found in biological living systems is a blueprint for building the organism, and reflects the life-form's evolutionary history since it includes the genetic adaptations that have occurred over time in the species' journey of survival through the millennia. In this sense, genes create organisms.

Consider next how social systems are created. The *memetic code* found in open, social systems such as societies, communities, and organizations, represents the blueprint for building culture, and reflects an entity's evolutionary history since it includes the memetic adaptations and innovations that have occurred over time in the entity's journey of survival and value creation through the years. In this sense, *memes* create cultures.

KOAN: WHAT IS A MEME?

Memes are ideas or clustered patterns of ideas that influence individual, group, and networked thoughts, behaviors, and activities.

As described by Richard Dawkins and other leading pioneers in the arena of the psychology and sociology of memetics, memes reflect one of the most important concepts in organizational dynamics in a very long time. Memes represent the ideas of individuals, groups, and networks and how these ideas are born, come "alive" within the organization, travel across organizational boundaries and morph and adapt in their applications along the way. Memes manifest themselves as spoken ideas, text messages, emails, blogs, symbols, videos, music, white papers, articles, slogans, brand logos, graphic illustrations, and all other artifacts created through human activity. An executive memo outlining a new broad-based incentive compensation program is a meme. The incentive program itself is a meme. The chatter and mistruths the memo generates at water coolers and in on-line chat rooms are memes. The subsequent Q&A document that Human Resources sends out to the workforce to dispel misinformation and improve overall understanding about the program is also a meme. And so on.

Memes evolve as they combine and interact with other memes and are affected by the same laws of natural selection as living organisms: memes that are more effective than others while requiring less energy have a greater chance of survival and transmission more broadly throughout an enterprise. Memes that do a better job are those that best resonate with people with respect to such things as solving a problem, making a decision, stimulating the senses, providing entertainment, and communicating desired information. Memes represent the foundation of cultural evolution within an organization.

Most organizations are probably unaware of the concept of memes and the study of memetics, which continues to gain momentum (as a meme itself!) and is slowly making its way into the public and popular domain. However, organizations *are* aware of the power of ideas and the speed at which information is disseminated in the age of email, instant messaging, texting, and social networking. And most would still acknowledge that they struggle with harnessing these tools and struggle with the issue of communications effectiveness in general when sharing information and shaping perceptions. It seems that no matter how much organizations invest in and focus on communications their people will say they want more.

While hard to define because of its breadth as a concept, communications in the context of organizations represents any planned activity that involves any form of information sharing. With this in mind, communications represents one of the most powerful sources of positive energy within the enterprise and is the foundation for creating the conditions that build consciousness to support value creation. Wise organizations understand very clearly that the organizational tableau is not much different from the rest of the outside world where there is constant competition for the "mindshare" of people.

Whether or not they use the terminology of memes and memetics, enlightened organizations cultivate and imbed important organizational information within the ways that work gets done and through the strategic use of images, messages, and ideas that are consistent with enterprise values. The strategic incubation, dissemination, syndication, and education about values-based memes within the organization are instrumental in building culture and achieving greater consciousness as a self-regulating system.

As an example of a planned and successful organizational meme, consider the experience of a petroleum company that learned through its climate survey that participants in the organization did not feel recognized or appreciated for the work that they did. Rather than implement a typical top-down employee recognition program, the company instead infused a process within the day-to-day work activity that helped people improve the quality of feedback they provided to others and reinforced how people should best acknowledge the work and recognize the contribution of a peer, direct report, or manager. This initiative was instrumental in creating a powerful meme within the enterprise regarding the importance of appreciating what people do in their daily work activities and how they contribute to enterprise success. Other examples of powerful positive organizational memes, among an *infinite* number of potential memes, include:

- The use of a highly creative **process** at an advertising agency that pushes traditional ways of thinking about consumer tastes, wants, and needs.
- The **principles** of building productive relationships used by a labor organization in engaging with the large employers of its membership.
- The playing of the same energizing **song** whenever a basketball sports franchise introduces its players at the beginning of a home game.
- The shared decision making **tool** used by a social service agency to collaborate with patients/clients in making good health-related decisions.
- The **brand logo** and tag-line used by a consumer products company whenever it communicates new wellness initiatives to its workforce.
- The consistent **activity** of reviewing and thoroughly discussing alignment with its core values before a government agency makes key decisions.
- The application of ten key **rules** used by an investment banking firm whenever it conducts due diligence during an acquisition process.

Unfortunately, not all memes are constructive or are in our best interest. Too often societies, communities, *and* organizations allow particular memes to invade our evolving memetic code that do not serve us well in the long run. While organizations should create memes that generate positive energy and reinforce values, harmony, and community, they often unconsciously spread and enhance memes that create negative energy and fuel the forces of entropy. Actual examples of powerful negative, organizational memes, among an *infinite* number of potentially negative memes, include:

- Confusing the concept of accountability with punishment for poor performance at a distribution company, leading to fear and anxiety among the workforce.
- The segmentation of small and large franchisees in reporting operating results at a large franchisor, leading to the feeling of second-class citizenship among smaller, but often very loyal, franchisees.
- The constant perception, based on the ongoing spread of misinformation, that the lead scientists at a research and development facility are underpaid relative to other similar organizations.
- The near-pathological use of email at a telecommunications organization where important, in-depth dialog and working sessions were conducted using email threads as opposed to face-to-face discussions.
- The over-use of a problem solving and project management framework at a petroleum company that slows down cycle time, stifles creativity, under-emphasizes results relative to process, and constrains decision making.
- A memo from the chief executive to the consulting staff of a professional services firm that offered no insight into how to effectively grow the business during a recession and, instead, requested that people simply work harder.
- The process of renewing employment agreements among faculty every year at a university that wasted institutional resources and caused dissatisfaction among both staff and faculty.

Not only does the enlightened enterprise carefully and strategically create and nurture memes within the organization, but it also carefully eliminates memes from its environment that are inconsistent with its value system and true nature and that conflict with its ability to generate positive energy and achieve its mission.

MY SAMADHI *A Personal Experience*

During the 1980s, there were several powerful memes shaping society and the overall business climate. At the same time that foreign companies were beginning to out-compete American firms in a variety of important industries such as auto manufacturing and semiconductors, there was a strong belief that our economy had hit an inflection point in its evolutionary life-cycle from a production economy to a services economy. Certain cultural memes took root in our psyche. One could find an article or a report almost every week on the decline of American competitiveness and the American worker We were also subjected to powerful new ideas, no more clearly shown than in the film, *Wall Street*, that making things was no longer necessary or important, that we had evolved to a new state of buying and selling things instead of creating things, and also that, in fact, "greed is good."

After several years of working with production employees on the shop floors of manufacturing facilities I learned the real truth: not that our work ethic was in decline, but that we had lost our way as investors, innovators, and leaders in ensuring the competitiveness of many of our key industries. Our work ethic had not eroded; our value system had.

During the 1990s, these new memes had evolved to once again dramatically shape our society and business climate. With rise of the Internet and the knowledge-economy, new cultural memes took root in our collective psyche: we learned that we could make billions of dollars without ever turning a profit, we learned that playing pinball and ping-pong at lunch meant one worked in an enlightened environment, and we learned that solid managerial capability no longer mattered; rather, creative chaos was the new reality and our new world was all about portals, search engines, information brokering, and cyber-commerce, despite the fact that little customer or consumer demand had emerged as yet to confirm this.

We were conditioned to think that sitting in cubes was the new way of doing work and that we no longer needed to talk; we could send an email instead. Perhaps no other film captures the negative energy of these memes gone awry than *Office Space*, where people do little real work and are subject to the misguided whims of silly consultants who have no real understanding or even interest in real value creation.

After several more years walking hallways and sitting with people in their cubes, I again learned the real truth: that there was something inherently wrong with the new soul-less business

models and that people still wanted to work hard, contribute, and find meaning in what they did for a living, but were being conditioned to believe that value creation and wealth were simply a matter of fancy websites, timing, marketing, and luck.

During the 2000s, these business memes had further evolved, and once again dramatically shaped our society and business climate. With rise of the real estate bubble, ever more sophisticated financial instruments, and the de-regulation of banks and risk management institutions, new cultural memes took root in our collective psyche: We learned we could make even more money by creating legal (or illegal) schemes that assumed infinite growth and ignored centuries of market wisdom regarding the natural cycles of growth and non-growth.

We moved further away from the ideals of value creation and focused on elaborate strategies for moving money—or simply the *idea* of money—around and believed that somehow the massive amounts of debt incurred would never be called due. Even in the most difficult economic period since the Great Depression, financial institutions have still not awakened to the wisdom of creating value instead of greed. Perhaps the film *Dirty Rotten Scoundrels* best represents the level of unconscious capitalism we have witnessed in this decade. Like many, I resisted the deceits and temptations infiltrating the memetic code of our society, and continued in my third decade of working with people in organizations to simply help make them better.

In these past few years of socio-economic turmoil, I did not learn any new truths per se. Rather, I had to fend-off or *unlearn* the negative patterns of our recent, collective experience, discard many invasive and destructive memes, and return to the timeless fundamentals and values of the enlightened enterprise: a long-term commitment to real value creation through integrity, quality, productivity, adaptability, and sustainability.

Leading with Strategic Sustainability

To paraphrase Albert Einstein, "We cannot solve our problems with the same level of consciousness with which we created them in the first place." His comment may have been given in the context of atomic energy and nuclear war, or some other great issue of his day, but it could not be truer with respect to climate change, the environment, and sustainability. Climate change has been described by some as the classic prisoner's dilemma as well as free rider problem rolled into one. At the core of the problem is the difficulty that comes with trying to fairly assign responsibility and allocate cost within collective activities, and trusting other parties to bear their appropriate share of the burden. And time and time again, history has shown us that one of the primary causes of ecological crisis is the nature of conventional, but wrong or ignorant, ideas about the role of humans and our relationship with and impact on our environment. With this in mind, there is no question that greater consciousness is required to tackle what has become the defining challenge of our age.

SUTRA LESSON *A Perfectly Designed Problem*[10]

In his April 19, 2010 blog in *Slate.com*, as reported by *The Week*, Felix Salmon states the challenge, with great insight and clarity:

"The U.S. government is trying to create incentives for businesses and their investors to plan for climate change. But climate change is a problem that is perfectly designed to make people do nothing: It happens far in the future; its effects will be felt most greatly by other people; and the efforts of any one individual are miniscule. Companies, too, tend to behave in predictably irrational ways. Executive should try to imagine their companies 30 years down the line, struggling with the deleterious effects of climate change on profitability and corporate survival. But they don't. That's the job for the next CEO's successor's successor. Right now there a million other things that seem much more urgent, starting with this quarter's earnings."

The enlightened enterprise understands that it has a shared destiny with its external environment. It understands that within the process of energy exchange and value creation, it must survive the challenges of its socio-economic ecosystem while also protecting, preserving, and even restoring this ecosystem and the broader natural environment. Fortunately, more firms are awakening to this reality. The key aspects of this awakening include a total commitment to the safety of people, an awareness of the vulnerability to climate change, a recognition of the wisdom of energy security, an emerging belief in sustainability as a catalyst for innovation, the realization of the risk to reputation and brand of the status quo, and a maturing sense of global responsibility.

The enlightened enterprise understands that value creation at the expense of the environment is short-lived, placing at risk its ability to perform and survive in the future. In this light, an organization actually increases its value creation by simply stopping certain practices, reducing its resource consumption and environmental pollution. But organizations need to go well beyond this initial step. To reinforce a greater awareness of the importance of sustaining the environment, an organization can reframe and broaden its definition of capital—which refers to all of the inputs used by the organization—to include financial capital, human capital, *and natural capital*, the natural resources it uses and touches in its operations. This awareness can accelerate the inclusion of sustainability as *inherent within the strategic intent* of the enterprise, along with the development of new imperatives and initiatives for achieving sustainable value creation going forward. Sustainability is not a program nor is it a responsibility. It is pure strategy for ensuring long-term survival and success. It is the conscious path we all must walk. And more organizations are moving from awareness to strategic action in this respect.

Consider, for example, the automobile production facility that has recently installed a solar power plant on the roof of the plant. This power station is able to produce sufficient energy for all the operations of the facility. In another example, a state-of-the-art office complex that is powered by solar energy is able sell surplus energy back to the main power grid. In a third example, a technology park currently under construction aims to power up to fifty office buildings by using only their own renewable sources of energy, including solar, wind, and hydropower.

With these examples in mind, we still have much work to do, and must leverage the power of community to influence those organizations that are not wise, that have not yet awakened to the reality of our shared environmental destiny. One of the largest corporations in the world, for example, is still resisting the move to more renewable sources of energy. While this highly profitable behemoth could be a global leader in shaping the future of clean energy on our planet, it has chosen to quietly and powerfully fight the proven truths of climate change and evade and prolong the inevitable move away from oil and non-renewable energy.

The good news is that a few prominent shareholders have awakened; there is a greater consciousness emerging among its constituents that this enterprise cannot ignore. People are pushing the giant company to invest more in renewable energy, to study the impact of its decisions and actions on the release of carbon emissions, and to assess the degree to which its *own resistance* to pursuing clean energy strategies and protecting the environment actually *threatens* the long-term success of the company itself, its shareholders, and their communities. This much-needed transformation will bring greater short-term financial success as well, as a recent study found that investors are already discounting the share prices of corporations that are not well positioned to succeed in a world of warming temperatures, shifting weather patterns, and new regulatory requirements.

KOAN: WHAT IS *SUSTAINABILITY*?

Sustainability reflects specific conditions of organizational activity where nature's resources are used at a rate at which they can be replenished naturally. A process is sustainable if it can be carried out consistently without negatively affecting the natural environment.

Enlightened organizations strongly believe in sustainability and rigorously practice it. A common view of sustainability reflects how to bring a higher quality of life (economic) to people (societal) without destroying living systems (environmental). In essence, practicing sustainability involves the creation of value for our world without destroying life, and the ecology of life, in the process. The enlightened enterprise is therefore committed to reducing and, ultimately, eliminating the extraction of natural resources, the buildup of toxic substances, and other practices that contribute to the general decline of nature. Organizations that truly believe in and practice sustainability will continue to demonstrate the following practices as integral to their strategic intent and organization model, *in addition to the baseline requirement of a safe workplace for all participants:*

- **Protecting and preserving biodiversity, the quantity and variety of plants and animals found in natural habitats.** This practice involves the preservation of the natural ecosystem, in its natural state, wherever the organization has operations. This practice is consistent with the philosophy of "leave no trace" wherever the enterprise has operations or is involved in significant activity.
- **Making sustainable use of renewable natural resources without affecting the natural ecosystem.** This practice involves the acquisition, use, and renewal of natural resources, such as timber or water, in a way that does not disrupt or alter in any way the natural state of the

ecosystem. When renewable resources are used, the organization is committed to either replacing/renewing the resource or off-setting its use in a way that is beneficial to the ecosystem.

- **Conserving non-renewable natural resources by reducing dependence through new productive practices, technologies, and energy sources.** This practice involves substantially increasing the productivity of natural resources through new, highly efficient, processes and technologies. This includes aggressive and ongoing action to conserve and continuously reduce the use of non-renewable resources such as oil and gas. It also involves the use of carbon-offsets and carbon capture and storage technologies that can dramatically reduce the amount of carbon dioxide that is pumped into the atmosphere, warming our climate.
- **Reducing and eliminating harmful waste, disposing of it through safe and responsible means.** This practice involves the reduction and treatment of waste in such a way that it does not disrupt or alter in any way the natural state of the ecosystem. This practice suggests that the organization is committed to the continuous reduction of waste from its operations with the ultimate goal of total elimination through the use of new resources that do not generate waste, the use of new processes and technologies that dramatically reduce waste, and/or the recycling of waste which is then used as a resource for other operations. As a start, some organizations are taking a close look at how some biological systems use natural resources without generating toxins or harmful waste in the process.
- **Restoring damaged habitats and ecosystems that have been affected by their operations.** This practice involves the active clean-up and restoration of the natural ecosystem that has been disrupted or altered by the operations of the enterprise in the past, with the goal of ensuring a healthy ecosystem that will survive into the future. This requires an enterprise strategy for investing in the natural capital of its ecosystem to ensure that future resource needs are met.
- **Working closely with other organizations they are linked to within their value networks to commit to similar sustainability practices.** This practice involves influencing and collaborating with other organizations to commit to the same rigorous principles of sustainability and meet the same standards of prevention, conservation, and restoration of natural resources. This typically involves the organization working with network partners to adopt a network

sustainability strategy that goes beyond individual organizational needs. In an exciting example, a global energy company with a history of poor environmental practices recently implemented a competition among its many suppliers to determine the organizations with the most effective sustainability strategies. It monitors, measures, and scores the environmental performance of these suppliers and awards contracts more often to the highest scoring firms.

SUTRA LESSON ***The Core Capabilities of Sustainability***[11]

In their timely book, *The Necessary Revolution: How Individuals and Organizations are Working Together to Create a Sustainable World*, Peter Senge and his co-authors write about crossing boundaries and thinking differently to achieve sustainability:

"These three capabilities—seeing systems, collaborating across boundaries, and creating desired futures—must continually develop in institutions as well as individuals, for, ... institutions, and the networks they create, shape how our present world operates and hold the greatest promise for systemic change."

Developing the Co-evolution Framework

Our civilization is an ecosystem of sustainable communities comprised of living organisms. Similarly, an organization and its networks is an ecosystem of sustainable communities comprised of its participants. The basic principles of ecology are therefore relevant to the enterprise and its environment. These principles include the interdependence of activities, the cyclical flows of resources, the fluctuating dynamics of competition and cooperation, and the entropy-fighting forces of flexibility, diversity, and adaptability. The enterprise itself is an ecosystem, where the same principles can be applied on a smaller scale. From an ecological perspective, a diverse organization is resilient because it contains communities comprised of individuals, groups, and networks that have overlapping capabilities and functions. In a diverse organization, information and ideas flow freely and openly, and the diversity of interpretations and learning styles enrich the entire community. This enables it to see a broader field of possibility and to adapt more easily to changing and challenging environmental conditions.

In the brilliant film, *A Beautiful Mind,* the main character is a genius mathematician who is constantly observing and studying the "governing dynamics" of socio-economic "systems" ranging from a flock of pigeons gathering food to the interactions of men and women at the local university tavern. In the end he is able to prove mathematically his all-consuming belief: that there are underlying dynamics within goal-based systems that favor some element of collaborative behavior over pure competition in achieving the best possible outcomes for the system.

Within natural ecosystems, the history of the evolution of organisms has also shown that it is cooperation, *and not competition*, between species that has been the most important to enduring success and survival. Similarly, in the domain of organizational dynamics, game theory, and social system evolution, strategies that begin with cooperation outperform in the long-run strategies that begin with competition. In this sense, the concept of "survival of the fittest" is often misunderstood; within the context of co-evolution, the fittest organizations are those that consciously flow with their environments and co-evolve intelligently with collaborators and competitors alike.

As an extension of its values and value creation strategy, the enterprise that understands the importance of co-evolution with its environment should consider using a co-evolution framework to develop a strategy that guides and monitors its evolutionary behaviors and actions. The framework suggests a specific set of strategic activities and capabilities that help enable the enterprise to evolve in harmony with the forces, trends, dynamics, and participants of its external world. The co-evolution framework has the following three elements: enterprise activities, ecosystem activities, and environmental activities:

- **Enterprise activities:** This first element of the framework reflects the key activities involved in ensuring that the organization has the *internal* ability and agility to effectively co-evolve with its socio-economic ecosystem and its broader environment. It is organized into three sub-elements, or key *capabilities:* enterprise intelligence, environmental analysis and scenario planning, and strategic learning. *Enterprise intelligence* represents the activities involved in capturing, understanding, and sharing information from inside the organization regarding the state of its internal climate (e.g., participant engagement levels), organizational capabilities (e.g., the quality of creativity and innovation), and culture-forming conditions (e.g., the degree of diversity) that enable the organization to adapt and transform both proactively and reactively on a continuous basis. *Environmental analysis and scenario planning* represents the activities involved in capturing information, building future scenarios, and prioritizing potential enterprise actions to negate, de-risk, respond to, or influence the external dynamics of the organization's ecosystem and broader environment. For example, a medical device company that primarily makes pacemakers would develop several scenarios regarding the potential growth of the pacemaker markets by taking into account health trends, technology trends, economic trends, healthcare trends, and activities of potential competitors. *Strategic learning* represents the activities involved in filtering, segmenting, and utilizing information from internal and external sources to inform, modify, and/or enhance the organization's evolving strategic intent and value creation strategy.

- **Ecosystem activities:** This second element of the framework reflects the key activities involved in ensuring the organization has the *internal/external* ability and agility to effectively interact with and influence its external web of activity, its socio-economic ecosystem. It is organized into three sub-elements, or key *capabilities:* ecosystem intelligence, network participation and leadership, and strategic alignment. *Ecosystem intelligence* represents the activities involved in capturing, analyzing, and sharing information from outside the organization regarding the state of the social, economic, and political climate, the state of the performance of its networks and other organizations with which it interacts, and the overall conditions that affect ecosystem health. *Network participation and leadership* represents the activities involved in the organization's participation in its external networks and the degree to which it is effectively performing its role within each key network, relative to the desired function of its consciously defined roles. For example, a non-profit environmental research enterprise would want to monitor its thought leadership and influence in specific areas, such as deforestation, that are required by its sources of funding. Moreover, this organization would periodically evaluate the degree to which it is partnering effectively with other entities to maximize the impact of the *overall system* in protecting woodlands and forests. *Strategic alignment* represents the activities involved in monitoring, assessing, and improving the overall alignment of the organization's evolving value creation strategy with the evolving external ecosystem and environment.

- **Environmental activities:** This third element of the framework reflects the key activities involved in ensuring the organization has the *internal/external* ability and agility to effectively understand, interact with, and influence its broader (global) environment. It is organized into three sub-elements, or key *capabilities:* environmental intelligence, environmental leadership, and strategic sustainability. *Environmental intelligence* represents the activities involved in capturing, analyzing, and sharing information from outside the organization regarding the state of its broader environment and its social, economic, demographic, and geopolitical trends, threats, and opportunities. *Environmental leadership* represents the activities involved in supporting the health and well-being of the broader communities, and their natural environments, in which the organization participates, especially those communities and regions that represent current and potential talent pools and sources of other resources for the enterprise. As an example, a petroleum refinery would actively play a leadership role in ensuring the well-being of its workforce, the surrounding community, and the natural environment by aggressively implementing new technologies to conserve resources, eliminating all forms of harmful waste, proactively keeping the natural ecosystem pollution-free, and engaging with other organizations to follow its lead. *Strategic sustainability* represents the activities involved in developing, executing, and supporting effective environmental sustainability strategies, including influencing the sustainability practices of external network partners and participants, as well as shaping governmental regulatory policies.

With these elements serving as the basic framework, the organization would develop an ongoing process for reviewing, assessing, prioritizing, and improving each element, and the overall integration of the elements as a whole, to ensure a conscious, collaborative evolutionary relationship with the external world.

In an inspiring example, consider the emerging storyline that is being developed at one of the nation's most prominent and powerful regional public agencies. This organization is investing substantial resources in the integration of its elevating value creation mission, strategic capabilities, belief in sustainability, and co-evolutionary activity. One possible storyline goes like this:

- As a public agency, we must transcend complacency and continuously evolve. As a regulated entity we must demonstrate the highest standards of our own accord. As a good performing enterprise we have the choice to become great. As a relatively young organization we have the opportunity to further create our legacy. As a steward of precious natural resources we have the responsibility to help shape an uncertain future.

- To realize this vision, we will pursue world-class science, engineering, and project management. We will continuously improve our organizational processes and workforce capabilities. We will be action-oriented, opportunity-driven, and focused in our strategy execution. We will demonstrate a strong commitment to environmental sustainability. And we will lead with highly ethical and collaborative governance.

The enlightened organization understands that the only stability in a chaotic universe is its own sense of self, its true nature as defined by the clarity and continuity of its purpose, value system, culture, and value creation orientation. The enlightened organization is aware of the need to co-evolve with its environment. It understands that a living system is better suited to survive and thrive in its environment if it appreciates the healthy, natural state of disequilibrium, and empowers its participants to break-down old patterns and co-create new ones. It facilitates learning and discovery from within, creates the conditions for new interactions and relationships, rigorously practices sustainability, and develops new and diverse capacities and capabilities to evolve successfully over the long-term.

THE TAO: Walking a New Path

In getting started on the path toward a more intelligent and successful co-evolution with the organization's environment, consider the following diagnostic questions:

- ***What are the organization's beliefs regarding its relationship with the external environment?*** Consider how the organization interacts with and attempts to influence its external environment today. Consider how these actions reflect an implicit or explicit belief system. Consider whether networks and the broader socio-economic ecosystem are explicit factors in strategic and operational planning.
- ***To what extent does the organization co-evolve with its environment as opposed to controlling its environment?*** Consider the organization's interactions with the external environment and the extent

to which they are integrating with and shaping the external forces and trends versus attempting to exert influence and control over them. Consider the degree to which the enterprise views itself as separate from its environment versus the various roles it plays in the networks and communities that make-up its ecosystem.

- ***Does the organization embrace and thrive on uncertainty and constant change?*** Consider how the organization discusses, prepares for, and reacts to uncertainty. Consider whether the organization works to actively narrow or widen its field of possibility. Consider how the organization plans for the unknown and the degree to which it attempts to flow with, adapt to, and influence, rather than control, environmental dynamics.

- ***How effective is the organization in capturing and transforming information into intelligence that supports the process of co-evolution?*** Consider how much the organization invests in learning from its environment. Consider how broadly information-related activities are distributed throughout the organization. Consider how open the organization is to sharing and syndicating—as well as interpreting—environmental information. How effective is the organization in creating knowledge from this information, and then applying that knowledge to best co-evolve with its environment.

- ***Does the organization truly believe in, and consistently demonstrate, sustainability in its activities?*** Consider what conventional, and potentially misguided, ideas are still embraced by the organization regarding the relationship between the enterprise and its environment. Consider how the concept of natural capital is applied in the organization's resource planning processes. Consider what actions the organization takes to protect, preserve, and/or restore the natural ecosystem(s) in which it operates. Consider how concepts such as preservation, conservation, waste reduction, and overall sustainability are woven into the values and culture of the enterprise.

FIVE

The Qualities of Productive Activity

Imagine that you are attending a recognition banquet hosted by your chief executive and her leadership team. There are hundreds of people in the cavernous hall—nearly the entire organization—to celebrate the success of the enterprise and acknowledge key achievements of high-performing individuals and groups. So far, enterprise leaders are doing a nice job of recognizing a broad and diverse group of people for their contributions, and you appreciate the way they talk about how different roles with diverse responsibilities affect the value creation of the organization. By the end of the ceremony, almost everyone in attendance has been acknowledged in one way or another, either individually or in a group. Then, in her closing remarks, the CEO makes an interesting comment: "My team and I have spent a fair amount of time trying to determine why productivity has increased so much this year." She goes on to say that after much consideration, she and her team believe that the collective effort of everyone in the room to invest more time and energy in how they engage and interact with each other has truly paid off. She closes with a request: "So now I would like everyone to stand up and acknowledge each other for this achievement. This should be easy since it is clearly something we already do on a daily basis." **This is satori.**

In this chapter we will explore important concepts regarding the properties of and conditions for highly productive activity, as summarized by the following principles:

- **Organizations that are more productive can create more value and have a better chance of success and survival over the long-term.**
- **The meaningfulness of work and the quality of the work experience are the most important determinants of productivity.**
- **The more engaged people are in the value creation process the more productive they are.**
- **The enlightened enterprise creates a culture of learning where all of its participants are both teachers and students.**

Each participant in an enterprise plays a unique role in the process of evolution and drive to generate and exchange energy and create value. When people do work as participants in the organization, they think, behave, act, and interact, thereby creating powerful energy fields. Each participant creates a local energy field that influences and interacts with the energy fields of groups, networks, and the enterprise as a whole. The overall quality of productive activity in doing work is therefore a powerful source of energy and a key determinant of the overall success of the enterprise.

Koan: What is *Productivity*?

Productivity reflects how well a system uses its resources—its financial, technological, human, and natural capital—to accomplish its goals, achieve desired results, and create value.

Defining the Nature of Work

Work is defined as coordinated and integrated activity that is carried out to perform the functions of the enterprise. At its most elementary level, the work in an organization involves applied energy frequencies, patterns, and flows. There are fundamental kinds of work activities that are performed by people in their roles, including analyzing, interpreting, communicating, operating, processing, observing, assessing, solving, creating, designing, facilitating, synthesizing, and deciding. Almost every role in an organization can be defined by using some combination of these categories of activity. The common themes that flow through these activities include information processing, problem solving, critical thinking, discerning, and decision-making, all of which are energy-transmitting, cognitive thought-functions.

Whether work is routine or non-routine, process-focused or knowledge-focused, manual or computer-controlled, creation-oriented or execution-oriented, the fundamental conditions for a highly productive workplace are timeless and absolute: dignity, meaning, involvement, freedom, capability, and accountability. As we have learned, successful organizations co-evolve with their environments rather than attempt to control their environments. Similarly, successful organizations do not attempt to control their internal environments either. Contrary to the traditional approaches of controlling the internal environment through hierarchy, policies, supervision, inflexible job design, and other constraining forces, the enlightened organization understands that the more people are meaningfully involved in a system, and the more they have freedom to act and make decisions within that system, there is actually *more* control in the system, *not less*. This is a defining principle of productive activity that is carried out in a self-regulating and open system.

SUTRA LESSON ***The Importance of Productivity***[12]

In his trailblazing book, *Maximizing Employee Productivity: A Manager's Guide*, Robert Sibson writes about the importance of productivity to the future of our society:

"Increasing employee productivity is the single most important economic issue in the United States. If we do not improve productivity a lot more in the next decade than we have in the recent past, ours will likely be a second-rate economic nation by the twenty-first century."

Exploring the Case for Productivity

It is an empirical macroeconomic fact that productivity is the primary differentiating factor *in the long-term* that determines the wealth of nations, societies, *and organizations*. Drawing from the work and research of Robert Pritchard, Robert Sibson, and others, we know that if the productivity of an enterprise is higher than its competitors over a sustained period of time, the organization has a much better chance of survival due to greater competitiveness and value creation. Very simply, productivity is the single most important factor in a firm's long-term survival, growth and profitability (in the realm of the social sector, profitability can be thought of as financial health). And in the global economy where knowledge and specialization are increasingly important, and labor cost/investment often exceeds capital cost/investment, the productivity of people is the most important ingredient. With this in mind it is beyond shocking how little attention is paid to true workforce productivity, especially in knowledge work environments such as financial institutions, research and development organizations, professional services firms, and centers for social policy development and implementation, just to name a few.

In examining the current state of productivity within an organization, a good place to start is by exploring the following line of questioning:

- How does the enterprise define productivity today? How does it measure productivity?
- What are the organization's beliefs, assumptions, hypotheses and facts regarding its current productivity levels?
- How competitive is the productivity of the organization with respect to its competitors? To what extent does this matter?
- To what extent does the enterprise understand what drives productivity improvement today and what will drive it in the future?
- To what degree are investments in the workforce linked to productivity improvement, either implicitly or explicitly?
- What is the business case for increasing the focus on productivity as a critical driver of value creation?
- How does the view of productivity change as the enterprise moves beyond a process, routine-work orientation to a network, knowledge-work orientation?

Defining Productivity

Productivity is a measure of how well an organization transforms inputs into outputs. From a value creation perspective, productivity must involve both the efficiency of work processes and networks, and their overall effectiveness in generating energy and creating something of real value. Productivity is not the simple sum of the productivity of individuals or groups; it entails the nature of the whole system and the interdependence and integration of information, processes, networks, technologies, people, and other resources. Productivity is not just determined by, or limited by, the organization's environment, strategy, or technology. The behavior of people, and how they interact in groups and networks, how they exchange information, and how they make decisions has a profound effect on productivity as well.

The most common theme in the vast amount of research on work and productivity is that meaningful work is the key, and yet very few organizations proactively focus on the nature of work activity and the meaningfulness of the work performed. Organizations are constantly re-organizing, restructuring, and reengineering their forms and structure, breaking down these forms into segments and separate parts, and rebuilding them to create new forms that are then broken down again. Similarly, organizations invest a great amount of energy in analyzing and redesigning business processes to eliminate non value-added activity, reduce variances, increase efficiencies, improve quality, and speed-up cycle time. *So why do organizations still experience levels of productivity that are much lower than what is possible?*

DHARMA LOG

The **unenlightened** organization often becomes obsessed with constant restructuring and reorganization that causes huge amounts of disruption, dissatisfaction, and discord. The **enlightened** organization is committed to creating and preserving the conditions that build organizational agility, flexibility, and productivity.

The problem is that too often the energy invested in restructuring and redesign activities intended to improve efficiency and effectiveness do not result in improving the fundamental nature and meaningfulness of work performed by people. For instance, customer service centers continually invest significant resources in utilizing new technologies and designing new processes to improve efficiencies, but rarely redesign the fundamental qualities of work done by service center representatives. Because of this, a large percentage of these organizations suffer from extreme levels of fatigue, burn-out, and turnover, negatively affecting service quality and customer satisfaction.

In another example, hospitals invest a lot of time and effort into attracting and retaining nurses, given the current shortage of nursing talent, and some institutions have redesigned work processes or restructured departments to be able to provide the minimal care necessary with fewer nurses. Yet, without changing the nature of the actual work performed by the nursing role, these initiatives fall short and will continue to do so in the future. Nursing is, of course, inherently meaningful work, but there remain opportunities to design the work activity to be less tedious and routine, and more fulfilling from the perspective of the participants.

SUTRA LESSON *Creating Productive Workplaces*[13]

In *Productive Workplaces Revisited: Dignity, Meaning, and Community*, Marvin Weisbord writes about the timeless conditions of productivity:

"We hunger for community in the workplace and are a great deal more productive when we find it. To feed this hunger in ways that preserve ... individual dignity, opportunity for all, and mutual support is to harness energy and productivity beyond imagining."

Understanding the Determinants of Productivity

The overall productivity of an organization is determined by the quality of productive activity that is carried out "inside" the organization and "outside" of the organization in its energy exchange with its environment. Based on significant research over the past few years by a number of organizations the most *engaged* participants tend to be the most productive. Not surprising, there are as many definitions of engagement as there are consulting firms who do work in this area. Simply put, engaged participants understand how the work they perform in their role contributes to the value creation process of the enterprise. They are typically committed to doing this work at high levels of performance. They know what to do when they are at work and typically have the elbow-room to do their work without much supervision. And they have the skills, tools, and other resources to complete their work activity and meet the high standards they set for themselves.

But there is an even more fundamental and important antecedent to productivity than engagement, and that is *presence*. Presence reflects the degree to which individuals, groups, and perhaps to a lesser extent, networks, are present in the moment as they interact and carry out work. Presence reflects an alert stillness as well as intensity in the "now" that enables participants to be highly focused and efficient, but also open and receptive, in their thoughts and actions. The degree of workforce engagement within an enterprise is therefore dependent on the degree of workforce presence, where participants are not overly encumbered by past challenges, current concerns and distractions, or future uncertainties. They are able to perform their work with extreme clarity, are much more open and able to respond to information, and are in-synch with the natural flow of events and situations inside and outside the enterprise. They are, in a way, more *conscious*.

There is an old saying in change "management" circles (perhaps change "guidance" is a better term?) that you need to "tell people, then tell them again, then tell them again" in order for them to "get it." And often this is true. *Why is this?* It is not because people are *unintelligent*; it is because they are often not *present*. They are not in the now; rather, their minds are somewhere else, either in the past or the future. In exploring the degree to which the workforce of an organization, including formal leadership, demonstrates presence, consider the following questions:

- To what extent do interactions, discussions, and meetings focus on and mobilize around present issues and challenges, and avoid spending too much time on past problems or future possibilities?
- To what extent are formal enterprise communications shared, received, understood, and acted on (i.e., information processed) in a highly efficient manner by participants, without the need for constant repetition of message?
- To what extent do enterprise participants consistently demonstrate active listening, alertness, patience (within reason), and empathy in most interactions (even when there are significant distractions)?
- To what extent are enterprise participants able to flow with unforeseen change and uncertainty, demonstrating a graceful agility in re-prioritizing key activities as needed and in real-time?
- To what extent do participants in meetings, working sessions, and other group settings utilize simple activities to help clear the mind and increase focus and presence, such as meditation, visioning, and breathing exercises?

When enterprise participants are present and engaged, they are significantly more productive, in large part due to their ability to communicate, learn, and adapt efficiently. Productivity is highly dependent on how people capture, receive, and process information, and how they transform their resulting thoughts and feelings into productive behaviors and actions. The enlightened enterprise establishes many of the conditions that support this translation, foster productive activity, and build productive workplaces.

Building further on these important concepts, the full continuum of qualities and conditions of a highly productive organization include:

- The understanding that the world is too dynamic, and that the organization itself is too complex, to tackle problems through hierarchical and expert-driven models, but rather through the creative energy of "open-system" interactions and community.
- The understanding that with the birth of the Internet, the world is so full of misinformation and false propaganda that the organization cannot control the quality of information that crosses its borders using a top-down model. Rather, the enterprise must equip and skill-up its people in how to best discern and apply discretion in the productive use of information.
- The development of broad-based business literacy, including the sharing of information regarding the external environment, enterprise strategies for value creation, the key drivers of value creation, the key drivers of financial health of the enterprise, and the performance of the organization relative to key goals and metrics.
- The inherent belief that people "deep" in the organization have a greater understanding of the challenges and solutions in increasing value creation. In our highly participative, networked model of the world, these are the people that are closer to the outer perimeters of value creating activity.
- An openness to and respect for the diverse interpretations of, and reactions to, information that is broadly shared throughout the enterprise (and a tolerance for allowing these reactions to be "organically" weeded out within enterprise groups and networks).
- An openness to and patience for curiosity, risk-taking, and experimental activity, along with making it safe for participants to evaluate and change limiting constraints into opportunities.
- The inherent belief that people are more likely to change their own behavior when they participate in the problem analysis and solution development regarding workplace challenges, and the understanding that they are more likely to carry out decisions that they have helped to make.
- The constant involvement of groups, networks, and the system as a whole in analyzing environmental threats and challenges and shaping

and creating potential strategies and processes for new ways to create value.

- The pursuit of fully integrating the activities of people (the social networks and systems) with the proven tools, technologies, and techniques (the technical system) used in doing the work of the organization to optimize the efficiency and effectiveness of key initiatives, processes, and networks.
- The constant, targeted development and application of new capabilities, competencies, and capacities (directly linked to enterprise strategic and operating capabilities) through on-the-job experiences and continuous learning opportunities.

DHARMA LOG

The **unenlightened** organization invests too much in leadership development and succession planning (based on hierarchy) and too little in workforce development and talent planning for the organization as a whole. The **enlightened** organization invests more in critical workforce planning, workforce development, and talent acquisition activities to ensure throughout the organization that the right people are in the right place with the right skills at the right time and at the right cost.

Enabling Optimal Work Experience

Productivity is driven by the degree of presence and engagement of the workforce, the technologies and resources at its disposal, and the quality of the work processes and practices it employs in performing work activities. The fundamental building blocks of work processes and practices are the work tasks, activities, and interactions that are performed at the individual level, within teams and groups, and across networks. The enlightened organization understands that the quality of the work experience, and the extent to which it helps cultivate self-fulfillment and self-respect, is critical to productivity growth at the individual level. Based on a significant amount of research over the past few decades from a wide variety of sources, including Eric Trist, Chris Argyris, David Hanna, and others, the qualities of optimal work experience are clear, timeless, and universal. They are summarized in the following statements:

- People are more satisfied and productive when they have clear goals and well-defined core responsibilities for doing work, interacting with others, and contributing to the overall organization.
- People are more satisfied and productive when their work involves clear linkages between personal goals, responsibilities, and enterprise value drivers, connecting the dots between what individuals and groups do and the success of the organization.
- People are more satisfied and productive when there is immediate and continuous feedback from the work itself as well as from peers, involving the formal and informal giving and receiving of feedback in their regular day-to-day activities.
- People are more satisfied and productive when their work involves some degree of variety, challenge, and wholeness of tasks and activities that provide desired levels of stimulation (this is true for both more routine and less routine work activities).
- People are more satisfied and productive when they have flexibility, autonomy, and freedom in carrying out activities and making decisions, within broad, but well-defined and clear boundaries.
- People are more satisfied and productive when there is continuous opportunity to learn and build capability on-and off-the-job that is fulfilling to the individual and directly linked to group, process, and network value creation activities.
- People are more satisfied and productive when their work activity is challenging, requiring them to apply and stretch their skills and abilities to complete the work, stimulating learning and growth in the achievement of work goals.
- People are more satisfied and productive when they have access to needed information, tools, resources, and technologies that enable them to do work efficiently and effectively.
- People are more satisfied and productive when they have opportunities to interact and build relationships within groups and networks that have shared goals and common interests.
- People are more satisfied and productive when there is support of and respect for diversity of thoughts and actions that allow for a broad range of ideas that, in turn, foster creativity and innovation.
- People are more satisfied and productive when they have the opportunity to (re)design work processes, make decisions about how work

gets done, evaluate the quality of work that is completed, and take action to correct and improve sub-standard work products and deliverables.

- People are more satisfied and productive when they have some degree of discretion over standard operating procedures and other work processes and protocols, enabling them to effectively deal with unforeseen organizational needs or situations when appropriate.
- People are more satisfied and productive when they do work that results in a product or service that is directly delivered to the customer, and/or when they collaborate directly with external participants/customers that benefit from the value delivered by the enterprise.
- People are more satisfied and productive when there are rewards that are clearly linked to their contribution to the success of the enterprise based on individual and/or group performance (rewards in this context includes both non-financial recognition and financial rewards, such as incentive compensation and bonus awards).

Improving the quality of work and work experiences within an organization may feel very challenging and even daunting. With this in mind, it may be helpful to think about the goal of enabling optimal work experience as not having a destination or an end-point; rather, it is a path walked with small steps that when strung together can travel a great distance. Instead of undertaking an overwhelming job redesign initiative (which is almost always destined to get buried under its own weight), an organization can reduce the amount of oversight and supervision that is built into the work system, re-assign people in supervisory roles to other roles, and begin to communicate the need for more real-time decision making among the broader workforce.

Instead of developing complicated and sophisticated processes and tools for exchanging performance feedback (which still places the emphasis on the wrong thing: the whiz-bang tool and not the actual conversations), the organization can conduct training that helps develop the fundamental skills among its participants for seeking, giving, and receiving feedback. And instead of developing and implementing a new diversity program (which, however well-intended, rarely makes a difference because it's a program), the organization can begin to publicly celebrate and privately reward those individuals and groups that embrace diversity, demonstrate an openness and willingness to explore a broader field of possibility in their creative process, and utilize diverse talent, methods, and ideas to get work done. There are many other pragmatic and common-sense "building blocks" that can be used to create meaningful work experiences and increase the quality of productive activity. The key is for each organization to walk its own path, one step at a time, setting down one block at a time.

Within every enterprise, participants play two roles: their functional role and their psychic role. In highly unconscious organizations, the psychic role of individuals often overshadows the functional role. The psychic role is an ego-based, self-defined role that represents the perceived importance of an individual, based on his supposed status, level, and authority (and also personality type, with respect to ego-driven control orientation). Too often, the work behaviors and activities of people are influenced by this form of self-imposed, and organizationally permitted, negative energy sink. The more conscious organization actively reduces the emphasis on psychic roles and increases the emphasis on functional roles, which focus on constructive work activities, responsibilities, and accountabilities.

More specifically, in creating the conditions we just explored for enabling optimal work experiences, organizations build a culture and internal environment where overly strong psychic roles have no real true power; they are not permitted and can gain very little traction within the webs of work activity. In a fascinating example, consider the highly successful family-owned packaging company where two sets of cousins (the third generation owners) diverged in their approach to influencing enterprise activity. One set of cousins, a brother and sister, primarily played their *psychic role* as family members and owners, and were consistently less effective in guiding the enterprise. The other set of cousins, also a brother and sister, primarily played their *functional role* as executives with specific expertise and as solid business people, and were consistently more effective in guiding the enterprise.

One way to facilitate more fulfilling and effective work experiences is to eliminate traditional job and role definitions and to develop new role descriptions that focus on the things that really matter when it comes to getting work done and creating value. Below is a general architecture for developing a more meaningful definition for a role—a cluster of jobs that have a similar scope of responsibility and do similar work activities—such as an experienced engineering role, a human resource generalist role, or a financial analyst role (only the *key responsibilities* would vary across the jobs that comprise each general role):

- **Purpose:** The general mission and high level goals of the role defined in the context of the value creation principles and strategy of the enterprise. *Purpose* reflects the way in which the true nature of the role aligns with the true nature of the enterprise, including why the role is important to the organization. An example of one aspect of a defined purpose for a senior engineering role might be: *Continually improves processes to increase productivity and the effectiveness of operational capabilities that directly drive value creation.*
- **Key responsibilities:** The most important work activities that the individual in the job is responsible for doing. *Key responsibilities* typically reflect those tasks, activities, and projects that directly relate to key organizational processes and value networks. An example of a key responsibility for a financial analyst role might be: *Prepares and presents a summary report each quarter to each of the business lines showing cash flow statistics, actual cash flow relative to business unit requirements, the implications for capital investments and outlays, and the barriers and enablers to improving cash flow to desired levels.*
- **Key drivers of value creation:** The influence the role has on specific drivers and/or organizational capabilities that directly (or in some cases indirectly) impact the strategy execution and value creation of the enterprise. An example of a statement in this part of the role description for a marketing/public relations manager at a government agency might be: *Directly impacts the public's awareness, demand for, and utilization of, primary agency services, resulting in increasing revenue for the agency and the state.*
- **Key relationships and interactions:** The important connections and interfaces that the individual has with other roles/people in performing the work of the role. The nature of these interfaces is defined within the context of the role's responsibilities and the related activities of other roles in the value network, and the degree to which the interface is a periodic interaction or a more robust relationship. An example of a key relationship for a human resource professional at a major university might be: *Interfaces continually with the associate deans of the school, develops a robust understanding of their management experience, capability, and approach, and works closely with them to develop shared expectations and norms of how the human resources function will best serve university staff.*
- **Key conditions for optimal productivity:** The information, frameworks, tools, technologies, environmental conditions, and other

resources that enable the individual in the role to perform the work at optimal productivity levels (assuming a solid level of general competence). An example of a key condition for a customer service representative at a professional association might be: *Immediate access to a summary of recent interactions with the association member.*

- **Standards and indicators of performance:** The explicit and/or implicit standards of performance that relate to the key responsibilities of the role. The qualitative and quantitative indicators—metrics, work products, decisions, customer or constituent experience/feedback, and other outcomes—that provide important information for assessing the overall contribution and performance of the individual in the role. An example of an important standard/indicator for the captain of an ocean freighter (a freighter is an organization to be sure) might be: *One-hundred percent accurate navigation of the ship along designated routes and within the defined range of coordinates, as measured by the navigation system and captured by the ship's navigational officer.*

Creating Value through Capabilities

So far we have explored the universal qualities of meaningful work design that drive highly productive activity. Next, we revisit organizational capabilities as another driver of productivity, and explore the degree to which there are capabilities common to highly productive work environments. Effective organizations constantly build and evolve internal capabilities to best meet the challenges of the environment and achieve their desired results.

As the environment increases in complexity, effective organizations will increase in complexity as well through innovation, differentiation, and integration. Recognizing environmental threats and challenges, building capability to meet those challenges, and responding to those challenges, all need to happen simultaneously, so organizational strategies and capabilities must co-evolve with the dynamic environment. For example, a distribution company, with many distribution centers and core capabilities in both logistics and customer service, needed to quickly respond to a dramatic increase in the price of fuel, simultaneously changing its distribution strategy and logistics and service capabilities to manage increased cost while also retaining top tier, profitable customers. Organizational capability therefore reflects a foundational source of powerful positive energy, productivity, and value creation as the organization evolves to best meet the challenges of its environment.

Distinctive from other sources of competitive advantage such as strategic insight, home-grown technologies, or product and service innovation, organizational capabilities—both strategic and operational—provide high leverage on enterprise performance since they are very difficult for competitors or imitators to transfer or replicate. Organizational capabilities are not linear processes, software programs, or key relationships. Instead, enterprise capability represents a web of integrated activity, processes, relationships, technologies, domains of skill and knowledge, and individual, group, and/or network interactions. The critical capabilities of high performance organizations include those that are specific to purpose and strategy, as well as those that are related to the effectiveness of the organization's day-to-day operations.

DHARMA LOG

The **unenlightened** organization invests too much in adopting unproven but often highly touted "best practices" used by other organizations. The **enlightened** organization invests little in popular best practices, choosing to invest significant resources in organizational capabilities that are uniquely strategic and operational to their specific external value proposition and value creation strategy.

There are a number of *operational* capabilities that remain critical to value creation and survival over the *life-cycle* of the organization, and that are also important to a meaningful and fulfilling work experience. At the conceptual level, these capabilities are very similar—again, almost *universal*—across a wide variety of organizations. At the execution level, however, these capabilities are unique to each organization in terms of their importance and specific make-up.

Based on extensive experience with organizations of all types, observations of their life-cycle experience, and the recent research in this arena, vital operational capabilities today (and in the future) include:

- Building and nurturing a culture of value creation by establishing, preserving, and reinforcing positive organizational action-schemas.
- Translating imagination into value creation through the freedom of creativity, the incubation and enhancement of the strongest creative ideas, and the efficient development of new innovations.
- Acquiring and disseminating important environmental and organizational information in broad-based as well as targeted ways.

- Managing knowledge, including the transformation of data into information and knowledge that is organized and easily obtainable by participants when carrying out their work activities.
- Establishing and preserving the conditions for healthy and productive interactions, relationships, and networks.
- Realigning operations as environmental conditions change, continuously synchronizing assumptions, information, priorities, resource allocation, and roles and responsibilities.
- Strategically cooperating with other organizations, some of whom may be competitors, to integrate diverse, advanced, and often highly specialized domains of knowledge.
- Practicing rigorous environmental sustainability while also promoting and reinforcing those practices among other organizations with whom the enterprise participates.
- Creating and disseminating organizational memes through diverse communication channels that reinforce values and culture, and increase harmony among people's thoughts, emotions, actions, and interactions.
- Eliminating and/or streamlining complex and inefficient decision-making and resource allocation processes that too often destroy value rather than create it.
- Observing aspects of ordered-chaos within the "whole system" and its networks and network patterns and understanding the webs of relationships and activities.
- Envisioning and socializing preferred future scenarios that will help the organization evolve successfully going forward.

Making Decision Making Easy

Much of the decision making that is conducted in organizations is fundamentally inefficient and broken. This is not to say that organizations do not make "good" decisions (however that might be defined). Rather, the process by which decisions are made and the quality of the decisions themselves are very often sub-optimal in nature. The opportunity cost from a value creation standpoint is much too high usually for the relative importance of the decision being made. In other words, organizations waste too much energy—and at times actually generate negative energy—

in taking too long to make too many unimportant decisions that add too little value. And chances are, too many decisions are made by too few people, a strong indicator of a control-orientation and a general lack of trust in people. In examining the current state of decision making in an organization, a good place to start is by exploring the following line of questioning:

- Who makes what important decisions and why?
- To what extent does the organization follow a decision making framework or process? If so, how consistently used is it?
- How are key decisions made? To what extent is decision making concentrated or distributed in the organization?
- How does the organization invest in improving its decision making capability and outcomes?
- To what extent do decision makers utilize a robust fact-base, identify solid alternatives, and apply criteria in a rigorous way to choose the best alternative(s) when making decisions?
- To what extent is the organization aware of the prevalence of distortions and biases that affect the quality of decisions?
- How does the organization know it is making good decisions?
- To what extent does the organization assess the efficacy of its decision making activities and the quality of its key decisions and outcomes?

SUTRA LESSON *Information and Decision Making*[14]

In his outstanding book, *Competitive Advantage through People: Unleashing the Power of the Workforce*, Jeffrey Pfeffer writes about people as a source of competitive advantage:

"Sharing information is a necessary precondition to an important feature found in many successful work systems: encouraging the decentralization of decision making and broader worker participation and empowerment in controlling their own work processes."

A leading telecommunications organization struggled with its decision making activities and effectiveness. Decisions were made too slowly, with too many steps, and with too many people involved. The organization studied these phenomena and found that there was a lack of clarity regarding decision-rights, a limited understanding of what consensus really meant, and an over-emphasis on influence due to status, level, and personality. There were too many unproductive decision-making meetings with too much lobbying outside of meetings, and a lack of an approach for resolving competing viewpoints and interests. It then proceeded to undertake an initiative to improve decision-making efficiency and quality that helped to speed-up key processes and better meet customer deadlines. Unfortunately, these decision making phenomena are not uncommon in other organizations. As a critical organizational capability, decision making in most organizations is not working very well.

The enlightened organization creates the conditions for highly effective and efficient decision making throughout the enterprise. *What is the secret to good decision making? How can decision making be easy but also effective?* In exploring these key questions, an organization should consider the following opportunities to improve decision making effectiveness:

- **Reduce the number of decisions and decision approvals that need to be made.** This is simply done through either eliminating unnecessary decisions altogether (organizations would do well to spend more time on identifying unnecessary decisions) or by infusing decisions into the responsibilities of specific roles and the actual activity of day-to-day work.
- **Eliminate steps in decision *making* processes.** Distribute decision making responsibility more deeply and broadly within the organization, trusting people at all levels to make good decisions under the right conditions and within simple boundaries. Ensure that relevant information flows freely across organizational boundaries to support distributed decision-making.
- **Eliminate steps in decision *approval* processes.** Eliminate meetings where participants present material to executive decision makers, especially when the participants themselves should be making the decision in the first place. Do not second-guess decisions that get made.
- **Develop and syndicate a decision rights matrix if necessary.** Outline what roles have input, influence, decision, and review/approval

accountability, but be careful not to over-engineer or over-complicate it. Again, do not second-guess decisions that get made.

- **Implement a decision-making review process.** Periodically, engage a slice of the organization to review decision making processes and key decisions and their outcomes, and develop strategies for improving decision making efficiency and quality.

DHARMA LOG

The **unenlightened** organization resists distributing the responsibility to make decisions under the banner that an organization is not a democracy and that leaders are there to, in fact, make decisions. The **enlightened** organization also understands that it is not a democracy, and that the role of senior leadership is to make critical decisions. At the same time, it believes that many decisions are best made at the outer perimeter in the organization, trusts in the judgment of well-informed people to make good decisions, and demonstrates a level of willingness, patience, and tolerance for the potential untidiness that comes with it.

Extending Capabilities to Competencies

Many organizations have invested a great deal of resources into the development of competencies—bundles of skills, knowledge, and abilities—that relate to specific roles, jobs, or even individuals. These are often an extension of organizational capability; they define what is important at the participant level given the strategic and operational capabilities that are critical to the enterprise. From a value network perspective, they define what capability is important at the role level, where a role can be thought of as a node in the network, a nexus where important activity is carried out, information is exchanged, or a decision is made.

There are many competency frameworks on the market and some organizations adopt these "pre-fabricated" models (they buy the single wide on wheels), while others supplement these models with competencies that are "made up" (they get the double-wide), while still others develop their own models based on internal research, analysis, and validation (they build the house), often with the help of an outside consultant or advisor.

Given the nature of the socio-economic ecosystems within which most organizations operate, characterized in this book through the concepts of energy exchange, complexity, disequilibrium, and evolutionary change, organizations should consider a whole new way of thinking about the competencies that really matter. Rather than putting a fresh-face on the old standby competencies like *communication, business acumen, problem solving, critical thinking*, and *teamwork*, an enterprise might consider an entirely new model that focuses on the critical drivers of effective co-evolution in a dynamic world. This new model would have the following competencies (an expanded model is further explored in Chapter 10):

- **Seeking:** This competency entails a passion for learning and understanding, demonstrating a near-boundless and genuine curiosity about the enterprise, its environment, and all things inside and outside the organization that may have some degree of relevance to its value creation process. It entails the ability to deeply and broadly investigate, filter, capture, and share information that is relevant and helpful to the organization in the short- and long-term. It entails role-modeling an orientation for constant learning. This competency involves seeking first to understand the ability to explore diverse alternatives, and the use of important information required to make good decisions for effective action.
- **Creating:** This competency entails the creation of innovative and highly productive memes—organizational ideas and artifacts—that are consistent with the true nature and value creation strategy of the enterprise. It entails the ability to generate new ideas, processes, programs, practices, and products that both reflect imagination and a rooted sense of reality. It entails the freedom to explore a breadth of topics and invent new ideas, combining both convergent and divergent thinking to make new connections. This requires the flexibility to apply multiple perspectives, and the cognitive agility to see new patterns and opportunities, and connect them to the value creation strategy of the enterprise.
- **Facilitating:** This competency entails the ability to move things forward in a harmonious and productive manner, at times involving diverse perspectives and conflicting priorities. It entails the ability to sense, support, guide, and nurture emergent ideas and activities with individuals and within groups and networks. It entails the ability to connect people, groups, and networks, and help them—while staying objective and somewhat detached—explore, challenge, and break-apart old patterns to create new directions. It entails the knowledge of

when and how to pursue appropriate forms of agreement, by finding common ground to achieve consensus, and make hard decisions. It involves the ability to effectively network, establish new relationships across internal and external webs of activity, and show that very little real value can be created and sustained without meaningful collaborative effort.

- **Integrating:** This competency entails helping to build and maintain connections between people, within networks, and across processes and initiatives. It requires a broad systemic perspective and involves understanding what makes interactions productive, which channels are best for sharing information, and which strategies work to gain needed alignment. It entails the ability to perceive patterns within a complex situation and apply this insight to the development and implementation of solutions. This competency often involves integrating technical systems with people systems to ensure the optimal performance of a process and/or network.
- **Regulating:** This competency entails the ability to continually observe, assess, and strengthen interactions, relationships, processes, groups, and networks to be more consistent with the values of the enterprise and in compliance with regulatory and other requirements. It entails understanding and applying indicators, metrics, and other objective measurement tools in a way that generates important, but carefully used, performance information. It entails understanding the difference between observation and assessment and the ability to influence people to improve processes, programs, and practices in a collaborative and non-threatening manner. This competency involves the subtle but critically important ability to understand how the enterprise flows in the currents of its environment while ensuring that its values are not compromised.

MY SAMADHI *A Personal Concern*

Over the past decade, researchers, thought leaders, and consultants have devoted a significant amount of psychic energy to the practices of discipline, execution, and measurement as critical to the enterprise in achieving superior performance. We are told that *discipline* is one of the fundamental differentiators of great organizations. We are told that in the best performing companies, culture and *execution* are one and the same. And we are told that highly complex and sophisticated *scorecard* systems are necessary to measure and truly understand what is going on inside on organization.

There is no question that the concepts and practices of discipline, execution, and measurement are critically important to an organization's effectiveness. At the same time, I perceive there are aspects to these concepts that are highly mechanistic in nature and that assume we live in a highly transactional (versus highly relational) world, full of constants, formulas, and standard operating procedures. If carried too far, these concepts can create imbalances between important, but also counteracting forces, such as efficiency and quality, protocol and flexibility, logic and creativity, goal achievement and goal resolution. Perhaps even most troubling within these three popular domains of advice and counsel, there is an implicit or explicit message that organizations must *confront* their environment head-on, *control* their internal dynamics, and *power* their way through in the search for the next plateau of stability and success.

My experience tells me that organizations need to be very careful in hanging their hats on single, powerful concepts and frameworks that can go too far in influencing workforce patterns of thinking and doing. Within the context of practices related to discipline, execution, and measurement, a Zen Master might suggest to an organization's participants something like the following: **enjoy freedom in discipline, be agile in execution, and take measure only in the present moment, for everything else is an illusion.**

Valuing Work in Meaningful Ways

Almost every organization has a need for an internal process that helps it place a "value" on work, jobs, or roles based on their main responsibilities. This valuation is typically done for several reasons, including the development of competitive compensation ranges for talent in the marketplace, and the creation of a simple job hierarchy that helps clarify guidelines for career paths, promotions, and job titles. To many people in organizations, however, the *process* of work valuation (also known as job evaluation) might seem unimportant or mundane. It is neither.

How jobs are valued, and how the compensation architecture—the number of pay structures, the number of pay levels (also called grades or bands), and the range of pay opportunities—is designed can have a significant impact, either positive or negative, on important organizational needs, such as:

- Supporting the movement of talent within the organization to foster a greater depth and breadth of knowledge and experience.
- Ensuring the competitiveness of compensation practices to help attract, acquire, and retain needed talent.
- Reducing the burdensome administrative (and often highly political) activity that is involved in assigning jobs to levels and making pay decisions.
- Increasing the return on compensation investment by ensuring that the top performers in the most important jobs/roles have greater compensation opportunities.

In an organization that is committed to achieving superior levels of productivity through high quality work design and optimal work experiences, the approach to valuing work, and compensating participants for doing that work, is critical. *In its most pure form*, a strategic approach to valuing work involves paying *more* for roles or jobs that drive competitive advantage and *directly* create value relative to general market practice. Conversely, roles or jobs that drive the operations of the enterprise and more *indirectly* contribute to value creation would be paid at a lower pay position relative to general market practice.

Regardless of the actual approach that is used, when these work valuation systems are designed and executed effectively, they are not prominent within an organization (although their outcomes are). But when these systems are broken, they become very prominent in a negative way and can cause significant distraction, confusion, and dissatisfaction in the workplace, negatively affecting productivity.

DHARMA LOG

The **unenlightened** organization over-emphasizes the external market and uses generic evaluation factors that are not tied to the business when valuing work and jobs. The **enlightened** organization uses the external market as only an input and uses internal valuation factors that are specific to the strategic intent of the enterprise.

In a nutshell, the enlightened organization uses a strategic and balanced approach to the valuation of work. It balances the external value of a job or role, based on a review of the market (only when high quality market data is available) with the internal value of a job/role, using valuation factors that are directly tied to strategic intent and impact, such as revenue growth, asset management, and customer experience (these are actual factors that were used by a major retailing organization). Other internal factors that are less strategic and specific, but nonetheless very important, include the scope of responsibility and the depth and breadth of skills and knowledge needed to do the work of the job/role.

In the case of a global medical technology company, a strategic approach to work valuation was used to "level" thousands of jobs worldwide into nine job groups, with specific compensation guidelines assigned to each group. The enterprise used a consistent process, involved many people around the world, and applied three primary factors to determine the relative value of jobs: *scope of responsibility*, which included sphere of influence and skills and knowledge, *impact on results*, which included degree of accountability and potential for financial impact, and *impact on strategic value drivers*, which included the potential for impact on revenue growth, operational effectiveness, and innovation. This valuation process was used primarily to determine annual and long-term incentive opportunities for people in professional and managerial roles across fifty countries.

The enlightened enterprise does not believe that its competitors should determine what value to place on work or how much to compensate its people, which is why it blends external and internal valuation in a way that reflects its own unique work system. The enlightened organization carries out its work valuation process with rigor, simplicity, and transparency. As a result, participants in the organization understand and appreciate the process and are able to easily focus on contributing to the performance of the enterprise rather than on the "fairness" applied in the valuation of their work. Furthermore, the organization as a whole achieves higher levels of *pay productivity*, the return on their compensation investment, by ensuring that more pay is delivered to roles and people that have a direct impact on the drivers of productivity, profitability, and value creation.

Reframing the Role of Technology

Organizations regularly invest in technology to enhance work processes and improve quality, efficiency, delivery and overall productivity. Unfortunately, many organizations have invested vast amounts of financial capital into technologies that have not lived up to their promise, such as enterprise resource planning systems. And today, organizations are still over-investing in technology and under-investing in people. Put another way, investment in technology that builds long-term competitiveness by helping to increase real workforce productivity has been entirely insufficient.

For many years, organizations have explored the concept of *socio-technical* work systems. Technologies and tools make up the technical system of the enterprise, and people, processes, and networks make up the social system of the enterprise. Socio-technical work design therefore represents the integration and optimization of these elements to achieve superior results. Regrettably, many organizations invest in major new technologies without investing in the associated social system in a collaborative design approach. These organizations make the major technology investment and then often make only minor changes to the nature of jobs/roles, and their associated work activities and practices, to better support the technology. Broadening this perspective further, in general, organizations tend to sub-optimize investments in technology due to a lack of integration with people processes.

SUTRA LESSON ***The Sociotechnical Systems Perspective***[15]

In his highly practical book, *Designing Effective Organizations: The Sociotechnical Systems Perspective*, William Pasmore writes very clearly about social and technical alignment:

"How well the social and technical systems are designed with respect to one another and with respect to the demands of the external environment determines to a large extent how effective the organization will be."

Consider, for example, the consulting firm that introduced a new, online relationship-management tool that was intended to do a better of job of helping client managers share information regarding current client engagements and new client opportunities. This new technology was highly ineffective due to a lack of investment in training system users, communicating user expectations, and clarifying the role responsibilities of the client managers and their assistants. Not only was the technology not syndicated effectively, but there was no discussion or activity to change work processes to better utilize the technology, nor was there any accountability designed into its utilization. The new technology did nothing to help the organization improve its business development activities or increase revenue. While this example is somewhat mundane in nature, it is also a perfect illustration of why organizations should lead with process and network redesign first and then support specific, desired behaviors and activities through the use of technology as a tool. This consulting firm would have had a much different experience if had taken a strategic look at the client relationship management web of activity first.

Dharma Log

The **unenlightened** organization places too much emphasis on capital inputs such as technology as the main driver of productivity, often confusing cost reduction and/or efficiency with productivity. The **enlightened** organization places more emphasis on human capital inputs and takes a more strategic approach to determining the optimal combination of technology inputs and people inputs to improve productivity.

The power of technology is often sub-optimized not only due to its lack of integration with the social system and work system of the enterprise, but also because of the focus of the technology in the first place. There is no question that technology has played a major role and will continue to play a major role in the productivity and health of organizations and societies. However, most organizations sub-optimize their investments in technology by investing too much in technologies that focus on cost and efficiency, and that have a lower return-on-investment, and investing too little in technologies that focus on innovation and growth, and that have a higher return-on-investment. Relative to most organizations, the enlightened enterprise invests a greater share of its capital in technologies that help unleash the potential of people and generate value creation over the long-term. And they do this in a way that is sound from a socio-technical standpoint, where the social system is well-designed to effectively utilize the new technologies.

Investments in technology can be segmented by the degree to which the technology drives greater value creation (from *low to high return-on-investment)*:

- **Resource planning, acquisition and allocation** technologies that support the efficient and coordinated acquisition and allocation of resources, including raw materials, hardware, software, durable and non-durable supplies, and (in some cases) people. These technologies are typically lower in their return due to their high cost, massive scale and scope, short-term emphasis, inflexible processes, and overall disruption to operations relative to their returns on productivity and value creation.

- **Operational efficiency** technologies that support the efficient operation of core organizational processes typically involving the production of a product or delivery of a service. These technologies are typically a little higher in their return, but still relatively low in return on investment due to their over-emphasis on linear processes and lack of emphasis on value creation networks. Moreover, these technologies are often not well integrated with one another within a network of activity, creating new variances and challenges at their points of intersection.
- **Project and program management** technologies that support the coordination and management of the portfolio of projects and programs carried out throughout the organization. These technologies are higher in their return, but are often sub-optimized and fall short of their potential due to their lack of integration with other technologies, such as resource planning or work scheduling systems, and with other key organizational processes and networks, such as strategic planning, operations planning, and workforce planning.
- **Information acquisition and sharing** technologies that support the acquisition and storage of important information from the external environment and the dissemination of this information to the right places and people inside the organization. These technologies are typically higher in their return due to their lower cost and minimal disruption to the organization relative to the power they create throughout the enterprise that enables people to broaden their knowledge base, make better decisions, collaborate more efficiently, and focus their contribution on the drivers of success.
- **Knowledge and learning management** technologies that support knowledge creation, storage, organization, access, communication/sharing, and syndication across the full enterprise. These technologies are higher in their return, again due to their lower cost and low disruption, and their scope of impact as people throughout the organization not only have access to information but also have the tools, resources, and opportunities to increase their knowledge base and build capability in the areas that directly influence productivity, competitive advantage, and value creation.

- **Relationship and network management** technologies that support the development, quality, and fluidity of the various types of interactions and relationships required to carry out the activities of groups and networks. These technologies are the highest in their return on investment due to their low cost and disruption relative to the long-term impact that comes from building capability within the workforce to have more healthy interactions, and stronger, more transparent and productive relationships between co-workers, organization participants and customers, as well as between organization participants and other external constituencies.

DHARMA LOG

The **unenlightened** organization invests too much in technologies that are used for controlling internal processes. The **enlightened** organization invests more in technologies that directly support the co-evolution of the enterprise with its environment.

Reframing the Nature of Learning

The enlightened organization understands that the process of learning—learning how to learn, actual learning itself, and then applying the learning—is itself a critical capability that perhaps more than any other capability is fundamental to long-term success and survival. A learning organization actively supports and facilitates learning throughout the enterprise through *formal and informal* activities and processes that develop, capture, segment, organize, disseminate, and apply knowledge in ways that enable it to co-evolve with its environment, shape its reality, and create value.

There are many enterprises that have invested vast resources in creating learning structures, or "universities" within the organization, with required and optional learning curricula and highly formal learning policies and processes. And there is no question that many of these internal institutions have brought and will continue to bring some benefit to the organization. However, there remains a question of the return on investment in this approach, which is once again a perfect example of creating form, content, and structure where perhaps a more organic and meaningful approach would be better. The conscious and evolving organization does not need to create a learning university within its boundaries; rather, it is in fact a university itself! Learning is its true nature. Its participants are both teachers and students, both creators and seekers. Its value creation networks *are* its curriculum. In this environment, a large amount of learning occurs on the job from the work itself through more broadly defined roles with larger scopes of responsibility, more meaningful work experiences, greater access to a breadth of information, and more discretion to decide how work gets done and what decisions need to be made. A large amount of learning also occurs through greater exposure to and interactions with colleagues, customers, and other constituents that comprise the value networks of the organization.

Organizational learning is a social process that involves formal and informal, and planned and unplanned interactions among people that lead to more well-informed decision making and more productive activity at a higher level of quality. The enlightened enterprise knows that each of its participants is at a certain place on his or her individual learning curve. It understands that the needs of the *role* along with the physical, mental, emotional, and spiritual needs of the *individual* require customized learning opportunities and experiences. And it knows that learning is much more effective when learning conditions align with learning needs.

As important, ongoing learning—true learning where the gaining of knowledge is translated into productive activity—requires presence and engagement on the part of enterprise participants. Many studies have shown that formal "classroom" training inside organizations has an extremely low efficacy, in part due to a lack of alignment with the ways in which people actually learn, but also in part due to their lack of presence with and engagement in the learning content itself. Presence equates to awareness, and a workforce with strong presence understands better that each interaction and activity is a learning experience. Moreover, in more formal settings, participants who demonstrate presence are able to focus better on the learning content and process it with respect to their own role and responsibilities. Engagement equates to commitment, and a workforce with strong engagement is more attuned to the needs of the organization and their role in its value creation; engaged participants are better equipped to apply what they have learned.

With these concepts in mind, there are three aspects of learning that are critical to building and sustaining a true learning organization:

- **Learning conditions** reflect the nature of learning opportunities and environments, including the degree to which there is *formal structured and informal learning, visual and auditory learning, concrete examples and conceptual frameworks, and individual and group learning*. While the enlightened organization builds learning into the way work is designed, it also understands the value of more planned, diverse learning experiences that can supplement what occurs on the job. It creates the conditions for these experiences based on the needs of the enterprise and the needs of the participants. A critical aspect of establishing learning conditions involves building and supporting a culture that reinforces the value of learning, a culture that replaces the phenomena of "mistakes" and "failures" (and the notion of blame) with the concept of constant opportunities for learning. In this culture, people actually make fewer mistakes due to less fear and tension, and more ongoing learning.

- **Learning processes** reflect the degree to which learning experiences involve *dialog, interaction, idea exchange, experimentation, open-ended problem-solving, linear versus systemic thinking, and task-based, data-based, and brainstorming activities*. The enlightened enterprise understands that different people learn in different ways and utilizes a combination of approaches in designing learning opportunities on the job and in supplemental learning experiences. For example, it may consistently reinforce specific principles in all brainstorming activity that supports mutual learning among participants as they generate and assess their ideas. It may formally require simple, but specific, guidelines be followed in project management activities for periodic review of progress and the infusion of key learnings in future project steps. And it may build-in feedback loops within its key value networks that help participants learn more efficiently during distributed idea exchange and problem-solving activities.
- **Learning experiences** reflect the types of learning experiences that are aligned with specific conditions and processes outlined above. Learning experiences can be thought of across a wide continuum of activity that include *observing, listening, reading, doing, practicing, studying, researching, coaching, mentoring, training, storytelling, and role-modeling*. The enlightened organization believes in continuous development, but also understands that periodically, it is worthwhile for participants to create/update development plans that identify specific learning needs as well as their counter-part learning experiences, with the understanding that some measure of diversity in learning is better. For example, a marketing professional at an internet company identified the need to learn more about search engines. He decided that multiple learning experiences made sense, and enhanced his

development plan with the following: Practice utilizing all major search engines on the web *(doing, practicing)*. Review sources of information that assess and rate search engines *(reading, researching)*. Attend an external workshop on search engine navigation *(training)*. Spend time with colleagues who regularly use search engines to do their work *(observing, studying)*.

Highly successful organizations understand that deep learning comes from internal feedback loops that serve to challenge the patterns that influence enterprise activity. Learning occurs as evolving beliefs guide better actions. The enlightened enterprise understands the importance of *unlearning* the assumptions, beliefs, and practices that can create negative energy and permit the forces of entropy to spread within the organization. Even in the most conscious organizations, imprinted patterns of thinking and behaving still exist, however dormant they may be. Energy sinks—pockets of entropy—continuously emerge that create obstacles and barriers to success. Destructive memes still materialize and evolve that invade and sabotage healthy, productive activities and interactions. Even the collective ego of the highly conscious enterprise would rather return to the easy days of unconsciousness than work hard to tenaciously break down conditioned views of reality and programmed ways of doing things.

The enlightened organization is not only in a constant state of learning, but also in a constant state of unlearning where it actively detaches from old assumptions that no longer fit with the changing environment, such as old paradigms of thinking, problem solving, and decision-making, and old war stories of the good ol' days that glorify how things used to get done.

Consider, for example, how a division of a global, non-profit financial institution made much needed improvements to its project funding, time recording, and budget management processes. Its first few steps were to educate division staff on the current practices regarding these administrative, but critically important processes, including the negative impact on staff and client satisfaction (clients in this case were countries to whom it lended money). Then organizational leaders began a long-term campaign at both the individual and group level—in both formal and informal ways—to break-down longstanding beliefs and assumptions regarding how to estimate funding needs, record time, and manage budgets.

Finally, the institution implemented new guidelines and tools to assist staff to adopt more realistic and transparent practices, while at the same time providing a safety net for the reputation of those professionals who now had funding or budgeting issues. It was clear in the transformation that the organization was more than just learning new ways of doing things; it was also unlearning old habits and behavior patterns that had accumulated over the years.

As an aside, the whole initiative was started by a "star" mid-level manager, who had noticed how these practices had evolved over time, wreaking havoc on the system as a whole. While a lesson in unlearning, this institution's experience also shows how harmful memes can infiltrate and evolve within a successful organization. And it clearly demonstrates the power that individuals can wield, regardless of their status, as strong localized energy fields in bringing change to the broader enterprise. In this transformation, the participants involved played the roles of both teacher and student in making the new ways of doing things stick.

In summary, the enlightened enterprise has a clear understanding that the quality of productive activity within the organization has a direct impact on its level of productivity, degree of competitiveness within its industry or social sector, and overall ability to create value. It builds strong internal capability to continuously learn those things that assist in creating value and unlearn those things that get in the way of creating value, contributing to the overall and enduring financial and operational health of the organization.

THE TAO: Walking a New Path

In getting started on the path toward increasing the quality of productive activity, consider the following diagnostic questions:

- ***To what extent are roles and goals aligned with the drivers of value creation?*** Consider how roles are defined and how goals are established. Consider the degree to which they are described in the context of the value webs of the organization, and the key activities and capabilities within those webs that directly impact value creation.

- ***To what extent do people experience immediate and continuous feedback regarding their contribution?*** Consider how work is designed so that the work itself provides feedback to the participant, through accessible performance information and customer feedback. Consider the degree to which there is built-in learning experiences in doing the work of the role that is meaningful to the individual and valuable to the enterprise.

- ***To what extent does work involve variety, challenge, and stimulation?*** Consider the extent to which roles in the organization are designed to include a variety of stimulating tasks, decisions, projects, and other activities. Consider the degree to which they require the participant in the role to moderately stretch the application of their skills, knowledge, and abilities.

- ***To what extent does the organization create the conditions for flexibility and freedom in carrying out work activities and making decisions?*** Consider how decisions are made in the organization and how concentrated versus distributed are the decision-makers. Consider how narrow versus broad roles are in terms of their responsibilities and accountabilities. Consider how much organizational activity focuses on supporting and enabling people in doing their work relative to activity devoted to monitoring and auditing their work.

- ***Do people have access to needed information, tools, resources, and technologies to work efficiently and effectively?*** Consider how well the organization syndicates information, knowledge, and proven practices that help people work more effectively. Consider how accessible the needed tools and technologies are and the degree to which participants can easily acquire and use them. Consider how resources are shared and the degree to which there is access to needed resources across organizational boundaries.

- ***To what extent do people know what to do at work to best execute strategy, be most productive, and create the most value?*** Consider how well participants understand their role and how it fits into and supports the broader value creation processes and networks. Consider the extent to which people are connected to the organization and have a passion for its purpose and strategic intent. Consider how involved people are in developing strategies and making decisions as part of their daily activities.

- ***To what extent does the organization support the diversity of ideas and actions?*** Consider how open the organization is to new and diverse ideas. Consider what informal and formal processes support the development and incubation of diverse and creative ideas. Consider the degree to which there are obstacles and barriers that reinforce only certain ways of thinking and doing to prevent the broadening of the field of possibility.

- ***Are people substantively recognized and rewarded for their contributions?*** Consider how well compensation programs and other financial reward systems reward people for their contributions to value creation to achieve the results that drive organizational success. Consider the degree to which people are recognized and acknowledged on a daily basis for their contributions.

- ***To what extent does the organization create the conditions for effective and continuous learning and unlearning?*** Consider how well the enterprise creates and supports effective learning processes and experiences that are infused into everyday work activities as well as provided through supplemental learning experiences. Consider how active the organization is in breaking down old ways of thinking and doing things. Consider how well the organization captures information, builds its knowledge base, and syndicates this knowledge throughout the enterprise to more effectively co-evolve with its environment and create value.

SIX

The Conditions for Collaboration

Imagine that you are in your study at home on a Friday afternoon. You are exchanging emails with several colleagues on a team chartered to explore new and innovative ways to reduce the cycle-time of developing new services for customers. You can hear your kids playing outside and look forward to joining them soon. But several very good ideas are emerging in the email thread and you wonder how these ideas should best be captured and syndicated, and who should do it. You know from past experience that ideas can get lost in the overwhelming email traffic that plagues almost everyone. A few more people join the email thread, adding more positive energy to the impromptu brainstorming. You wonder if you should volunteer to capture the information and summarize it in a memo to the leadership team, when one of your kids walks into your study asking you when you can come out and play. Thinking quickly, you suggest to your email cohort that your assistant can send out the full thread to the whole marketing and operations group and schedule a top-priority web-conference for early Monday morning to further expand the network of ideas and activity and develop a plan for mobilization. This organically builds in a process for greater collaboration and learning while also creating a forum for exploring what might have the most impact. They agree. As you put on your blades to go play some street hockey with the neighborhood kids, you smile and think to yourself: The same principles we apply to reduce the cycle time of developing new services can be applied to how we brainstorm and decide on the best cycle time reduction strategies in the first place. ***This is satori.***

In this chapter we will explore important concepts regarding the nature of and conditions for effective groups and networks within the enterprise, as summarized by the following principles:

- **Organizations are learning more and more that much of the important work of the enterprise is carried out by networks, or communities, of people.**
- **Effective organizations consciously and carefully utilize formal and informal groups and networks to carry out a wide range of organizational activity.**
- **The enlightened organization creates enabling conditions and provides continual support for effective groups, networks, and large-scale communities.**

There are many forms of collaboration that take place within organizations and across their permeable boundaries with other organizations. The very definition of an organization requires that some degree of collaboration take place in order for it to exist in the first place. For that reason, the quality of collaboration is very important as a key determinant of organizational effectiveness, and, not surprisingly, the actual *quality* of collaborative activities within an organization can span across a wide spectrum. Unfortunately, we must return briefly to the nature of the egoic mind and remember that the ego does not believe that the more easily people can work together the more successful they can be. Cooperation is a foreign concept to the ego, unless it believes that it can further itself through this type of activity. Therefore the quality of enterprise collaboration is constantly affected by the degree to which individuals within the organization are conscious themselves, and can transcend the sabotaging nature of the egoic mind.

While the informal collaboration of individuals in their daily interactions with each other is critically important (covered to some extent in the following chapter), the heart and soul of collaboration within organizations involves participant groups and networks, and the degree to which the enterprise establishes the right conditions in creating a strong collaborative climate to maximize their potential effectiveness. One of the key conditions—and perhaps the most important one—is that of trust. Without trust, it is difficult for people to work with each other in meaningful ways to create value. In the enlightened organization, trust is a natural phenomenon due to the strong presence of integrity, and other antecedents, including openness, honesty, consistency, dignity, and diversity, the conditions that create a meaningful work environment in the first place.

SUTRA LESSON ***Trust and Teamwork***[16]

In *Teamwork: What Must Go Right/What Can Go Wrong*, Gary Larson and Frank LaFasto write about how their extensive research revealed the antecedents of trust, a fundamental element of collaborative work systems:

"Our content analysis of the data indicates that trust is produced in a climate that includes four elements: (1) honesty—integrity, no lies, no exaggerations; (2) openness—a willingness to share, and a receptivity to information, perceptions, ideas; (3) consistency—predictable behavior and responses; and (4) respect—treating people with dignity and fairness."

Exploring Group Effectiveness

One of the most important areas of organization effectiveness that has rightfully received significant attention from researchers and practitioners is that of team and group effectiveness. Organizational groups reflect a vast array of collections of people grouped together to accomplish a specific goal or task or set of goals or tasks. Common groups from across a wide variety of organizations include surgical teams, product branding teams, production cells, sports teams, six-sigma teams, technology implementation teams, customer service pods, military platoons, movie casts, study groups, and so on. There is no question that a significant amount of the work done by an enterprise is done through the collaboration of individuals in groups, where the most productive methods of value creation involving interdependencies and interrelationships cannot be practically or efficiently performed by a single individual. Many organizations view the effectiveness of their teams and groups as a primary engine of their respective business models.

Regardless of the type of group, there are fundamental and timeless conditions for, and elements of, group effectiveness. High performing organizations place great emphasis on the effectiveness of both formal and informal groups. The conditions and elements of group and team effectiveness include:

- **Sponsorship and guidance:** Effective groups typically have a sponsor that provides clear direction in the forming stages of the group as well as ongoing and constructive guidance during the group's life cycle.

Ineffective groups often have no sponsor, an inactive sponsor, or inconsistent sponsorship that can fluctuate from directive types of activity all the way to disinterest and unresponsiveness.

- **Purpose and goals:** Effective groups typically have a clear and elevating purpose (or mission) as well as shared, well-defined goals and desired outcomes. Ineffective groups often have an ambiguous purpose and a lack of clear goals or a set of goals that are too broad or too narrow in scope.
- **Roles and responsibilities:** Effective groups typically have some degree of role definition within the group where specific roles and responsibilities are defined and assigned to group members, as collectively agreed upon by the group. The degree to which roles and responsibilities are specific and detailed is based on the nature of the group and the complexity of tasks and activities. Ineffective groups often have unclear, undefined, or unassigned roles and responsibilities that lead to confusion among group members and poor execution of work activities.
- **Capability mix:** Effective groups typically have a complementary set of skills and knowledge among group members that is well-matched to the goals and activities of the group. Based on the nature of the team, the degree to which capabilities need to overlap may vary, and the degree to which capabilities need to be broad or deep in specific areas of expertise may also vary. Ineffective groups often have a suboptimal mix of skills and knowledge with either capability gaps, too much capability redundancy, and/or capability overkill.
- **Contribution levels:** Effective groups are able to create a working environment where members have a relatively equal opportunity to contribute to the group process and outputs. This typically occurs due to the group's investment in planning work and inventorying skills and knowledge, and then best aligning work activities with capabilities. Ineffective groups often have a significant imbalance in the contribution levels of members, where a small minority of members does the majority of the work.
- **Enabling resources:** Effective groups are able to define their resource requirements and typically have access to, and are able to acquire, the resources, such as tools, technologies, and information, required to perform the work of the group. The access to and acquisition of resources can come through various supporting and

well-defined channels from inside the organization, such as from the group's sponsor, or outside the organization, such as from an advisor or consultant. Ineffective groups often are unable to define resource requirements, do not have access to needed resources, or may not understand how to gain access to and acquire resources within the organization. For one or more of these reasons, these groups often underperform due to a lack of resources.

- **Internal dynamics:** Effective groups develop a positive and productive dynamic over time, characterized by a shared imperative to achieve the group purpose, a healthy and constructive as well as challenging dialog, an ongoing attention to group process, a methodology for group-based consensus and decision-making, the active capture of feedback from external stakeholders, a comfortable approach to addressing any emerging conflict, a discipline in carrying out group activities relative to a plan, and a commitment to carrying out accountabilities with agreed upon standards of quality. Ineffective groups often have uneven internal dynamics, with varying levels of commitment, sub-standard facilitation of group process, undisciplined habits in carrying out group activities, a lack of interest or appreciation in getting feedback from external sources, and an avoidance of accountability or conflict. These groups are susceptible to an overwhelming leader, engaging in groupthink and follow-the-leader behavior.
- **Norms of participation:** Effective groups develop implicit and explicit norms of behavior over time, typically reflecting the characteristics of honesty, trust, openness and receptivity to feedback, mutual respect, acceptance of new ideas, encouragement of group members, and teamwork. Ineffective groups often have few explicit norms or implicit norms, and the few that are present are practiced inconsistently. If explicit norms are present, there is inconsistency in practice and a general disregard for the importance of and follow-through of these norms.
- **Performance tension:** Effective groups typically have a strong, but healthy, performance tension in the group that serves to keep the group focused, efficient, and disciplined in conducting its work and achieving its goals. Deadlines are consistently met and deliverables are on-time and at expected standards of quality. Ineffective groups often have little to no performance tension, even though some participants on the team may have high performance standards as

individual contributors. Therefore, there are inconsistent levels of commitment to the purpose and goals of the team. These groups can be inefficient and unfocused as well as inattentive to progress or results. Deadlines are often missed and deliverables vary widely in their level of quality.

- **Integrative activity:** Effective groups typically conduct their activity within a broader context of the organization, paying attention to the interactions, relationships, interdependencies, and points of interface of the group with its environment. These groups tend to engage in collaborative behavior with lateral and vertical stakeholders, such as other work groups or decision-making teams to produce deliverables that are fully integrated with other related work products developed outside of the group. Ineffective groups often conduct their work in a vacuum, view themselves as islands of creativity and performance, and/or mistaken their membership as representative of the broader organization thereby neglecting the interdependencies with other organizational entities and processes.

DHARMA LOG

The **unenlightened** organization over-utilizes formal teams and groups (and under-utilizes networks) to get work done, often chartering an extensive number of teams concurrently that result in too much time spent in the forming and norming stages of the group life-cycle and too much time in unproductive meetings. The **enlightened** organization creates the conditions for effective groups and networks that often emerge as well as dissipate organically, and invests less time and energy in formally managing the portfolio of these entities.

When the conditions just outlined are present, even to varying degrees, working groups and teams will typically perform at higher levels of quality and productivity than if these conditions are not present. In some cases, though, in climates of both low and high levels of collaboration, groups can suffer from ego-driven behavior that can significantly reduce their effectiveness. In situations where groups are highly cohesive, insulated or isolated, and homogenous in make-up, the group-ego can manifest itself in several ways. Groups may feel they are unassailable and that their work is more important than it really is. They may suppress conflict and create an illusion of strong unanimity. They may achieve consensus too easily or too quickly without the necessary data, discourse, and diversity of ideas. And they may reject needed interaction, support, and guidance from outside the team. Groups and teams should always be aware of the potential for ego-driven behavior and groupthink, encourage constructive and challenging dialog, encourage creative and divergent ideas, and engage an outside party to periodically observe and review the process, decisions, and deliverables of the group to ensure it is not falling into one or more of these traps.

Exploring Network Effectiveness

One of the most important areas of organization effectiveness that has received less attention from researchers and practitioners alike is that of network and community effectiveness. As we have already explored, an organizational network reflects a web of interactions and relationships that cut across traditional organizational boundaries and that generates value through dynamic exchanges and transactions between participating individuals and groups.

A common type of network includes *practice networks*, where participants working in similar disciplines or with interest in similar domains share knowledge and exchange ideas. Other common types include *value networks* that link individuals, groups, and other networks in the direct value creation activities of the enterprise, such as a six sigma/lean operations network, *communication networks* that syndicate and socialize information, and *internal/external networks* that reflect the productive relationships the enterprise has with its external environment, including alliances, partnerships, and consortiums. *Organizational communities* are typically a stronger form of network involving more face-to-face interactions, a greater proximity of work activity, and often more personal relationships.

Regardless of the type of network, there are fundamental elements and conditions for network effectiveness. High performing organizations place great emphasis on the effectiveness of both formal and informal networks. The conditions and elements of network and community effectiveness include:

- **Network facilitation:** Effective networks typically have a built-in facilitation function that is performed by a participant or a designated facilitator, and/or by a feature of the technology being used that helps transmit the free flow of information and provides a user-friendly method for interaction among network participants. Ineffective networks often rely too heavily on technology to facilitate the development of productive outcomes from ongoing network communication (and do not have a defined role for helping network participants draw conclusions, make decisions, or develop well-formed ideas or recommendations).

- **Network governance:** Effective networks typically have some form of regulating system that monitors network activity to help ensure that desired levels of quality and productivity are met with respect to interactions and information exchange, while also preserving the desired format and "organic" mode of the network. Network governance also involves assistance in the periodical measurement and validation of the performance of the network. Ineffective networks often have no visible or even invisible regulating system to help guide the "organic" nature of network activity in productive directions. Moreover, some networks may have too many "gatekeepers" or "anchor" nodes that prevent the fluid flow of information sharing and decision-making.
- **Norms of interaction:** Effective networks typically develop implicit and explicit norms of behavior over time, reflecting the characteristics of openness to new ideas and sharing information, responsiveness to network activity, an understanding of the dual-roles of knowledge seeker and knowledge contributor, agility to capitalize on emergent ideas from the external environment, and self-management in using technology as a tool for interaction. Ineffective networks often have few norms of interaction and there is very wide range of the nature of participation in network activity, slowing down or even preventing the network from adding value in efficient ways.
- **Enabling technology:** Effective networks typically utilize some form of technology, such as email, instant messaging, chat rooms, or other web-based tools, to enable information exchange and other interactions, given the high number of participants who are working at different times and in different places. Ineffective networks often do not have a technology platform (beyond just email) that enables the network to efficiently interact and productively exchange information.
- **Network intelligence:** Effective networks have built-in processes and practices for transforming information into knowledge and, in essence, learning as a total system so that new ideas and new information can be constantly integrated, and the overall knowledge of the network

continuously updated. Ineffective networks often do not learn; there is no mechanism for capturing data or the integration of data into important information or syndicating this knowledge across network participants.

- **Participation and composition:** Effective networks typically have a preferred degree of participitation with formal or informal guidelines for the desired composition of the network, including who can join and participate, and how and when they can join and participate. Some networks are managed almost as closed systems when it comes to membership, while others are totally open systems with no barriers to participation, and others have some limited guidelines for membership. Ineffective networks are often either too closed and myopic, or too open and broad, both ends of the continuum being suboptimal in terms of the quality of network activity.
- **Participant expectations:** Effective networks typically have explicit and/or implicit expectations regarding the contribution of network participants relative to the purpose and goals of the network, the day-to-day intensity of their activity in the network, the nature of roles and responsibilities that come with network participation, and the expected demonstration of network norms and behaviors. Ineffective networks are typically unclear about participant expectations and allow for a very wide-range of participant involvement that at times can undermine overall network productivity.
- **Network interfaces:** Effective networks typically have an extensive reach inside and/or outside of the organization, need peripheral vision to integrate with organizational activity both laterally and vertically, have a clear sense of their points of interface with other groups and networks, and monitor and manage their interactions. Ineffective networks often do not pay any attention to their interfaces and therefore poorly leverage the work and their activity with other networks. In some cases, networks allow smaller webs of activity within them to "drift" away from the core network, causing distraction and inefficiency.
- **Learning conditions:** Effective networks typically involve a wide variety of informal learning opportunities through high quality day-to-day interactions. They have organic feedback loops (e.g., through explicit norms of interaction for giving feedback) that iteratively improve the quality of knowledge used within the network, and also implement formal learning experiences within the network to consolidate,

enhance, and syndicate knowledge through periodic meetings, on-line forums, webinars, chat-rooms, and video conferences. Ineffective networks often do not have the means to capture information or syndicate knowledge. Feedback is treated too organically, with little responsibility for creating feedback loops. And there are very few if any planned, formal learning experiences.

- **Measurement and assessment:** Effective networks typically have a built-in methodology for measuring and assessing network performance through the facilitation and/or governance function supporting the network. This includes a methodology for sharing information about network performance with participants and improving the performance of the network over time. Measures may or may not be specifically defined or even well-understood in some more informal networks, but at the very least there is a process for gaining member/participant observations regarding the usefulness and success of the network. Ineffective networks often have no interest in or methodology for measuring and assessing their effectiveness (and interestingly, participants may not see this as an issue, since their perception of a network is highly informal and purely organic). A lack of any kind of assessment, however, prevents the network from learning, evolving, and improving, even through informal and organic means.

When the conditions just outlined are present, even to varying degrees, networks will typically perform at higher levels of effectiveness than if these conditions are not present. Nevertheless, as in the case with groups and teams, network effectiveness may be substantially reduced when there is little to no formal oversight. Similar to the need for more than just the belief in the "invisible hand" in macro-economic systems (which we recently and very painfully have relearned), there is a need for more than natural network forces to ensure optimal network performance. There are several "watch-outs" that may indicate the need for improved network performance from increased oversight, including a lack of identifiable deliverables and/or outcomes from ongoing network activity, a lack of interactive information exchange (a lack of true communication involving forms of dialog and discussion), a highly uneven distribution of focus and activity with respect to the work of the network, the emergence of min-webs or isolated webs within the network, and a lack of clarity regarding network membership, composition, and expectations.

MY SAMADHI *A Personal Revelation*

Over the past several decades a few organizations have moved beyond the traditional use of project teams, implementation teams, and key initiative groups to larger-scale, fast-cycle, community-based change methodologies. In the early 1990s I explored these approaches, studying the works of Marilyn and Fred Emery, Marvin Weisbord, and David Axelrod, pioneers of a process given many labels over the years including "open systems change," "future search," and "direct participation."

In a nutshell, these high involvement processes are large-scale interventions that involve engaging a broad, diverse, and high number of organization members, as well as external stakeholders, in a multiple-day, highly interactive, self-managed "conference." Over the course of the conference, participants go through a well-planned, thoughtfully-designed, carefully facilitated, but also very flexible (with limited boundaries) experience. This process includes getting the whole system "in the room," gaining a broad perspective on the past, establishing a sense of community among participants regarding their current reality, finding common ground on the issues, opportunities, and potential actions, creating a "preferred" future with respect to new directions, and achieving public commitment on the part of all participants to the actions agreed upon.

I worked with several organizations using this type of process, focusing on challenges such as strategy execution, organizational efficiency, work system and business process redesign, performance culture development, workforce diversity, and reward system change. The process was highly successful given its underlying principles: that real change can happen in real-time when you involve the "whole system" in a singular and shared experience, and engage people in solving the problems that they confront on a daily basis. In contrast, most organizations depend on the judgment of executives, who are often detached from the day-to-day realities, or depend on project teams and that typically have a narrow perspective and limited implementation authority, to tackle key organizational challenges.

While the "whole system" methodology has been proven to be highly effective in achieving significant change in a short period of time, it also has several fundamental weaknesses given its typical application in the context of the traditional and mechanistic model of change. In other words, this process is still applied in the context of a static and discrete model of change where participants take precious time away from their "regular" jobs and practice the art of unfreezing and refreezing, committing to do things differently, but going back to the same old job they had before, and at times with limited follow-through.

In the future, the most successful and enlightened organizations will weave this approach into the core of their operations, utilizing communities to quickly develop ideas and move them to implementation on a continuous basis. But perhaps more powerful than that—and this reflects my learning after several years of doing this work—**organizations will understand that whole system methodology not only results in a shared vision of a potential future, but creates an awesome positive energy field that substantively affects the internal energy field of the enterprise and influences and alters the external energy field of its environment.**

This energy, sent out into the universe, changes the flow of things, and enhances the value creation potential of the enterprise. The collective awareness that is generated enables the enterprise to more easily walk its own path.

Exploring Community Effectiveness

The mesmerizing and epic film *Crouching Tiger, Hidden Dragon* explores several different types of communities and their interrelationships in ancient China. The masters of the Wudan community have been the protectors of goodness, purity, truth, and justice through centuries of practicing white magic, martial arts, meditation, and expanded consciousness. Hidden high in the mountains of the country's interior, the community embraces the principles of living and learning together in harmony, principles practiced by many enlightened communities across those lands and, later, in the Zen monasteries of Japan. These timeless principles include existing together under the same conditions, observing the same rules, speaking carefully to avoid dispute, sharing gratefully one's possessions, sharing openly different points of view, maintaining physical, mental, and spiritual health through discipline, and creating common ground to sustain the joy of daily community life.

SUTRA LESSON ***Building Community***[17]

In his classic book, *The Different Drum*, M. Scott Peck suggests that the principles of good communication are the same as community-building, and explores the use of broad rules as critical to the process:

> **"The rules of communication and community-building can be simply taught and learned with relative ease. This conscious learning allows people to remember the rules and practice them at a later date."**

He goes on to say:

> **"As with other things, the rules of communication and community-building are best learned experientially. If they know what they are doing, virtually any group can form themselves into a genuine community."**

Over the years, in western society, organizations have tried different ways to build community. One path has involved the conducting of large-scale interventions that involved either the whole enterprise (that is, the "whole system") or large communities within the enterprise, in a highly collaborative exercise to achieve major organizational goals in a very short period of time. These interventions helped to engage and mobilize the whole workforce, or a large portion of the workforce, in real-time to support the implementation and execution of complex change. The critical success factors for these experiences almost always included clear and straightforward goals, simple ground rules for participation (such as openness, personal respect, and constructive dialog), broad but specific boundaries regarding the scope of the effort, and action plans for mobilization that were immediately and publicly committed to.

At the center of many of these large-scale change processes are multi-day conferences where groups of people bring highly diverse perspectives to bear on difficult organizational challenges, led by a team of facilitators who guide the flow of the experience in a firm, but typically hands-off way. Within these community experiences, small and large groups and networks form, accomplish specific tasks, and disband in real-time. Some continue this over the course of the whole event. Others continue their work well-beyond the close of the conference.

These experiences are essentially microcosms of the enlightened organization. They are designed with many of the conditions necessary to unleash the power of positive and productive energy of the organization. They are fishbowls of people swimming in the flowing relational energy fields of the enterprise who, while always present, are too often not fully tapped into. In these conferences, participants from within the organization swim together with other constituents from outside the organization. Executives talk openly with front-line workers. Diverse teams organically emerge to complete a specific task and then disband. Community leaders brainstorm with training managers at the same time a group of customers and sales professionals explore future scenarios. New affinity groups and networks self-organize and self-regulate to examine complex topics more holistically.

At the same time, every conference has a backbone, a carefully thought out strategic design, carefully guided by conference facilitators, to ensure that the collective activity of participants is moving in the same direction, albeit at different speeds and levels of efficiency depending on the time in the life-cycle of the experience. The strategic *design* is to a conference what the strategic *intent* is to the enterprise.

This high involvement in community experiences can be messy, frustrating, and emotional, requiring patience and tolerance, not unlike how the real world works and how things can feel within an enlightened organization that is co-evolving effectively with its environment. Moreover, these large-scale collaborative methodologies do not replace the need for expert input, analysis, and advice, or executive decision-making. The organization does not transform into a democracy for three days, but certainly employs democratic ideals. It is still an organization that has participants in formal leadership roles for a reason: to make key decisions and be accountable for key outcomes. But with subject matter experts and senior executives in the same room as everyone else, participating in the same experience, there are many opportunities to access these resources and utilize their expertise and authority to get things done when needed and in real-time during the experience.

Sutra Lesson *The New Collaborative Model*[18]

In his engrossing book, *The Empathic Civilization: The Race to Global Consciousness in a World in Crisis*, Jeremy Rifkin explores how large groups are demonstrating superior results:

"These new flat collaborative learning environments mobilize the collective wisdom of crowds, and their track record is impressive when compared to traditional hierarchically organized corporate learning environments."

As an example of an organization that has invested in high-involvement, community processes, a global energy company conducted a series of large-scale interventions involving enterprise communities of people from around the world to develop strategies for increasing diversity (for the corporation as a whole), identify substantial cost savings (for the shipping company), develop new performance measurement processes (for the chemical company), and identify leadership opportunities for minorities and women (for the information technology division). Over several years of repeatedly conducting these experiences, the company found that not only had it achieved important goals very quickly, but that it had also developed new levels of trust between senior management and employees. It substantially increased the commitment and loyalty of participants, and gained momentum in reinforcing the ideals of openness, broad-based information sharing, collaborative problem solving, and collective accountability within the enterprise.

The enlightened enterprise understands the magnitude of the challenge in engaging whole communities in face-to-face transformative processes. It also understands that change is not "discrete" nor can it be "managed." Change is continuous and can be guided and shaped. In the future, then, conscious organizations will seek to create the conditions for weaving this practice and methodology more organically into the fabric of the culture and the day-to-day operations of the organization. In essence, the flowing currents of these amazing and meaningful experiences will no longer take place in a fishbowl, but will flow in the sea-currents of the enterprise as a whole on a more regular basis.

In the future, large-scale initiatives that require high levels of interaction in real-time will involve less formal planning, design, and preparation, will entail greater utilization of advanced technologies to bring large groups together as a community, and will be utilized more frequently and organically as a more natural way in which work is done. Rather than spending months gaining approval, inviting participants, designing conferences, planning logistics, conducting conferences, communicating outcomes, and syndicating action plans, enlightened organizations will create the conditions for large groups and communities to more fluidly and productively self-organize, self-regulate, and collaborate to achieve superior and inspiring results.

Incenting Collaborative Activity

There are many factors and conditions that support and reinforce collaborative goal achievement within the enterprise. Many of these are non-financial in nature, ranging from how work is designed (to be more meaningful) to how performance is assessed and recognized (to be more motivating). Over the past twenty years, there has been much debate in public and private circles of both commercial and social sectors regarding whether financial incentives actually work, and whether they can support or detract from the collaborative achievement of results. Whether individuals are working primarily in small teams, broad-based groups, or in broader-still communities, the short answer to the question of whether monetary incentives work is, of course: *it depends*. In this context, be warned of anyone who suggests that financial incentives *always* or *never* work. They are wrong.

There is significant research that has been conducted over the past three decades clearly showing that group incentives, *when designed effectively*, can significantly influence participant behavior and the achievement of improved results in the areas of quality, productivity, cost, cycle time, revenue, and value creation, among others.

There are many kinds of financial incentive programs, also called variable pay or pay-for-performance, that are used at different "levels" of the organization (strata in the hierarchy) and with different populations. Over the years it has become very common for executive groups as well as sales functions to participate in performance-based compensation programs. More recently, however, organizations have increasingly begun to explore and implement performance-based reward programs for other groups that constitute the remaining *vast majority* of the workforce.

Around the turn of the millennium, several studies indicated that more than fifty percent of American companies used some form of group-based incentive pay. Group-based incentive programs, at the most fundamental level, are simply programs that award predefined groups additional compensation for the achievement of predefined goals and results. In examining a cross-section of for-profit organizations, it would not be uncommon to see many types of groups participating in incentive programs, including R&D functions, software development teams, assembly lines in production facilities, hotel management staff, distribution center shift teams, customer service teams, development and fundraising groups, and so on. As an example of the prevalence of these programs, but perhaps not entirely unusual, a medical device enterprise that operated in many countries around the world found that there were over two-hundred incentive programs in effect throughout the organization, with unfortunately little oversight or coherence.

While the purpose of this book does not include an extensive exploration of group incentive programs, it is important to view these programs as a potential factor in or condition for supporting and even driving effective group behavior and performance. An effective incentive approach involves using performance-based compensation as a strategic process and tool for incenting collaborative goal achievement. *So what does this really mean?* Consider the following practices that have been empirically demonstrated over time as critical to the success of variable pay programs for groups:

- **Clear purpose:** The purpose of the program must be clear in terms of whether it is intended to motivate specific behavior, drive enterprise results, communicate priorities, share in the financial gain of the enterprise, or some combination of these. Consider, for example, the photo-processing company that used group incentives to clearly communicate and reward for improvements in processing and service quality (no other metrics were used).
- **Definite participation:** The incentive must include clear guidelines for who (which groups) participates in the program and at what range of compensation opportunity. The scope of participation is typically based on the purpose of the incentive program(s), the array of groups that have direct influence on desired performance, and the degree to which variable compensation is a prominent part of the organization's internal value proposition for its people. Consider, for example, the global pharmaceutical organization that provided its regions and divisions with a design framework that enabled them to determine incentive participation based on more local competitive practice and business needs.

- **Coherent Design:** The incentive design—how the program works—must support and align with how work actually gets done. It should also align with the internal value proposition of the enterprise in terms of the prominence of compensation relative to other elements such as *association* with the values of the organization or opportunities for *development*. Finally, if there are multiple programs within the enterprise, focused on different groups, there must be points of alignment among any interdependent programs. Consider, for example, the financial services institution that introduced incentives to directly reinforce its re-engineered, group-based loan processing operations, measuring and rewarding results at both the group and unit level.
- **Meaningful metrics:** Determining what will be measured and rewarded with respect to group performance is one of the most important elements of incentive design. The most effective incentive programs focus on two to three measures that reflect *key value creation drivers*, such as asset utilization and cycle time, and/or reflect *key result areas* that are more downstream, such as service quality, cost reduction, productivity, revenue growth, and customer satisfaction. Note that a major study of incentive program effectiveness conducted several years ago reported that the most effective programs had both at least one operational measure (e.g., value driver) and one financial (e.g., results area) measure. The other most important consideration in determining program metrics relates to the degree to which group participants can significantly impact the measure, and whether the metric should be measured at the group *and/or* enterprise level. Consider, for example, the furniture production facility that incented its assembly groups on waste reduction and its distribution groups on efficiency, and the whole facility on on-time delivery.
- **Sensible Goals:** The most overlooked aspect of implementing effective incentive programs, and yet extremely important, is the process used to set performance goals or ranges for each program metric. A good process will typically build a fact-base upon which to set goals for a finite period of time, such as three, six, or twelve months. The fact-base that helps determine stretch, but still realistic goals for the group can include past performance levels, past variability and cyclicality trends, competitive benchmarks (if available, but not required), business objectives going forward, and the financial contribution to the enterprise (in hard or soft dollars) if incentive

goals are met or exceeded. The goal setting process should have a built-in feedback loop so that program managers can learn from each performance period to set goals—often in partnership with the actual group participants—that create a sound and strong relationship between program awards and overall group and enterprise performance. Consider, for example, the insurance company that goes through a facilitated, rigorous methodology each year to ensure that performance ranges are aligned with historical performance levels as well as future goals and financial requirements.

- **Improvement infrastructure:** One of the most common and hazardous traps in implementing group incentive programs is a lack of program connection to, or simply the inexistence of, a continuous improvement process or culture that supports the actual improvement needed to help groups "move the dial" on key metrics, achieve stretch goals, and earn rewards. Organizations often make the mistake that the incentive program *itself* is enough to dramatically improve results, but this is the case only if the enterprise *actively* uses the tool to develop strategies for improvement and help group members understand how they can work differently to contribute more value. Rarely does the simple existence of variable pay open the gates to whole new levels of performance. Consider, for example, the consulting firm that enhanced its partner bonus plan to reward more handsomely for cross-practice business development. The program failed to move the dial significantly because there was very little internal training or coordinated activity to foster cross-practice synergies among the business developers.
- **Rigorous review:** It is critical for the organization that has implemented one or more incentive programs to periodically review program effectiveness and make modifications to the design as needed, in a transparent manner, ensuring that group participants understand why the changes are being made. In some organizations, participants may actually be involved in the review process for their own plan. Program effectiveness reflects the degree to which the incentive is achieving its purpose, the degree to which there is a desired pay for performance relationship, and the degree of overall return on investment to the enterprise. Due to ongoing review, effective incentive programs are more like incentive *processes* and should be managed as thus. Consider, for example, the durable goods manufacturing company that uses a statistical model to determine the return on

investment of its incentive plans on a quarterly basis. This information is then used to determine if new performance ranges or new metrics are needed.

The enlightened enterprise may or may not utilize performance-based compensation processes to incent group collaboration and results achievement. While there has been an increasing trend to move away from fixed compensation to more variable compensation, incentive-based rewards are not required to achieve superior performance levels and value creation. The conscious organization uses incentives strategically and judiciously. It ensures that incentive programs are purpose-based, straightforward, well-understood, and aligned with other programs and processes of the enterprise. Finally, it rigorously assesses the degree to which incentives directly impact enterprise performance, help create value, and bring a substantial return on investment to the enterprise.

THE TAO: Walking a New Path

In getting started on the path toward improving the effectiveness of groups and networks within the enterprise, consider the following diagnostic questions:

- ***How are groups and networks used to do work?*** Consider the various activities that groups and networks perform for the organization, and the degree to which they are involved in strategic, operational, and tactical work. Consider the role that groups and networks play in carrying out the activities of key business processes. Consider the role that groups and networks play in serving the customer and/or interfacing with key external constituents.
- ***To what extent are groups and networks formally chartered?*** Consider whether the organization has a formal and consistently-used chartering process for groups and networks. Consider the degree to which formal and/or informal chartering activity establishes clear objectives, boundaries, and performance metrics for groups and networks.
- ***To what extent are groups and networks primarily formal or informal entities?*** Consider the different types of groups and networks in the organization and the degree to which they are formally chartered entities versus organic entities. Consider how formal groups and

networks differ from informal ones regarding the type of work they do, their life-cycle, their membership, and their performance levels and actual contribution to the value creation of the enterprise.

- ***Does the organization know how effective its groups and networks are?*** Consider how the organization monitors and measures group and network effectiveness. Consider how the organization supports and enables groups and networks to perform at optimal levels. Consider how disciplined the organization is in taking action to improve, re-charter, or dissolve under-performing groups and networks.

- ***How does the organization monitor and manage its portfolio of groups and networks?*** Consider how the organization inventories its groups and networks and the degree to which these entities are managed as a portfolio of assets. Consider the degree to which there are processes or practices in place to help manage the portfolio from either a centralized source or in a decentralized manner. Consider the degree to which there are formal roles in the enterprise that have responsibility for sponsoring, supporting, and/or guiding groups and networks.

- ***To what extent does the organization facilitate the collaboration of large communities toward specific objectives?*** Consider how communities within the organization collaborate today. Consider what opportunities exist for large groups of organizational participants to collaborate in real-time and face-to-face. Consider what strategic imperatives and initiatives might benefit from large-scale involvement and mobilization. Consider what enablers and barriers exist, given the organization's culture and history, to fostering more productive collaboration among large groups, such as business units, divisions, and functions.

- ***How does the enterprise use financial incentives to support, reinforce, and/or drive group performance?*** Consider how and to what extent the enterprise uses performance-based compensation (variable pay) for groups and units within the organization, beyond senior executive and sales populations. Consider to what extent these programs are aligned with respect to their purpose, measures, and focus on value creation. Consider how well the enterprise understands and applies good incentive design in creating and implementing these programs. Consider the degree to which the enterprise assesses the performance of these programs and periodically refreshes them to ensure the desired degree of alignment, effectiveness, and return on investment.

SEVEN

The Harmony of Healthy Interactions

Imagine that you are volunteering at your organization's annual charity picnic and carnival for a local shelter that serves families who have fallen on hard times. You enjoy this event every year and love to be outside on a cool, clear autumn day doing something good for the community. You always feel that you should do more volunteering but never seem to find the time, and yet, your cynical side wonders how much this event actually helps, and what the return on investment is for your organization. This year, you and a colleague are running the dunking booth and you can't wait for your turn to take a few plunges into the ice-cold water for a good cause. You enjoy getting to know your colleague, who is new to the organization, as you both work the booth. You have heard that he is really doing well in his new role and is already highly respected for his collaborative approach, original ideas, and a deep empathy for the well-being of his co-workers. You openly share your thoughts with him, wondering aloud about the true value of the event. Your colleague listens intently and introduces his wife to you who has walked up to the booth to say "hi." His wife seems excited to be there and thanks you for hiring her husband, even though you had nothing to do with it. As her husband smiles, she says: "After my husband's terrible battle with depression, we lost almost everything. He is a well-educated, hard-working man, but if it was not for this shelter we would not be here right now." **This is satori.**

IN THIS CHAPTER WE WILL EXPLORE IMPORTANT CONCEPTS regarding the nature and importance of healthy interactions within the enterprise, as summarized by the following principles:

- **The most successful organizations have the most healthy and collaborative people, relationships, and communities.**
- **Improvement in the quality of interactions and relationships represents the greatest opportunity to generate more powerful energy fields and create greater value.**
- **Improvement in the physical, mental, emotional, and spiritual health of people is required to improve the quality of interactions and relationships.**
- **Rather than control the interactions of people, the enlightened enterprise creates the conditions that foster more open, authentic, collaborative, and creative relationships.**

In the future the most effective organizations will create, support, and reinforce the conditions for healthy interactions and strong relationships among their participants, enabling them to harmoniously achieve the reality they conceive and collectively turn their vision into superior value creation. In essence, the most successful organizations will have the healthiest participants, the strongest relationships, and the most collaborative communities. The balance of this chapter explores these ideals and further explains their importance.

We are all spiritual beings living a human experience. Each of us is born and lives with the universal spirit as an inherent part of our being. The notion that some of us are more spiritual than others is an illusion. Growing a cool pony tail, going to yoga at the cliff-side spa, surfing and becoming one with the wave at lunch-time, or roughing it in a desert ashram does not a superior spiritual being make. Each of us expresses the same true nature of spirit, but does it in different ways. We are already of *spirit.* And we should not compare our degree of spirituality or limit how we see and accept each other with respect to our individual life-situations. Each of us struggles and each of us succeeds. Each of us represents a center in the universal field of energy, the unified field of intelligence and spirit, and together we create the reality of our world. In our quest to achieve greater community, we seek unity, not uniformity. Mindful of all of this, it is true that some individuals are more awake than others, more conscious, if you will. They are more aware of and attuned to the artificial and imaginary veils with which we have covered our world.

While we participate in the creation of our own *real experiences*, we also allow a whole host of illusions to stand in the way of seeing and experiencing a richer and more meaningful *reality*. The human mind creates its view of the world through the experiences, memories, and behavioral patterns that have been imprinted within it over time. When an event occurs, the human mind uses these historical-based constructs to observe and process the event. The mind subjectively captures data from what is observed and adds meaning based on personal beliefs and values, forming a deeply personal perception. Each of us sees people, places, and things similarly but also in our own unique way. The mind makes assumptions and draws conclusions from its perceived reality, and in turn demonstrates behavior and takes action, imprinting subjective beliefs and judgments further into the psyche. Each of us acts on our own perceptions in different ways. Each of us possesses our own perceptual framework. This ongoing loop of observation, perception, and action at the individual level is the foundation for all behavioral interactions within social systems.

It is important, then, to remember that organizations are fundamentally open, self-regulating, social systems. Each participant in the social system of an organization has a unique set of attitudes, motivations, beliefs, priorities, preferences, and dreams. Each of us can, and often do, misuse these energy patterns causing misinterpretation, misunderstanding, and other ego-driven behaviors that are often destructive. This behavior plagues organizations every moment of every day.

But there is good news. As we become more conscious, we can leverage our understanding of these patterns to break-down biases, re-interpret information and other stimuli, reframe our thought processes, and better integrate more rational, less impulsive, behaviors and actions with other participants in our communities. In this way we can move beyond thinking to awareness, and move into a higher level of consciousness, a higher vibrational frequency of mind. Even then, when demonstrating new levels of consciousness, we will still need to be aware of the "old tapes" constantly being played in our disarmed, but still potent and forever present, egoic and unconscious mind.

KOAN: WHAT IS CONSCIOUSNESS?

Consciousness reflects the state of awareness where an individual is able to transcend the thinking of the mind. Thinking and awareness separate, a strong presence in the moment occurs, and there is a renewed spiritual connection with energy field of the universe.

Unleashing the Potential of People

Understanding the dynamics of human behavior at the individual and group levels is profoundly important to improving organizational performance. These dynamics affect the degree to which every single interaction in every single part of the organization at every moment in time is either generating positive and productive energy or negative and destructive energy for the enterprise.

Understanding what makes an organization more effective, and striving to achieve the extraordinary potential of the organization, means understanding the people that make-up the organization. And every person is different in some way with respect to how they listen, process information, learn, communicate, solve problems, and generate new ideas. We understand intellectually that this innate diversity can be a wonderful source of fresh ideas, creativity, and innovation, and yet, our minds, at a more unconscious and ego-driven level, often lead us to making easy rationalizations, unhelpful distinctions, heavily biased judgments, and erroneous evaluations. Through our inherited assumptions and filtered thought processes we invent all sorts of resistances, evasions, and justifications in our daily interactions, often without even knowing it. In this way our imprinted patterns of thought can and do get in the way of leveraging the power of curiosity, objectivity, and diversity in working well together to achieve enterprise results.

Consider how the ego-driven mind develops and sustains the following irrational, and yet *universal*, human beliefs that have been identified and studied for years, by pioneering experts like Albert Ellis and others, to better understand how the inherent states of the ego—fear, want, safety, separation, and time—can unproductively affect belief systems and states of mind:

- **The ego tells us we must have approval.** The mind must feel that it is appreciated by others as being capable and competent. The perceived lack of this can cause strong feelings of anxiety and insecurity that manifest as toxic behaviors within the enterprise. Think about your own mental programming in this arena and what you observe in others on a daily basis. *How often has an important interaction inside of an organization, or an important project or initiative, been undermined by an ego-driven sense of lack of appreciation?*

- **The ego tells us we must have fairness.** The mind must feel that it is treated by others in the way that it expects to be treated: with justice and equity. The perceived lack of this can cause strong feelings of irritability and hostility that manifest as toxic behaviors within the enterprise. Think about your own mental programming in this arena and what you observe in others on a daily basis. *How often has a growing relationship inside an organization, or the dynamic of a working group or team, been impaired by an ego-driven sense of lack of fairness?*
- **The ego tells us we must have convenience.** The mind must feel that it is able to exist in comfort, free from struggle or hassle. The perceived lack of this can cause strong feelings of intolerance and discontent that manifest as toxic behaviors within the enterprise. Think about your own mental programming in this arena and what you observe in others on a daily basis. *How often has an important activity, meeting, or appointment inside an organization been subverted by an ego-driven sense of lack of accommodation?*

With these irrational beliefs in mind, consider how each participant in the organization brings a unique (and continuously developing and evolving) set of personality characteristics and traits that affect all of his or her interactions and relationships both positively and negatively. Each unique personality involves a different mix of mental (rational), emotional (relational), physical (practical), and spiritual (transcendental) energies that determine the nature and quality of a person's expression and the degree to which she represents a positive energy source within the organization.

In the disciplines of behavioral psychology and human dynamics there is an extensive amount of research and knowledge on the various and diverse personality types that affect behavior, activity, interactivity, and communication. These personality dynamics reflect a broad array of differences in the nature of values and beliefs, emotions and behaviors, approaches to discovering and learning, interests and affinities, and interpersonal communication styles. Embracing this diversity is critical for creating the conditions within the organization's environment for healthy and productive interactions and relationships.

SUTRA LESSON *Conscious Interdependence*[19]

In their groundbreaking book, *Human Dynamics: A New Framework for Understanding People and Realizing the Potential in Our Organizations*, Sandra Seagal and David Horne write about our need for increased consciousness when communicating:

"In the future, understanding the diversity of human functioning will play a central role in the success and sustainability of both organizations and societies."

In large part due to the unconscious state of ego-driven thinking, the vast majority of interactions between people are of lower quality than they could and should be. This is true of interactions that occur in all facets of an individual's life-situation, *including* the interactions at work, which are clearly very important in developing the relationships that do the work of the enterprise, generate energy, and create value. The low quality of organizational interactions is the primary obstacle to—and therefore the greatest opportunity for—the generation of powerful and positive energy fields. Organizational interactions are constantly disrupted and thwarted by the cognitive snares of the ego and the associated negative thought patterns of the mind. Consider the whole continuum of ever-present causes of and conditions for low quality interactions, organized below by key aspects of the egoic mind (some of these are richly explored by David Burns, David Myers, and other pioneering psychologists who study these phenomena).

Ineffective actions and interactions are often caused by *biased* ways of thinking, such as:

- Viewing events or situations in black and white or all or nothing absolutes, without the ability to consider the "grey area" between two ends of a continuum of possibility.
- Drawing conclusions very quickly or being unduly influenced based on limited or anecdotal data (that often support one's own initial assumptions or hypotheses).
- Assuming and predicting outcomes based on insufficient information or incomplete personal experiences, sometimes called fortunetelling.
- Allowing preconceptions, biases, beliefs, and other mental patterns to affect or control the interpretation of data/information.

- Misremembering past and recent experiences in self-enhancing ways that are then applied to influence current situations.
- Mistakenly perceiving in oneself or others that experience equates to knowledge, tenure equates to capability, and (over)confidence equates to leadership ability.

Ineffective actions and interactions are often caused by *exaggerated* ways of thinking, such as:

- Dwelling on the negative characteristics, or discounting the positive characteristics, of an event or situation.
- Making too much of or too little of the relevance or impact of an event or situation, often termed magnifying or minimizing.
- Overestimating alignment or contriving consensus from a filtered or biased view of the group/interaction dynamic and the degree to which there is real convergence or agreement.
- Overestimating one's capabilities relative to others, judging others more critically than oneself, and seeing one's own defects as common while one's virtues as rare.

Ineffective actions and interactions are often caused by *irrational* ways of thinking, such as:

- Conforming to custom, ritual, or imprinted past practice (a mindset of *it has always been done this way*) when the situation requires original or creative thinking.
- Applying specific characteristic patterns of particular events or situations too often to other independent events or situations, often termed generalizing or stereotyping.
- Misperceiving correlation with causation, and using this perceived cause and effect to attempt to predict or control outcomes.
- Concluding what someone else is thinking about you or a situation with no real data or fact-base, sometimes called mindreading.
- Over-focusing, or anchoring on one single solution to multiple and diverse problems, often based on hindsight and past perceptions of cause and effect.
- Learning only through direct experience as opposed to learning from the experience and teachings of others or other resources such as books or other media.

- Labeling a person or situation in a way that over-generalizes negative qualities and/or equates an individual's true nature to a specific quality.

Ineffective actions and interactions are often caused by *defensive* ways of thinking, such as:

- Holding oneself accountable for situations that are outside of one's control, sometimes called personalizing.
- Defending one's actions and demonstrating denial even when there is objective evidence to support another solution.
- Not taking personal responsibility for one's actions and constantly blaming others for less than desirable outcomes (accepting credit for success and blaming others for failure).

The prevalence of these thought-patterns is staggering inside organizations; it is truly a testament to the human spirit and our perseverance that we can accomplish the things we do, given the minefield between our ears that extends across our meeting room tables! Quite simply, it is through greater consciousness that this pervasive and treacherous minefield will dissolve and disappear, unleashing a whole new era of communication, interaction, and collaboration. Improving the quality of organizational interactions is therefore critical to the generation of powerful energy fields. Here is the good news. There are specific cognitive and behavioral strategies that enable individuals and groups to avoid or transcend prevalent cognitive traps and distortions, create new patterns of positive thinking, and achieve healthier interactions and relationships. These strategies include the following:

- **A constant awareness that cognitive distortions exist** and act as strong energy sinks during interactions between people. The art of self-awareness and the non-judgmental awareness of the egoic mind of others is the foundation for improving the quality of interactions.
- **The avoidance of impulsive responses, reactions, and decision-making** by pausing to examine the moment with the perception of an observer. Perhaps the most important attribute of the conscious individual as well as the conscious organization is the ability to rise above an interaction or situation and dispassionately and objectively observe its dynamics. This is best done on an ongoing basis but can also be used at critical milestones, where people involved can "press the pause button" and transcend the often chaotic interplay, take a breath, and more consciously walk the best path.

- **The practice of objective, non-judgmental curiosity,** seeking first to understand the nature of the topic, event, or situation that is in focus. Demonstrating genuine curiosity not only helps to better understand the perspectives of others, but also goes a long way in establishing a sense of personal interest and mutual caring between people.
- **An understanding of the difference between "objective" observation and "subjective" assessment,** where *observation* reflects a degree of personal perception and *assessment* reflects a degree of personal judgment. Understanding when and how to apply observation involves using confirmable data to make a point and has a lower probability of triggering an unwanted defense mechanism. Understanding when and how to apply assessment involves sharing a point of view that may have a higher probability of triggering an unwanted defense mechanism.
- **The replacement of blaming and personalizing with critical thinking and problem solving,** where commonly-used tools such as force-field analysis, diagnostic questioning, and scenario building can be used to identify root issues and quality solutions. Blaming and personalizing serve no constructive or productive purpose in the art of value creation. Instead, more positive applications of energy involve the open reception, active absorption, and detached concentration of specific ideas, alternatives, and strategies.
- **The active focus on areas of agreement rather than disagreement,** where the elements of the activity/interaction are segmented to identify areas of common ground. One of the most prevalent barriers to productive progress is the amount of time that individuals and groups spend on topics where there is disagreement. In most cases, significant progress can be made when areas of agreement are identified and used as a springboard to move forward in developing recommendations or making decisions.
- **The capture and collection of useful data to build a relevant and robust fact-base** that can be infused into ongoing dialog and work activities. One of the most powerful ways to neutralize negative energy in interactions is through the use of high quality data from objective sources.
- **The proactive disabling of old and unhelpful memes, preconceptions, patterns, and practices** by practicing the act of unlearning and reframing automatic thoughts into more rational actions and

responses. This strategy involves moving beyond simple awareness into a more active identification of the specific cognitive distortions that may be in play. In an environment that can be open about these natural phenomena of the mind and educates itself about how they manifest themselves in every-day communications (and through organizational memes), participants can directly and non-judgmentally identify these energy sinks together and reframe them to improve the quality of the interaction.

- **The removal of obstacles that stand in the way of shared goals, and/or discovery of whether alternative goals may be more appropriate,** resolving differences and leading to the possibility of different alternatives and solutions. Unconscious organizations often "power through" barriers to achieve goals at any cost, in part influenced by a fear of failure that itself is an illusion. A more conscious strategy at times is to slow down to speed up, and take a more pragmatic approach to remove obstacles or reframe what really needs to be achieved.

DHARMA LOG

In the **unenlightened** organization, executives and "leaders" attempt to manage, control, incent, and coerce people into behaving in specific ways that have been deemed appropriate by the powers that be. In the **enlightened** organization, executives and "leaders" create the conditions that reinforce healthy thinking, interactions, and relationships through the role-modeling of empathic and conscious actions.

We are all immersed in the sea-currents of our own thinking, the cumulative energy field of all that we have ever thought, said, and done. Our capacity to act, interact, and flow among the currents is limited by our level of consciousness as participant and observer. The motives and biases imprinted in the mind actually affect what is seen and heard, and furthermore, affect our responses and reactions. With this in mind, we also know that these lifelong patterns of wrong or unconscious thinking can be consciously unlearned and neutralized, and an entirely new mental and emotional state can be established in the mind. We can reframe and rewire our minds by observing our thought patterns and emotions, examining assumptions and belief systems, and reviewing our thinking and decision-making processes. We can swim more easily among the flowing energy currents of the organization and its environment, create new flows of productive interactions and harmonious relationships, and ultimately achieve far superior results for the enterprise.

Achieving High Quality Interactions

Almost every interaction among individuals and groups can be improved in its overall quality, productivity, and strength as a source of positive energy. This can be done using a single framework of conscious interactions (applied to almost any situation, such as meeting, conference call, one-on-one conversation, performance review, customer lunch, etc.) described as follows:

- **What is the topic and objective of this interaction?** Early in an interaction it is important to be aware of the general topic(s) being discussed and the emerging potential outcome of the interaction, such as idea and knowledge exchange, brainstorming, problem solving, and/or decision decision-making.
- **How would the nature of the interaction be described?** Throughout the interaction it is important to consider how an "objective" bystander might characterize the nature of the dialog in terms of the degree of positive/constructive versus negative/destructive energy, the degree of one-way versus two-way information transfer, the degree of active and appreciative listening, the degree of balanced contribution, and the degree of potential individual benefit versus mutual benefit.
- **To what extent is the nature of the interaction consistent with our values?** Throughout the interaction it is important to be aware of potential conflict with the values and beliefs of the organization and to raise these concerns in a non-threatening manner.
- **What assumptions and belief systems are shaping the interaction?** Throughout the interaction it is important to be aware of the assumptions and beliefs applied during the course of the interaction and the degree to which there is openness and interest in constructive challenging, sharing diverse ideas, and a reasonable breadth in the interpretation of ideas and information.
- **What potential cognitive distortions are at work in this interaction?** Throughout the interaction it is important to be aware of the natural patterns and distortions of thinking that are reflected in the dialog and that may negatively affect the nature, direction, and/or outcome of the interaction.
- **To what degree would more information and/or a fact-base improve subsequent interactions on this topic?** At key points in

the interaction, it is important to pause and explore whether more information is required to continue to the dialog or to engage in productive future interactions on the same topic(s).

- **To what extent are there areas of agreement and common ground?** At key points in the interaction it is critical to highlight where there is agreement, consensus, or common ground emerging to confirm progress and help gauge the quality and productivity of the interaction.
- **How does this interaction support the purpose of value creation?** Throughout the interaction it is important to consider how it directly or indirectly contributes to value creation, such as contributing to the execution of work within a value network or generating new knowledge that will help in a specific organizational decision-making process.
- **What can be done to improve the quality of this interaction and future related interactions?** Toward the end of the interaction it is important to recognize what has worked well and not well and what might be done to improve the nature of the interaction with respect to the assumptions being applied, additional information that may be needed, the dynamics of the interaction, and its alignment with values and potential for contributing to value creation.
- **What was learned from the full interaction?** After the interaction, or set of interactions, it is important to review what was learned in terms of the process of the interaction and its outcomes.

Building Positive and Productive Relationships

High quality and productive *interactions* are the foundation for building high quality, productive, and healthy *relationships*. Relationships are not simply a series of interactions, however. Even high quality interactions can be somewhat *transactional* in nature, characterized by the prevalence of distance between participants and the degree to which contractual exchanges, negotiation and persuasion, infrequent contact, and a lack of personal investment may exist. Strong relationships, by definition, are typically more *relational* in nature, reflecting a highly charged relational energy that vibrates at a different frequency than the energy involved in more simple transactions. Strong relationships occur over time and involve shared benefits for participants. Relationships are vitally important because they involve a vested interest in mutual success, and are the foundation for achieving overall greater alignment, resonance, and harmony within the enterprise.

But strong relationships are critical for another reason. Throughout this book we have explored our ability to change and influence the nature of reality. We live in a participatory universe. Our participation affects our experience, which is our reality. Reality is not constant or permanent; it is dynamic and continuously emerging as entities co-evolve in relation to each other through the flow and exchange of energy. In other words, our reality is not defined by singular, independent phenomena. It is defined and explained only in how things *relate to one another*. The true nature of our reality, then, is one of *relationships*, and the stronger and deeper these relationships are, and the more harmonic their energy frequencies become, the more effectively we can create our desired reality. In the case of the enterprise, on a smaller scale, healthy relationships are therefore critical to walking a sustainable, successful path into the future.

In addition to requiring high quality interactions as a foundation, strong relationships are developed under many of the conditions that naturally evolve in an organization that creates positive energy for its environment. Some of the elements/conditions that reflect strong relationships include:

- A measure of consistency and continuity in personal and face-to-face contact. Not all interactions are in-person, but participants possess a degree of proximity and/or capability to communicate beyond voice-to-voice or through voicemail, email, and other interactive modes.
- A higher degree of investment and interdependence in defining and accomplishing shared goals and achieving mutual benefit from the relationship.
- A higher frequency of contact and degree of ongoing collaboration and dialog required to do more complex work, explore alternatives, resolve differences and accomplish shared goals.
- A greater openness in and commitment to sharing information, developing shared expectations, trusting personal agendas, and periodically discussing the effectiveness of the relationship to improve its overall quality.
- A measure of mutual learning that occurs, with participants benefiting from the experience of the relationship itself and the value exchange that comes from ongoing interaction.

Moving Beyond Diversity to Multiversity

The more diverse an organization is the more potential it has to be more open to new possibilities, make manifest its strategic intent, and demonstrate resiliency in its co-evolutionary activities. Once again, though, we find a need to move beyond established concepts into a new realm that better reflects the complexity of our interconnected global village, the *multiversity* of our world. Within our universal field of energy there are a vast number of determinants that greatly affect the productivity of our interactions and the health of our relationships within the organization. Consider just some of the elements of multiversity that affect our thoughts, behaviors, and actions every minute of every day (and these are not at all mutually exclusive): ethnicity, geography, culture, family type, personality type, values and belief systems, religious and spiritual traditions, politics, socio-economic class, educational experiences, work experiences, communication style, value propositions, and personal goals and priorities.

These elements of multiversity inform and influence our daily activities. Everything we think, feel, and do begins with our own personal, perceptual framework forged from the history and current state of our life situation and from our evolving degree of consciousness, our ability to transcend the memories, patterns, assumptions, and beliefs that impulsively and subjectively guide our mind. The more conscious we are, the more we are able to adapt our perceptual framework to a given situation, transcend destructive or irrelevant patterns, and achieve a productive interaction or activity. The more conscious we are, the more we understand how the elements of multiversity influence the perceptual framework and shape the actions of ourselves and of others. How each us think about the world, translate our thoughts into actions, manage our egoic mind, and in general perceive the nature of reality—all of which involve applying our perceptual framework—affects many aspects of being and doing in the organization. We must take care in our being and doing in an enterprise of relationships by being highly aware of several fundamental aspects of multiversity. These include the following:

- **The nature of our spiritual orientation:** Each individual in the organization is guided by their own religious and/or spiritual beliefs. These beliefs often translate into a degree of consciousness, empathy, and compassion that each of us brings to the workplace, which in turn affects the nature and quality of our interactions and relationships. In addition, spiritual orientation can influence one's interest in and ability to perform organizational activities at certain times or in certain ways. There is great sensitivity among most people regarding their spiritual (or religious) beliefs and traditions, since these are often hard-wired with their overall value system. Each of us has a strong and powerful spirit, but the extent to which we allow that spirit to shine through for the goodness of the enterprise dramatically varies by person. Some are farther along on their path to consciousness and enlightenment than others. Among all of the elements of multiversity, spirituality most of all requires awareness, tolerance, and acceptance.

- **The nature of our time orientation:** Each individual participates in the activity of the organization with a personal sense of time and pace. Depending on the situation, there is a range for each person within which this pace can be increased or decreased. An individual who works at a pace that is viewed by others as "fast" may perceive that he is working too slowly, while an individual who is viewed by others as "slow" may perceive that she is working fast. When a situation requires an increased pace, there are also differences in the degree to which an individual perceives the sense of urgency and changes pace accordingly. Moreover, some individuals are guided by an "event" orientation, where the sense of time is primarily anchored to events, such as a presentation that is coming up in three days, while others are guided by a "clock" orientation where there is close alignment of actions with the incremental flow of time, as measured by minutes and hours. In some cases, there are people who, for whatever reason, have very little sense of time at all.
- **The nature of our quality orientation:** Each individual in the organization has a personal sense of quality, and what constitutes good versus sufficient versus poor quality. Some individuals are very detail-oriented while others are more big-picture; some are perfectionists while others often apply the proverbial 80/20 rule. Due to the nature of products and services of some organizations, this perceived range of quality may be very narrow with few outliers. For example, quality can be measured quite precisely in many consumer products companies. For other organizations, such as universities and professional services firms, quality may be more subjective, and the perceptual continuum broader. Moreover, it is important to view differences in quality orientation not just with downstream *products* and *services*, but with upstream *activities*. In fact, it is the quality of

activity that permeates throughout the enterprise at all the nodes in its value creation networks that determines the overall quality of the organization, and much of this activity involves information transfer, process execution, and network navigation. In this context, quality is extremely difficult to define when it comes to knowledge-based work, which makes it even more important to understand how the perceptions of quality vary across individuals.

- **The nature of our authority orientation:** Each individual in the organization has a personal sense of the meaning of authority and its relationship to hierarchy. Some individuals are guided by a sense of equality and perceive that power is created through one's actions and contributions, while others are guided by a sense of authority and perceive that power is created from formal roles and vertical chains of command, or accountability. Based on where an individual falls on this continuum, there is variation among organization participants regarding the measure of immediate and ongoing respect, trust, and commitment that is given to people in formal/functional versus informal/psychic roles of authority and power.
- **The nature of our collaborative orientation:** Each individual in the organization has a personal preference and capability when it comes to working individually or collectively, how often, and in what context. Clearly, some people like to work by themselves while others prefer to work in groups. There are many different reasons for the difference in this orientation; some reasons are perhaps more legitimate than others. Regardless of one's orientation, we do know that organizations have increasingly become more collaborative entities and that the *ways* in which collaboration occurs is increasing as well, in part due to technological advances, such as teleconferences and web-based meetings. With this in mind, there still remains a continuum of preference regarding individual and group-based work, and it is important that these differences are understood.
- **The nature of our risk orientation:** Each individual in the organization has a personal comfort zone and set of boundaries with respect to risk as it pertains to their own safety, security, status, and success. Some individuals enjoy taking risks and embrace uncertainty while others are more comfortable with more routine and less uncertain activities. Clearly the risk profile of individuals changes (at least for most) as we move along the continuum from safety and security to status and success. Most people are risk-avoiding when it comes to

safety and security, while some avoid risk across the whole continuum. Others are more inclined to take risks when it comes to status and success. Often, an individual's risk orientation as it pertains to status and success is directly linked to the perceived risk/reward ratio. But even this varies among individuals where some are comfortable in taking big risks to earn great rewards (financial or non-financial) while others are not.

- **The nature of our loyalty orientation:** Each individual in the organization has a personal definition of what loyalty means, to what or whom it applies, and how it influences one's daily activities. There are different types of loyalty and within those types, different magnitudes of loyalty and different ways in which loyalty manifests itself. Much has been written over the past two decades about the "death" of loyalty on both the part of the organization and the part of the participant, but it *is not* very productive to try to understand what this really means. What *is* important is understanding that each person has a particular strength of *association* with the organization (an element of their value proposition) and a personal concept of loyalty that guides his level of ongoing commitment and engagement, as well as willingness to adapt to temporary dynamic situations where enterprise and individual values and needs fluctuate and become more or less aligned.
- **The nature of our motivational orientation:** Each individual in the organization is motivated by a mix of intrinsic and extrinsic phenomena. Individuals are intrinsically motivated along a wide continuum; for some, intrinsic motivation—the internal desire to achieve and excel—is very strong. Others are more motivated by a balance of intrinsic and extrinsic factors (other aspects of the value proposition such as strong relationships or career growth), while others appear to be motivated only by extrinsic rewards such as money. Not only does the mix of motivational drivers vary by individual, but so does the magnitude of the motivation itself, which is correlated to association, loyalty, and engagement, as shown in several large-scale studies over the past ten years. One's motivational orientation also can fluctuate with things that are going on in his or her life situation, such as the long-term illness of a loved one or with life-stage (early versus late in one's career).

In the dramatic and moving film, *The Power of One*, the main character is a boy who grows up as an orphan and who continually finds himself in situations where he does not fit in. As he grows into manhood, he learns how to thrive in the face of violence, prejudice, and unrest. He learns how to defend himself, speak multiple languages, fight injustice, and help others even when others are raging against him. At the same time he retains his sense of who he is—his true spirit—and where he came from. As the title of the film suggests, his path involves becoming a leader, originating not from his status but from his inherent sense of empathy, while also blending in with different cultures to embrace the unity that comes from being human.

As we have already explored, the creation of a positive and harmonic resonant energy field in an enterprise that achieves superior value creation does not come from uniformity, but rather unity. It is ineffective and unwise to attempt to "manage" multiversity, or too-tightly "control" the boundaries around productive network activity within a multi-cultural enterprise. Instead, the enlightened enterprise achieves unity of purpose and intent along with acceptance and appreciation for differences. Throughout the book we have touched on several key drivers and conditions that create unity and build community. Earlier in this chapter, for example, we explored strategies for establishing new patterns of positive thinking. Consider, then, the following summary of drivers and conditions for *embracing multiversity* and harnessing its incredible power to create a unified field within the enterprise:

- **Respecting our humanity:** Each of us has a unique life history and life situation, characterized by a vast array of experiences that have occurred over time. These experiences continuously shape the nature of our physical, mental, emotional, and spiritual well-being. It is therefore impossible and irresponsible to think we can pigeonhole or stereotype an individual based on a single external variable, such as ethnicity or perceived wealth or life stage. We must embrace each other's life story, with all of its imperfections, mistakes, achievements, and challenges. The only thing, and the most important thing, that universally binds us is our shared experience of *being human*.
- **Seeking first to understand:** It is imperative that in respecting our shared humanity we seek first to understand how our perspectives and viewpoints are similar and different. Many interactions and fledgling relationships are either slowed or killed by our propensity to attack different views from our own without understanding how and why an individual has these views This prevents us from our own learning and perhaps gaining productive insights. Curiosity leads to discovery, and

discovery leads to innovation, while at the same time this seeking establishes the foundation—a sense of personal interest and mutual caring—from which healthy relationships can grow.

- **Finding common ground:** It is a universal truth that we are all the same at the spirit level in our shared *humanity*. Beyond our common spirit-consciousness, however, we diverge and differ in many ways, forming our individual perceptual frameworks and the multiversity of our world. As we have already discussed, our differences can be enormous. At the same time, it is always surprising how similar we actually are in our "quest" for safety, security, meaning, fulfillment, happiness, and love. In fact, across a wide array of cultures and religions, there is significant evidence that the vast majority of us actually share a basic value system involving fundamental concepts of life, liberty, honesty, fairness, work, responsibility, tolerance, and community. It is therefore easier than we think to find common ground, even in challenging organizational situations where there might be heated debate and argument, and seemingly insurmountable differences. When we can identify shared experiences and values, and when we can focus on areas of agreement rather than disagreement, we will almost always move forward collaboratively and productively.
- **Applying objective data:** In almost any situation where differences in viewpoint and perspective can create barriers to progress, it is good practice to reduce the emphasis on subjective perception and replace it with good, hard, solid facts. High quality data—not necessarily quantity of data—can help create a foundation for efficiently finding common ground among differing perspectives. It is therefore critical that people have the opportunity to help build the relevant fact-base and/or have exposure to the conditions for its validity.
- **Transcending old patterns:** We are wired to perceive, behave, and act in a consistent way with our internal patterns and perceptual frameworks—the ruts in the road of our mind—created from our past experiences. We have discussed the need to transcend these patterns, to get out of the ruts, become more self-aware, and view the world more openly and objectively. The activities of a highly diverse enterprise require the constant awareness of our own biases, prejudices, and filters, and our subsequent ability to overcome these patterns and engage in healthy interactions and build productive relationships (and in the meantime create new, healthier patterns).

- **Understanding value drivers:** Similar to the collection of data, the more individuals possess a shared understand of how the business works and the key value drivers within the network of organizational activity, the more than can use a common language to interact and do work productively. Organizational literacy, especially as it pertains to value creation, enables individuals to more efficiently break-down barriers and overcome obstacles (that come from a multiversity of perspective) to have a constructive dialog, solve problems, and make decisions. The more in depth organizational knowledge is broadly shared, the more focused the participants can be in their interactions.
- **Rallying around the customer:** Customer requirements represent an effective platform for finding areas of agreement and common ground, even when there are highly diverse viewpoints and perspectives in play. Through an emphasis on the specific needs of the customer, interactions become less about the organizational participants (and their biases) and more about what truly matters, the organization's external constituents. By rallying around the customer, helpful boundaries are established that allow for a reasonable degree of multiversity, but also help to focus the collective efforts to more efficiently deliver value.
- **Communicating non-judgmentally:** Each of us has a unique personality and communication style, and this element of multiversity should be valued and respected. At the same time, there are characteristics of effective communication that each of us can adapt to, especially in situations that involve highly diverse perspectives and views. These characteristics are timeless, and reflect many of the concepts already outlined above, but perhaps the most important one is to communicate without judgment and to demonstrate a genuine openness to and acceptance of what others think and say and believe. This does not equate to agreement; rather, it is communication that involves curiosity, objectivity, and empathy.

Experiencing Fulfillment within the Organization

Healthy interactions and fulfilling relationships begin with healthy and fulfilled participants. The enlightened employee/member understands his role in the organization and the nature of his contribution. As a participant in the organization, he creates positive energy through full engagement in the strategic intent, culture, and community of the enterprise. He can see how his behaviors and actions influence and affect the health and value creation of the overall entity. He is able to observe his interactions and relationships and transcend the programmed reactions that are hard-wired in his unconscious mind. Through presence and engagement, this person is awake, aware of both the simplicity and complexity of organizational life, and finds meaning, joy and fulfillment in his *varied* contributions to the success of the organization.

SUTRA LESSON *The Modalities of Awakened Doing*[20]

In *A New Earth: Awakening to Your Life's Purpose*, Eckhart Tolle writes about three active modes of doing, their alignment with the creative forces of the universe, and how critical they are to realizing serenity and fulfillment in the workplace:

"The modalities of awakened doing are acceptance, enjoyment, and enthusiasm. Each one represents a certain vibrational frequency of consciousness."

He goes on to say:

"If you are not in the state of acceptance, enjoyment, or enthusiasm, look closely and you will find that you are creating suffering for yourself and others."

For the enlightened participant in an organization, the degree to which the work experience is fulfilling and meaningful involves three important concepts. *Acceptance* brings peace in the understanding that some activity simply needs to be done. The participant is taking responsibility for—and therefore finding meaning in—an activity that may not create enjoyment but serves a purpose and contributes to the whole. *Enjoyment* comes from doing an activity that unleashes intense creativity and is a catalyst for one's own sense of being and contributing. The participant takes pleasure in doing the activity itself, based on its inherent qualities. *Enthusiasm* involves performing an activity toward a defined goal or desired outcome. The participant is fully engaged in the enjoyment of the activity and the elevating experience of achieving a needed result.

Regardless of the nature of their job or role in the organization, participants can find enjoyment in their work by being present in the moment and conscious of the importance of that moment; nothing else exists except for each single moment of being and doing. In one insurance organization it was clear that the assistant salad makers (yes, this was a real job title!) in the cafeteria kitchen showed greater acceptance, enjoyment, and enthusiasm in doing their work than the corporate controller in the executive suite who made twenty times their salary. Organization participants who have the greatest awareness and congruence in their thoughts, feelings, and actions are the most conscious. Regardless of how routine an activity is, these participants constantly set goals (however minor), become immersed in their activity, connect the dots of their activity to other activities within the organizational web of activity, and learn to appreciate their immediate experience and the inherent value of productive activity. In some cases goals may not be met, but the conscious participant will find harmony in goal resolution and the creation of new pathways to success.

At a mid-sized consumer products organization, the environmental health and safety (EHS) employees consistently enjoy the modalities of awakened doing and find meaning and fulfillment in work that most participants in most organizations consider too repetitive and routine, and reserved for the lowest skilled people in the enterprise. At this company, this perception could not be further from the truth. EHS employees have developed over time a very strong sense of pride in what they do and believe that their duties, which include cleaning, eliminating waste, and ensuring the safety and purity of raw materials, are absolutely critical to the success of the organization,. They have proactively expanded their duties to include environmental sustainability practices and challenged the organization to consider their work as more impactful and valuable than traditionally viewed in most organizations. People in other departments comment on the enthusiasm and quality of orientation that EHS members bring to work every day. Through awakened doing, these people have generated a strong, positive energy field and are highly productive.

Emphasizing Health and Well-Being

One of the most critical and challenging issues regarding organizational effectiveness is the health and well-being of people. Unfortunately, many organizations do not have the wisdom or the courage to take a real interest in and invest in the health of their people. There are many reasons why organizations abdicate from the good "business" practice of promoting good health among their participants, including questions of the legality of rewarding good health, a perceived (but wholly mystifying) lack of a clear return on investment (ROI) of wellness programs, and the convenient belief that a person's health is simply a personal matter and not a matter of concern for the organization. This is unfortunate and unwise. Possibly more than any other factor, organizational performance and value creation suffer from untapped potential due to the poor health of enterprise participants.

The health and wellness of an individual involves the nature of their physical, mental, emotional, and spiritual fitness. In many "modern" societies and communities, where enterprise of all types are enormously important to the socio-economic ecosystem, the people who make-up the organizations suffer from an astonishing number and range of illnesses, disorders, addictions, and ailments. In general, people are eating in a less healthy way and eating more, taking too many medications, exercising less, and engaging in an array of other unhealthy activities including smoking, drinking, and using other mind-altering and addictive substances. Often these activities coincide with mental or physical health issues that are not adequately diagnosed or treated, such as depression, chronic pain, sleep deprivation, or poor nutrition.

Unhealthy people do *not* spontaneously become healthy when walking through the front doors of an organization. We should pause here and think about this. *How can it be any other way?* There is no right or wrong here, no blame or shame, just the objective reality that the vast majority of people are suffering. Not only are people often absent due to poor health, but when they are present, they bring their poor health with them, and this substantially affects the quality and productivity of their individual contributions, interactions, and relationships. *With this as our reality, how can organizations ignore this epidemic of poor health?*

They cannot. Our professional and personal lives have always been intertwined to some degree, and with the increasing complexity of our daily lives, it is even more true that we tend to spend more time "at work" than we do any other organization, activity, or at home, given our fragmented lives. Furthermore, with the invention of the internet and the increasing use of telecommuting and other flexible work practices used by some work environments (not as many as one might think, however), our work and non-work activities are even more intertwined and our boundaries less-defined. The concept of work/life balance today is even more confusing than it was ten years ago. Do we have more or less? Has technology helped or hurt? Does any of this matter? It is unclear. What matters is that each individual finds the right balance within a healthy lifestyle, and that organizations understand it is good practice to enable and support this personal process.

Life is a long and winding journey for most of us. We set sail on the ocean currents of our shared energy fields and chart a unique course, experiencing the ebbs and flows of our own personal adventure. Along the way we learn that there is no such thing as "normal." We learn that following rules and complying with policies do not help us be any more healthy or productive. We learn the art of conformity and lose our innate spirit of self-expression. We are bombarded with destructive memes that tell us to get a grip on ourselves and shape up, when we should be seeking help from others (and they should be offering more help to us). And most organizations reinforce this phenomenon when their executives spend hours and hours in meeting rooms deciding if it makes sense for the organization to do more to promote good health and be more active in the well-being of its people. The enlightened enterprise understands the insanity here. It does not question or debate the importance or value of this effort; it simply does it.

The good news is that, more and more, research studies—and the experiences of the few organizations that have awakened to the reality of this issue—show that there in fact is a substantial return on investing in both the mental and physical health of people in organizations. Some of the compelling findings from these studies and experiences include:

- A clear link between the use of wellness programs and decreases in employee disability, annual medical costs, workers compensation, sick-time, and unwanted turnover.
- A clear link between the enterprise participants who seek out and participate in organization-sponsored wellness programs and those who are consistently the most productive.
- A clear link between increases in productivity (as measured by output, days missed, and on-time arrivals) from employees who suffer from mental health disorders, such as depression, and their participation in organization-sponsored treatment programs.

My Samadhi *A Personal Journey*

The concept of enlightenment holds a special meaning for me as a spiritual being assigned to a highly imperfect human form. As a successful management consultant for over two decades I am blessed with the experience and expertise that comes from working with many organizations and people over the years. Over this period of time, I was asked somewhat regularly what the keys were to my success. I consistently responded by saying that self-awareness and a lack of ego were the most instrumental characteristics in my effectiveness and advancement. I now know that this was only partially true, that certain aspects of my health and well-being were in dire straits. Unaware of my ego's grip on me, I lived much of my life from a place of ego-driven fear and anxiety.

And like millions of other Americans, I struggled with significant physical, mental, and spiritual health problems. I found no peace in the countless airports, airplanes, and hotels that were my home. I found no respite in the endless client meetings and conference speeches that gave me my false identity. My passion for life was swept away by the winds of irritability and resentment. I injured my integrity and, a few times, neglected my duties, at least by my own high standards. I was eventually abandoned by some of those that I thought I could count on: people who might have been more helpful had they been more conscious, and less judgmental, themselves. I was lost in the wilderness of the mind and felt spiritually empty. The reality of my life was that I was profoundly *unconscious* in many ways, performing my roles as a family man and a business person with little real self-awareness and oppressed by fears contrived by my ego and the obsessions of the mind it had created.

One day I decided that I could no longer tolerate this situation. And after a period of time trying to take "control" of my life, and failing, it became clear to me that I needed to "let go" instead and fundamentally change my life experience. Through self-study, professional care, hard work, and a strong commitment to my mental and spiritual well-being, I have broken down many of the imprinted patterns of my mind and their associated destructive behavior.

I have *awakened* to a new level of *consciousness* that releases me from many of the negative memes of this world. **This process of renewal has helped me unlearn many of my perspectives and let go of many of my beliefs. It has enabled me to perceive the world more objectively and transcend the cognitive distortions and fear-based pathologies that had affected my life for so long.** I am no longer a prisoner of my mind and see more clearly the substantial opportunities for people and organizations to also transcend their self-imposed limitations, experience their inner happiness, and achieve far greater things than they think possible.

Today I often experience the natural serenity I once had, and that we all have, when we innocently enter this world with *beginner's mind* and a *pure spirit*. Each day I try to cultivate my consciousness by how I live and through the simple and practical activities of daily life. It is not always easy, and at times I fall prey to the old, destructive patterns, and I allow myself to be dragged into the world of form and the many unconscious forces and beings that inhabit it. But I do not dwell on the past or worry too much about the future. I rejoice in the presence of today. I practice rigorous honesty, and work hard not to judge others. I do not maintain anything close to spiritual perfection, but I remain committed to spiritual progress. I try to keep things simple and let things go. I try to act with discipline and live with passion. I care about people and give to receive. I am committed to creating positive energy and realizing a life of joy and abundance that each of us in this world deserve.

The most fundamental source of positive and productive energy within an organization is its people. Healthy people have healthy interactions and relationships and are highly productive. The enlightened enterprise invests significant resources in the physical, mental, emotional, and spiritual health of its members. These investments are both "hard" and "soft" and include the development of wellness programs and practices *within* the organization, the easy access to programs *outside* of the organization, and the flexibility for participants to pursue good health *on their own as part of their work-day*. They include the reinforcement of good health practices in key organizational memes, such as through enterprise values, communications, and operating principles. And more and more, there is a spiritual nature to this practice, a desire to experience peace and harmony through a more conscious connection between the spirit in each of us and the world as a single, interconnected organism.

These kinds of investments undoubtedly bring significant returns to both the organization and to the organization's broader environment. Moreover, the stakes are getting higher and the potential returns greater given the demographic trends that are shaping the workforce of today and tomorrow. The workforce is aging. The pool of employable talent in many professions is decreasing. The global marketplace for talent is becoming more competitive. And these trends will remain with us for years to come. In the context of this reality, organizations must do more to help their people be healthy, productive, and fulfilled. Consider again the telecommunications company that sponsors spiritually-based workshops; a key goal for this investment was to help improve health and wellness, which subsequently decreased sick-time and drug costs, and also improved productivity.

The enlightened organization does not discriminate against physical or mental disease in the attraction or retention of capable and talented people, but reaches out to them in meaningful and altruistic ways to educate them on good health practices, invest in their well-being, and help them in their disease management and recovery activities when assistance is needed. The enlightened organization does not avoid or abdicate from the sensitive and serious issues and challenges that surround the health of people and the healthcare system that is supposed to improve it. The enlightened organization understands that the health and wellness of its people are the most important and fundamental ingredients in its ability to exchange energy with the environment, influence its own reality, and achieve superior value creation.

DHARMA LOG

The **unenlightened** organization often demonstrates a stunning ignorance regarding the best strategies for dealing with health issues in the workplace, and believes that it is good practice to cast away people who are unhealthy, or perceived to demonstrate unhealthy practices, believing that simply replacing talent is the best policy. The **enlightened** organization understands the goodness of helping quality talent—especially talent that has demonstrated loyalty, commitment, and contribution over time—who may need and desire assistance and support in improving their health (and the organization understands the positive energy this creates in the workplace).

Enabling Healthy Creativity

As spiritual beings, all people are creators, and as creators, we see each day as a field of possibility, a field of potential activity to create new energy flows of reality. The values, culture, and work environment of the organization represent the enabling conditions for unleashing creativity, through continuous opportunities for learning, brainstorming, idea generation and incubation, and the application and integration of new concepts and paradigms. Healthy and conscious people in the work environment therefore represent powerful positive sources of creative energy.

Unfortunately, most organizations stifle creativity and innovation, erecting barriers through policies, processes, and work/job design that decrease, rather than increase, those opportunities for creativity and creative thought and expression. For example, a professional services firm would not allow one of its divisions to implement its own internal and external value propositions developed from a significant creative effort from a large number of people, due to a "one company" philosophy that made little sense (since the division did very different work, and attracted very different talent, from the other divisions).

In another example, this same organization would not make a relatively minor investment in a specific role that would have *reduced* the amount of administrative work of its partners and *increased* the opportunity for them to create new and leading-edge intellectual capital, a key component of their business development efforts and new revenue generation. In a third example, senior leadership rarely approved any "soft" investment in the creative process of developing new strategies for changing the firm's business model to better co-evolve with its changing and more challenging environment. It is not surprising that for this firm growth has been slow, value creation sub-optimized, and that the firm finds it harder and harder to attract top talent and differentiate itself from competitors.

A culture of innovation requires the conditions for creativity and support for the creative process throughout the organization, not just in traditional functions in the organization, such as marketing and research and development. As an integrated web of interactions, the organization that enables and places value on creative activity in all functions and at all levels has a better chance of success and survival in the long-term.

Organizational cultures that support creativity and foster innovation typically have the following qualities:

- Freedom to organically develop and explore new ideas among individuals, groups, and networks.
- Formal and informal processes, forums, and practices for developing, incubating, sharing, exchanging, and testing new ideas at all levels of the organization.
- Accessibility to new and cutting-edge domains of knowledge that is directly or indirectly relevant to the purpose and value creation of the enterprise.

- Stimulating learning experiences that involve creative activities for exploring both depth and breadth of specific knowledge domains.
- Broad (not narrow) filters for selecting and further developing potential ideas that can increase organizational capability and drive value creation.
- Networks and/or network facilitators within the organization that monitor the evolution of new ideas and support the activities involved in the creative process.
- Identification and nurturing of creative talent within the organization, and the freedom and resources for them to explore new ways of working, developing new products, and delivering new services.
- Substantive financial investment in formal and informal creative activities that drive innovation of new products and services and the ongoing co-evolution of the enterprise with its environment.

THE TAO: Walking a New Path

In getting started on the path toward improving the health of organization's people, relationships, and the overall well-being of the enterprise, consider the following diagnostic questions:

- ***Do people know how to listen and speak to one another?*** Consider the quality of formal and informal interactions across the wide variety of settings within the organization. Consider the degree to which diverse participants interact effectively and embrace, internalize, and take action on diverse ideas. Consider the degree to which people communicate honestly, directly, and respectfully. Consider how well participants are able to give and receive feedback, and have potentially difficult conversations with each other.

- ***Do people have free access to one another throughout the organization?*** Consider how accessible people at all levels in the organization are to other people. Consider the degree to which artificial barriers, such as geographic, functional, and hierarchical boundaries limit access and/or prevent discourse.

- ***Do people have free access to needed and helpful information?*** Consider how accessible important internal and external information is to a broad array of organizational participants. Consider how easy it is to access or acquire information that is required for specific tasks, projects, or decisions. Consider how technology is used to either enable or prevent the access to and use of information. Consider the degree to which people are trusted with proprietary and important information.

- ***Do people care about each other?*** Consider how individuals and groups mobilize when a colleague is in need. Consider the degree to which physical and mental health issues are treated with disdain and stigmatized, versus treated with compassion and support. Consider the general nature of interactions and relationships and the degree to which people naturally show a caring interest in each other.

- ***Does the organization support and invest in the health and wellness of its workforce?*** Consider the degree to which the enterprise provides programs that reinforce the mental, emotional, physical, and spiritual health of its participants. Consider the degree to which the principles of health and wellness are hard-wired into the daily activities and routines of the organization. Consider how the organization handles situations where contributing participants have health-related challenges and needs, and how well the organization supports their desire to improve their health.

- ***Does the organization embrace multiversity as a critical element of current and future success?*** Consider how open, receptive, and positive people are in the organization with respect to the many different aspects of diversity. Consider how far the organization goes beyond traditional definitions of diversity and leverages different views and perspectives. Consider the degree to which the organization understands and cares about how multiversity can impact its ability to co-evolve and achieve superior and sustained value creation. Consider the extent to which the organization measures and assesses diversity/multiversity and the degree of alignment between what it says it values and what it actually does.

- ***Is creativity truly supported, appreciated, and rewarded?*** Consider how well the organization nurtures, reinforces, and recognizes creative and innovative actions and behaviors both formally and informally. Consider the degree to which the organization invests resources in creative processes and talent development. Consider the degree to which reward systems reinforce the creative process and the development of new products and services that generate new sources of value.

EIGHT

The Path of the Enlightened Participant

Imagine that you are attending a mandatory training class—one of those classes that you have found to rarely be a good use of time. To make things worse, the organization has asked one of its engineers (of all people!) to teach the course, and you question the value of this, given all of the other priorities on your plate and the plates of others. The course has the mysterious title of Exploring Our Memetic Code, *so your interest is piqued, but again you wonder if this class will be another waste of enterprise resources. The instructor is an expert in genetics and you gradually discern that she is teaching material that actually may be of real value. She defines* memes *as the building blocks of culture, the ideas and clustered patterns that influence individual, group, and networked thought systems in the enterprise. She continues to compare this internal* memetic code *as similar to the genetic code in biological organisms, and goes on to discuss how memes evolve and interact in ways that substantially affect how well the organization creates meaning for its participants and how well it creates value for its constituencies. The most insightful concept, which comes toward the end of the class, is the idea that each participant in the enterprise is actually a sort of* memetic engineer, *with the intrinsic power through ongoing thoughts, behaviors, and actions, to influence and shape the culture of the enterprise on a daily basis. As you sense a growing awareness of this concept inside you (a new meme!), you raise your hand and ask how you can better wield this power. She responds that your thoughtful question has already started the process.* ***This is satori.***

In this chapter we will explore important concepts regarding how participants in organizations can most effectively contribute to the enterprise in ways that bring personal meaning and fulfillment, as summarized by the following principles:

- **The most important key to long-term success for the participant in any organization is the discovery and development of self-empowerment.**
- **Increasing one's contribution involves the growth and demonstration of competencies that directly link to key organizational capabilities.**
- **The conscious participant shapes enterprise culture and creates enterprise value through greater awareness, attention, and courage to proactively change unproductive and restrictive organizational practices.**

Each participant plays a unique and important role in contributing to the energy field of the enterprise and its creation of value. Throughout this book we have explored energy and value creation from an organizational perspective, but have recognized along the way that enterprise success is directly dependent on the contributions of individual participants. It is true that much of the work done inside organizations involves collaborative activity in teams, groups, networks, communities, and so on. Yet, even the effectiveness of collaborative activity begins with the individual and his/her behaviors, skills, knowledge, abilities, and actions. In this respect the most fundamental "unit" of any enterprise is the individual and his or her ability to maximize contribution in a way that is also personally meaningful and rewarding. The balance of this chapter will explore how individuals can best participate in and contribute to the conscious and high-performing organization, from the enterprise participant perspective.

Ascending to Self-Empowerment

The most important key to long-term success for the participant in any organization is *self-empowerment*. Unfortunately, the concept and term "empowerment" was very trendy a number of years ago and its overuse led to its ultimate demise in the organizational lexicon. The term was most often used in the world of organizations as a concept for creating the conditions within an enterprise that liberated and enabled people to work in new ways and contribute more to overall enterprise success. The concept itself is timeless, and fundamental to productive work design, but the context for empowerment during this period was that of a top-down process, or even worse, a program, where the organization was driving its application. And like many trends that emerge from within organizations, there was no shortage of irony and mishap as leaders *pushed* empowerment down into the workforce.

Consider, for example, the global consumer products company that preached empowerment to its production employees but was unprepared and unable to support needed work system change as individuals and teams evolved and developed new value propositions and new expectations for how work should be done and the financial rewards that should go along with it. In another example, consider the university that pursued empowerment among its administrative staff groups but did not provide the learning experiences and skill-building necessary for staff members to be able to actually increase their contribution, although they were given the green light to do so, causing dissatisfaction and anger among people in key roles.

Those organizations that were successful with the concept during this era created the conditions for empowerment to emerge from the bottom-up and from the periphery, and created demand—a *pull* rather than *push* strategy—for more freedom and autonomy within the workplace, transforming the way in which work got done. For most organizations, however, empowerment was eventually buried in the graveyard of good ideas that failed from a lack of real insight into the factors for its success in the first place.

Self-empowerment is a completely different concept. It is essentially the art of self-actualization within the organization setting. The most present, engaged, productive, and effective individual in the organization of today and in the future is the person who is committed to her authentic self, without being unduly influenced by the artificial limitations, controlling factors, suffering egos, and constraining boundaries that all too often are imposed upon her by the enterprise. In her quest to contribute the most she can to the enterprise while also experiencing the most personal fulfillment, she does *not* seek to climb the organizational ladder (the more trendy term these days is “lattice”) as her primary goal, but rather she seeks to climb the ladder of consciousness and in so doing consistently expands her field of possibility and increases the value she brings to the efforts of the enterprise.

KOAN: WHAT IS *SELF-EMPOWERMENT?*

Self-empowerment is the development of a more conscious level of participation in the organization. It reflects the power that comes from one's own commitment to his or her authentic self and the ability to be present, aware, and focused in every situation and activity. The self-empowered person is humble, but also confident, courageous, but also rational, in his or her ability to support and significantly contribute to the success of the organization.

The key to self-empowerment, that is, achieving power within the organization originated by one's true self, is the consciousness that comes from physical, mental, emotional, and spiritual balance and well-being. It is an awareness that transcends the pathological and unproductive impulses and actions of the egoic mind. It is the generation of constructive, positive energy while navigating the (at times) treacherous waters of the organization, and detaching from, and then helping to transform, its pervasive obstacles, barriers, and energy sinks. With consciousness comes power in many forms, and the organization participant wields this power in different ways, depending on the degree to which the enterprise as a whole is walking a more conscious path itself, with a high performance orientation and a strong value creation culture.

So how does one become self-empowered? What does self-empowerment look like and feel like? How is self-empowerment different from self-centeredness? There are important strategies and practices that an individual participant can and should embrace to achieve a degree of self-empowerment that will not only unleash new levels of performance and contribution, but will also result in new degrees of meaning, fulfillment, and joy. These include:

- **Actively practice good health and wellness:** As a participant who interacts and collaborates with other participants, and helps create the social and cultural fabric of the enterprise, the individual must focus on the state of his physical, mental, emotional, and spiritual well-being. Health and well-being begins at home, and the enterprise participant should first focus on a healthy lifestyle in general. Without good health, in any one or more of these four areas, challenges and problems will arise in the participant's personal life that will erode his focus and attention in the workplace, and ultimately reduce his overall effectiveness. Sound body, sound mind, and sound spirit are each equally important for an individual to achieve and sustain peak performance in the organization in the long term. The conscious participant understands that the health of individuals determines in large part the overall health of the enterprise.

- **Consistently demonstrate the spirit and values of the enterprise:** As a participant who creates his own energy field that affects the overall energy field of the enterprise, the individual must constantly create positive energy through thoughts, behaviors, and actions that reflect and reinforce the spirit and values of the enterprise. Every thought, behavior, and action vibrates at a certain frequency, and the more these vibrations are in-synch with the frequencies of the enterprise's true nature—*who it is*—and its values-in-action, the greater the potential for superior value creation. The conscious participant understands the vast potential of the enterprise that comes from the alignment of values-in-action and the positive energy field that this creates.
- **Understand enterprise internal and external value propositions:** As a participant who exchanges value (i.e., energy) with and contributes to the value creation of the enterprise, the individual must have a solid working understanding of both its internal and external value propositions. With respect to the *internal* value proposition, and its elements of association, relationships, development, activity, and rewards, *alignment* is most critical between what the organization provides the individual participant and what the participant values and expects as an employee and/or member. In other words, the internal value proposition is a two-way street, where substantial value exchange must flow both ways between the participant and the organization. With respect to the *external* value proposition, and its elements of impact, experience, and advantage, *commitment* is most critical for the organization to realize its value proposition and for the individual in contributing to that realization. The conscious participant pays close attention to the implicit and explicit nature of these organizational value propositions and periodically assesses the actual versus desired degrees of alignment and commitment to ensure that he is fully engaged, effective, and fulfilled in his work and ongoing contributions.
- **Understand key enterprise value creation processes and networks:** As a participant who does work for the enterprise, the individual must have a solid working understanding of the key organizational processes and networks that contribute most to its

overall value creation and delivery. This involves taking initiative to constantly learn about the roles, resources, interdependencies, technologies, process flows, and other strategic and operational activities that make-up the internal and internal/external networks that create value. In other words, this involves the participant taking \responsibility to gain organizational *literacy:* to know how the organization works and functions, how it serves its varied constituencies, and how it creates value. There are multiple ways in which this knowledge can be gained and applied over the long-term through individual initiative, including self-driven research, formal and informal discussions with other participants (in other roles), training courses, educational classes, observation, job swapping and/or job shadowing, and so on. The conscious participant understands the key to his ability to consistently maximize his value to the enterprise is his knowledge of the key leverage points within organizational processes and networks that most directly impact value creation, so that he can focus a greater share of his efforts and influence on those areas relative to other activities that have less impact.

- **Transcend the egoic mind:** As a participant who influences the overall effectiveness of the enterprise, the individual must continuously strive to transcend the distortions, traps, and illusions of his ego, and in so doing, dramatically improve the overall quality of interactions, communications, and relationships within the enterprise. As we have explored, the ego wishes to be special, separate, and in control. It is the primary cause of human suffering as well as the primary cause of negative energy and energy sinks within the enterprise, including hierarchical and control-based behavior, poor quality communication, unproductive politics, destructive competitiveness, and insufficient collaboration and a lack of community. It is also a primary cause of ignorance, arrogance, hubris, and greed, all of which are dangerous enemies of the enlightened enterprise. The ego creates negative states of mind that require the insecure needs for approval, unreasonable ideas of fairness, and undermining notions of superiority. The conscious participant transcends his ego. He rises above his egoic mind and is not imprisoned by its false assumptions, obsessions, and impulses. He understands that true power does not come from formal authority, psychic roles, or even functional roles. True power—the result of self-empowerment—comes from informal authority that is created through the ongoing demonstration of the timeless qualities of true leaders and influencers: authenticity, integrity, dignity, humility, confidence, initiative, passion, tolerance, compassion, and unity, among others. The conscious participant understands that by guarding against the ego's distortions and traps, detaching from the ego-driven behaviors of others, and continuously developing and demonstrating these qualities, his actions and contributions *over time* will far surpass in impact those that remain imprisoned by their egos, and he will contribute far more to the overall consciousness and performance of the enterprise.

- **Actively practice the art of conscious interactions and relationship building:** As we have already explored, a conscious interaction involves the *application of mindfulness to the interaction itself*, where the participants are actively engaging as well as *observing* the nature of the interaction as it unfolds. The observation of critical elements of the interaction, such as whether the nature of the interaction is consistent with enterprise values and the degree to which cognitive distortions and ego-driven behaviors are present, enables the participant to change the nature of the interaction in real-time to increase its overall positivity, quality, productivity, and value. Practicing the art of conscious interactions and diligently and consistently using the framework will build stronger relationships and dramatically improve the performance of the organization. The conscious participant recognizes the importance of high quality interactions as the foundation for solid working relationships, and strategically selects relationships that he actively builds and sustains over time through open information sharing, shared goals and collaborative work activity, frequent communication, mutual learning opportunities, and personal contact and interest.
- **Actively pursue and monitor learning and unlearning:** As a participant who is responsible for the continuous development of new skills, knowledge, and abilities that increase his value to the organization, the individual must actively pursue new learning opportunities. This entails understanding the learning conditions, processes, and experiences that are best suited for her to continuously learn and develop new competencies that enable her to perform her role with excellence, and that also support and strengthen the key value creation capabilities of the organization. The conscious participant seeks constant learning on the job as well as more diverse learning experiences that involve such activities as self-driven study,

research, coaching, mentoring, and formal training/education. Moreover, and very importantly, the conscious participant is aware of how assumptions, beliefs, perspectives, and other patterns can influence his behaviors and actions, and thus overall effectiveness, and seeks to constantly unlearn, deprogram, and disable these unproductive mindsets and destructive memes.

- **Consistently embrace the three modalities of doing:** As a participant committed to the realization of the organization's mission, value proposition, and value creation goals, the individual is most productive, and also most fulfilled, when he is aware of the appropriate modality of *doing* in each enterprise situation. Recall that the three modalities of awakened doing, as outlined in a previous chapter and defined by Eckhart Tolle, are *acceptance*, *enjoyment*, and *enthusiasm*. Each has a positive energy frequency, or vibration, associated with it. Each require and involve the energy of attention, a concentration in the present moment on the specific activity that is being carried out. The conscious participant is highly aware that he flows in and out of each of these modalities throughout his day, and uses this awareness to find meaning in each activity, recognizing that not all activity involves enjoyment or enthusiasm per se, but he can still do his best work through presence and acceptance, an immersion in whatever needs to be done at that moment in time.
- **Show courage in creating positive energy:** As a participant who contributes greatly to the overall energy field of the enterprise and helps create the social fabric of its culture, the individual should be courageous in demonstrating specific action-schemas that create positive energy. Several key action-schemas that are particularly effective at the individual level include trusting people to do their best, working with passion on the value proposition of the enterprise, demonstrating courage in being creative and taking reasonable risks, compassionately recognizing the goodness in others, actively listening and seeking to understand, reframing problems as opportunities, replacing judgment and blame with collaborative critical thinking, searching for areas of agreement rather than disagreement during interactions, and proactively being of service to others inside and outside the organization. The conscious participant is in a constant state of positive energy creation and vibration, and practices and applies positive behaviors and actions that energize the organization in highly productive ways.

- **Consistently perform at high levels of excellence:** As a participant who performs a defined role, carries out specific responsibilities, and contributes to the results achievement of the enterprise, the individual must aspire to consistently perform at high levels of quality, productivity, and overall excellence. In the conscious and high performing organization, excellence is defined in the context of impact on value creation. In this broader frame, success and performance have a more inclusive definition than is typical in most organizations, and includes financial, operational, customer, owner, social, and environmental outcomes. The conscious participant does not fear performance expectations, feedback, review, or assessment. Moreover, he understands that performance and contribution transcend standard, narrow definitions of goal achievement. He is less concerned about ratings and position in performance distributions, and more concerned about the performance of the enterprise, and how he can best optimize his contribution to it and to its value creation efforts overall.

SUTRA LESSON ***Conscious Participation***[21]

In *The Art of Power,* Thich Nhat Hanh writes about the power of consciousness and the importance of mindfulness in transforming one's professional life:

"Mindfulness is the energy of attention. It is the capacity in each of us to be present one-hundred percent of the time to what is happening within and around us."

He goes on to say:

"If every day you produce positive thinking and good ideas with understanding and compassion; if every day you practice active listening and caring speech; if every day you do good actions, your value will reveal itself to the people around you."

Exploring Competencies that Foster True Power

The strategic and operational capabilities of the enterprise are critical to its competitive advantage, co-evolution, and overall value creation. These capabilities are often translated into competencies at the individual level, bundles of skills, knowledge, and abilities that relate to specific roles, jobs, and individuals. Each competency is a mix of things that, when learned, developed, and demonstrated by the enterprise participant, integrate with the competencies of others and help build and/or strengthen organizational capability in key areas for success.

The conscious enterprise invests significant resources in the identification of the *unique* bundles of skills, knowledge, and abilities that drive high performance (and are difficult to imitate or replicate by other entities), infusing these competencies into organizational processes, including work process design, role design and definition, network design, formal and informal learning activities, performance assessment and improvement efforts, and growth and development activities. The conscious participant understands the relative importance of various competencies given her role, responsibilities, career trajectory, and overall sphere of influence inside and outside the enterprise.

As an example, a biotechnology company developed a competency model where individuals were expected to select three to four competencies to focus on as part of their ongoing performance development activity. Each participant selected her competencies based on her role and functional area, level (sphere of influence and associated performance expectations), and career path (technical or management). The degree to which the participant invested energy into these select competencies was furthermore determined by the participant's current levels of competency, key areas of responsibility, and specific individual goals. In essence, individuals used the framework to determine specific competencies to further develop based on personal *and* organizational needs. In this way, the organization was consciously and effectively creating the conditions to help its people increase their impact on key enterprise capabilities and value creation drivers.

Each organization that directly links individual competencies to organizational capabilities in a serious way will typically create its own unique framework, based on several sources of input. These sources include, but are not limited to, executive input, subject matter expert input, organization capability requirements, the traits and abilities of top performers, gaps in the skills and knowledge levels of the workforce, and the expertise of outside consultants or advisors.

With this in mind, it is still helpful to consider a number of competencies that, *regardless of the specific commercial or social sector*, are of particular importance to the success of the enterprise participant who pursues new levels of consciousness, self-empowerment, and informal leadership, and strives for new levels of performance and value contribution. Moreover, these competencies are also critical for success given the uncertainty, complexity, and dynamics each of us face in the ever-changing and evolving world. It is important to note that they are not mutually exclusive or collectively exhaustive, and their relevance can vary based on role and the nature of responsibilities. Twelve key competencies include seeking, creating, facilitating, integrating, regulating, engaging, collaborating, executing, adapting, daring, attracting, and unifying (note the first five have already been explored to some degree from the organizational perspective in a previous chapter). These twelve are described as follows:

- **Seeking:** The conscious participant who is strong in this area demonstrates a passion for learning and constant curiosity about the enterprise, its value creation drivers, its environment, and other role-specific or project-specific activities. Individuals who embody the competency of *Seeking* take initiative to expand the field of knowledge in order to expand the field of possibility and influence reality. They capture information, build knowledge, and syndicate this knowledge within the enterprise. They challenge the status-quo and break down old patterns, debunk old myths, weed out misinformation and other destructive memes, and constantly search for new ways of understanding the dynamic world and the implications for doing things more effectively. They search for information and knowledge that can be used *with insight* to apply greater wisdom for the benefit of the organization. They do not necessarily seek truth in its pure form, since that is too abstract a concept, but instead prefer to replace judgment with an empirical fact-base as a solid foundation for action. *Seeking* is essential to the creation of positive energy fields and the ongoing process of co-evolution.
- **Creating:** The conscious participant who is strong in this area demonstrates the ability to generate new ideas, processes, programs, practices, and other innovative memes that generate positive energy for the enterprise. Individuals who embody the competency of *Creating* balance an active imagination with a practical sense of reality to invent new things. They find real fulfillment in self-expression and the creative process. They often see the world differently and therefore conjure fresh ideas and envision new possibilities. They possess a cognitive agility to see past constraining influences, boundaries, and ingrained patterns to conceive new ways to improve the

value creation capability of the enterprise. They are often at the forefront of transformative activities that are sparked from new ways of perceiving, thinking, and doing. Highly effective Creators understand and work within the creative culture of the enterprise; they are able to not only generate new ideas within relevant domains of knowledge, but also help nurture and incubate these ideas through the natural screens, filters, and gatekeeping that exist as part of the co-creative process of the enterprise. *Creating* is essential to innovation, the development of new processes, products, and services, and the co-evolution of the organization with its ecosystem and environment.

- **Facilitating:** The conscious participant who is strong in this area demonstrates the ability to help groups, networks, and communities more efficiently and effectively interact to achieve shared goals. Individuals who embody the competency of *Facilitating* are able to stay objective and detached in a wide variety of situations and with highly diverse issues and challenges. They are able to incorporate diverse perspectives, rigorously explore alternatives, and manage conflicting priorities to help find common ground, achieve consensus, make difficult decisions, or determine a new direction. They effectively apply a broad stakeholder model to optimize value creation activities, by assisting in the prioritization and balancing of the requirements of all enterprise constituencies, including employees, owners, investors, customers, communities, and ecosystem entities. They effectively navigate within and across enterprise structures, functions, and networks to help establish and sustain meaningful, collaborative activity. They role model the behaviors that foster productive interactions and healthy relationships. *Facilitating* is essential to the strategic and scenario planning, decision-making, and collaboration activities of the enterprise.
- **Integrating:** The conscious participant who is strong in this area demonstrates the ability to make connections and create alignment (when needed) between seemingly disparate ideas, phenomena, systems, processes, networks, and entities. Individuals who embody the competency of *Integrating* possess a broad, systemic perspective and are able to see patterns, linkages, and interdependencies within complex situations and environments, and apply this insight into improving the performance of the whole. They are excellent analyzers and problem-solvers. They also utilize a breadth and depth of

knowledge across multiple domains to help ensure the seamless flow of resources and help others make systemic decisions that are in alignment with enterprise values and value creation strategies. *Integrating* is essential to the co-evolution of the enterprise in an increasingly complex socio-economic ecosystem (recall the definition of complexity is the co-existence of differentiation and integration).

- **Regulating:** The conscious participant who is strong in this area demonstrates the ability to observe, monitor, analyze, and assess situations in the context of alignment with organizational values, environmental forces and requirements, and the efficacy of value creation strategies. Individuals who embody the competency of *Regulating* understand and apply the use of objective criteria, indicators, metrics, and other measurement and assessment tools to generate important and useful performance information. They utilize both observation and assessment to influence people in the improvement of organization processes, programs, and practices. They demonstrate a passion for, and are typically involved in, developing and infusing standards of quality and efficiency into the operations of the enterprise as well as among the enterprise and its network partners and constituencies. They are well-positioned to play the role of (and act as) stewards of the enterprise, leading the way in ensuring the organization manages risk appropriately and complies with regulatory and legal requirements. *Regulating* is essential to ensuring that the enterprise demonstrates its values and that it complies and/or aligns with internal and external standards of operation.
- **Engaging:** The conscious participant who is strong in this area demonstrates the ability to effectively interact and communicate with people in widely diverse settings with highly dynamic conditions. Individuals who embody the competency of *Engagement* practice the art of mindfulness, and are able to focus their full attention on the present moment. They are role models of presence. They are consistently aware of their surroundings, and highly alert to what is happening at any given point in time. Due to their mindfulness, along with their communication skills, *Engagers* are very proficient in effective observing, listening, speaking, and interacting, and do these things with significant tolerance, detachment, and non-judgment. They are able to concentrate and be very productive in diverse situations, especially when there is a perceived sense of urgency. They often help to strip away distractions and organizational clutter to help

groups execute efficiently. They help to energize the behaviors and actions of others. They are typically able to share and exchange information in a captivating and engaging manner in one-on-one, group, and community (large group) settings. *Engaging* is essential to organizational awareness and strategy execution; as the degree of engagement in interactions increases, so too does the overall consciousness of the enterprise and its ability to influence its reality.

- **Collaborating:** The conscious participant who is strong in this area demonstrates an inclusive and cooperative approach to getting work done and achieving specific organizational goals. Individuals who embody the competency of *Collaboration* are passionate about co-creation, co-evolution, and other collaborative efforts where the synergies associated with coordination and teamwork can produce superior results. They are able to work with others in diverse settings and under diverse conditions both inside and outside the organization. They bring to a collective effort an organic sense of leadership and facilitation that supports a group in developing its own operating norms and work strategies. They are able to foster teamwork even when there are highly diverse and/or diverging personalities, work styles, views, and goals. They thrive in the organizational multiverse. They are skilled in giving and receiving feedback, both formally and informally, and show an appreciation of the efforts of others. *Collaborators* enjoy working with others, are highly cooperative with their colleagues, and can be very influential through their positive energy and inclusive tendencies, even when there is limited contact and limited opportunity for collaboration. They consistently balance personal and organizational needs when working with others in groups and networks. *Collaborating* is essential to achieving productive interactions within the enterprise, building healthy relationships, and sustaining vital communities.
- **Executing:** The conscious participant who is strong in this area demonstrates the ability to efficiently and effectively carry out and follow through on activities as outlined in project plans, work plans, and implementation plans. Individuals who embody the competency of *Executing* exhibit the ability to get things done with efficiency, quality, accountability, and within timelines. They do not blindly comply with plans, but, assuming that the expected work is sensible and constructive, they commit and apply full attention to the art of getting things done and rarely settle for excuses for not meeting a

deadline or achieving a needed outcome. They are very action-oriented and break-down bottlenecks, barriers, and obstacles to efficiency. They often serve as formal (or informal) process owners or in key network node roles to help ensure processes and practices effectively complete needed work activities. *Executing* is essential to the ability of the enterprise to carry out strategic and operational plans that ultimately result in delivering the products and services that create value for the organization's various constituencies.

- **Adapting:** The conscious participant who is strong in this area demonstrates the consistent flexibility and agility needed to navigate and "flow" in the currents of the organization and its networks. Individuals who embody the competency of *Adapting* are highly accepting of any situation and avoid judging phenomena and conditions in terms of their "rightness" and "wrongness." Rather, they accept the "isness" of each moment, and are able to re-frame a problem, barrier, obstacle, or crisis as an opportunity for change either internally through their own behaviors and actions or externally through influence over specific conditions. They are typically unbiased in their perceptions and are able to effectively discern productive pathways through complex situations or scenarios that are best for the enterprise and its constituencies. They apply objective critical thinking to most situations. They adapt to specific conditions in real-time as well as adapt to, and also influence, organizational and environmental conditions that consistently evolve over time. They choose to *flow* rather than fight, flee, or freeze, and help to mobilize others in urgent or uncertain situations. *Adapting* is essential to the co-evolution of the enterprise within its socio-economic ecosystem.
- **Daring:** The conscious participant who is strong in this area demonstrates the courage necessary to take risks, envision new possibilities, experiment with new ways of doing things, and confidently take initiative and action when required. Individuals who embody the competency of *Daring* do not spend much time concerned about the perceptions of others and do not work and live in fear of misperceptions, misunderstandings, or mistakes. They do not worry about failure; in fact they believe that most fear, especially the fear of failure, is an illusion. They do not need constant approval from their bosses or co-workers. They are bold in their actions, but in a sensible, reasonable, ethical, and practical manner. They often lead programs, initiatives, and special projects because they are

willing to walk a new path, and can lead others due to their informal authority that comes from an energizing courage, spirit, and fortitude. They are authentic in their passion for positive change. They like big challenges and big ideas and view difficult situations as adventures. They understand the value and wisdom of boundaries but will push them when viewed as too narrow or constraining. They often are non-conformist but at the same time do not disparage conformity. They understand hierarchy but believe that power comes from within and is earned through quality behaviors and actions. They are role models for self-empowerment. *Daring* is essential to the social fabric and culture of the conscious organization, and it is one of the fundamental building blocks for the creativity and innovation of the enterprise.

- **Attracting:** The conscious participant who is strong in this area demonstrates the principles of the timeless and universal law of attraction. Individuals who embody the competency of *Attraction* have a strong belief in the ability of individuals, groups, and communities to realize the preferred futures that they envision. They consistently contribute positive energy to the enterprise, envision potential desired futures, help others to conceive and contribute to these futures, and heavily influence the organization's co-evolution with its environment through the thought patterns they create. They call action and outcome into existence through consistent and committed thinking, asking, believing, and receiving. They are often leaders in the process of scenario planning. They educate others on the universal law of reflection: that what we send out into the universe comes back to us as if a reflection in a mirror. They understand that negative energy cannot possibly help the enterprise in any way. They are role models of creative visualizations. They help create clarity, and determine priority about what the organization must do to create value and be successful. They are pivotal in helping to create breakthroughs in thought, behavior, and action that manifest as new paradigms, new energy fields that act as a kind of magnetic attraction to other internal and external forces. *Attraction* is essential to the fundamental energy sources of awakening and consciousness, and critical in the co-evolutionary process.
- **Unifying:** The conscious participant who is strong in this area demonstrates an unyielding commitment to the development of harmonious relationships, systems, and networks. Individuals who

embody the competency of *Unifying* create orderly, coherent, synchronized, and unified arrangements from complex and seemingly disparate or opposing elements and forces. They believe in the simplicity, beauty, and elegance of harmonious systems. They are typically selfless, non-defensive, humble, caring, and forgiving in their interactions within the enterprise. They are committed to principles that go beyond self-interest and that reflect the needs of the whole. They bring together groups of people to solve problems, often serve as the glue within formal and informal networks, and help create unity within larger communities. They show a compassion and empathy for others and understand that those enterprise participants who act as gatekeepers, blockers, disrupters, turf-defenders, and control-freaks are doing so because they are *suffering*, most likely due to something unhealthy in their personal lives or due to some form of mental illness, or are simply *unconscious*, not because they are inherently bad people. Furthermore, individuals who role-model *Unifying* are able to transcend their own egos. They are productive employees who come to work each day as a friend, supporter, and teammate to their colleagues and coworkers. They embrace multiversity, show how it creates strength and not weakness, but will also disagree or dissent when appropriate. They do this to achieve the ultimate goal of unity and common ground, not to create or reinforce destructive adversity. *Unifying* is essential to creating a healthy workplace and organization where there is low negative stress and tension, and few energy sinks or sources of entropy. Instead, *Unifying* establishes a unity of purpose, *not uniformity*, but harmony through multiversity, constructive debate and dialog, and elegant complexity—the integration of differences, the collaboration of specialists, and a strong sense of community.

MY SAMADHI *A Personal Examination*

Over the years as a management consultant with extensive exposure to other organizations, I observed countless individuals enter and exit organizations. Moreover, within my own firm, I had significant leadership responsibilities involving hiring, mentoring, coaching, developing, and firing activities. Unfortunately, even within my own firm, I observed many individuals come and go, in part due to the extremely high standards we established as a premiere professional services enterprise. But just as often, it seemed that we hired very smart, talented, and well educated people who simply were not conscious enough to succeed within our demanding business model.

It was remarkable to me over the years in observing who "made it" and who did not. And over time, I began to see recurring patterns and common themes with respect to the determinants of success and "failure." To be clear, failure is the wrong term, since many of the individuals who did not thrive at the firm went on to be very successful in other roles with other organizations. That said, those that did make it and were successful, demonstrated consistent qualities, and these therefore gradually evolved into identifiable determinants of success.

In summary, the determinants of success in my own organization and I believe in many other organizations, include the following qualities:

First, a **boundless and natural curiosity** about the world, the nature, strategies, and operations of the firm, and most importantly, the characteristics and requirements of clients and customers. Second, a **very strong quality orientation** with naturally high standards but that does not cross the line into fear-based perfectionism (the most common career killer). Third, a **desire to continuously learn**, develop new competencies, and improves regardless of past performance or current status in the hierarchy.

Fourth, the **ability to transcend the ego**, be self-aware, and objectively analyze and assess situations where natural biases typically play a role. Fifth, a **willingness and ability to give and receive constructive feedback** in the spirit of openness, receptivity, and accountability (including the critical elements of being non-judgmental and non-defensive) in both formal and informal settings. Sixth, the **ability to creatively, critically, and collaboratively think and problem solve** using multiple tools and frameworks to develop alternatives and determine optimal solutions.

Seventh, the desire to proactively take initiative and challenge the status-quo when necessary, and the **courage to walk a different path** when it is more aligned with the value system of the enterprise (and when forces, trends, and inertia threaten to move the enterprise away from its true nature). Eighth, an authentic—not artificial—humility and **service orientation in working with others**. Next, a **self-empowered confidence** that communicates a measure of balance with flexibility, and self-management with integrity.

And finally, a **passion for the mission and work of the organization**, a disciplined approach to doing the work, and an elevating, positive attitude in all situations regardless of the issues and challenges at hand.

Self-diagnosing Emerging Consciousness

Self-empowerment is inherent within the consciousness that comes from physical, mental, emotional, and spiritual groundedness, balance, and well-being. It is characterized by an awareness that yields incredible power, the power that comes from concentration, attention, focus, and insight. But self-empowerment is not achieved in a vacuum nor is it independent from its environment. As we have explored already, we are all connected in this universe of energy. We are all players in the participatory world. The individual does not evolve or transform independently; rather the individual and the organization are a single unit of co-evolution, just as the organization and its constituencies and networks are a unit of co-evolution in the broader socio-economic ecosystem.

Understanding this *interdependence*—not to be confused with *dependence*—is important context as the individual walks his own path. *How can this be? How can an individual walk his own path when everything is so interrelated?* The key is to remember that we are free, regardless of the illusions of borders, boundaries, and controls that many of us allow to be our own personal prisons. The conscious participant is able to engage and detach at the same time; she acts *as if* she is free, is flexible, adapts, and creates her own reality through a deep connection with her authentic self. This is true power.

Unfortunately, many people tend to sleepwalk through their day, resigned to the illusions of fear that cause suffering. The enlightened participant is awake and finds fulfillment and meaning as she contributes to the value creation of the enterprise in her daily activities. The key to sustained fulfillment and success for the individual, therefore, involves the periodic review and assessment of the state of her health and well-being (and the ability to create positive energy), the alignment and satisfaction she has with the organization's external and internal value propositions, and the state of her performance, competencies and value contribution potential relative to the organization's evolving needs.

Consciousness has been defined in some circles as *awareness with detachment*, the ability to transcend the ego-based delusions of the mind, eliminate the clutter, and observe the objective reality of one's current life situation. The conscious participant is able to do this on a consistent basis, using self-diagnostic skills and personal insights in the process. Those individuals with the clearest minds are the ones that can be most present and most productive. The following question sequences are intended to assist the participant in this important and ongoing undertaking.

With respect to the state of one's *health and well-being and the ability to create positive energy* in the organization, consider these key diagnostic questions:

- To what extent am I in good health, physically, mentally, emotionally, and spiritually?
- To what extent do I actively take good care of my body, my mind, and my spirit?
- How does my health affect my personal life? How does my health affect my professional life?
- To what extent does my health and well-being affect my ability to create positive energy? And what can I do to improve my health and well-being?
- What can I do to become more positive, and contribute more positive energy, in my personal and professional life?

With respect to one's *alignment and satisfaction with the external and internal value propositions of the organization*, consider these key diagnostic questions:

- To what extent is the organization realizing its value creation goals and strategies?
- To what extent is the organization honest and realistic about its actual impact on its constituencies relative to its desired impact?
- To what extent am I excited and inspired by the potential and/or actual impact and value creation of the organization?
- To what extent is the organization a leader in its commercial or social sector and how important is this to me?
- To what extent am I proud to participate in, and be associated with, this organization?
- To what extent do I share the same value system and value its culture, and how important is this to me?

- To what extent are my interactions and relationships in the organization positive, high quality, productive, and fulfilling?
- To what extent do I have ongoing opportunities to learn, grow, and develop in ways that are meaningful and fulfilling, and how important is this to me?
- To what extent does the organization's work environment enable me to do my best work?
- To what extent do my role, responsibilities, and day-to-day activities reflect variety, challenge, flexibility, freedom, and other conditions that I find meaningful?
- To what extent am I appropriately rewarded/compensated for my work and the value I contribute to the organization, and how important is this to me?
- In general, how compelling is the overall value proposition at this organization to me?
- What can I do to increase the degree of meaning, fulfillment, and satisfaction as a participant in this organization?

With respect to the reality of one's *performance, competencies, and value contribution potential relative to organizational needs*, consider these key diagnostic questions:

- What is my performance relative to my personal goals, key responsibilities, and organizational expectations?
- How is my performance and contribution viewed within the organization by key leaders and influencers?
- What can I do to improve my overall performance and value contribution in the short-term and over time in the longer-term?
- To what extent do I possess proficiency in and demonstrate key organizational competencies?
- To what extent am I evolving in terms of my own consciousness and self-empowerment?
- What can I do to improve and/or continue to evolve in this way?
- To what extent am I doing what I should be doing to co-evolve with the organization and ensure my ability to contribute value in the future?

Dharma Log

The **unenlightened** particpant in an enterprise does not practice self-awareness, typically participates in political and power-based organizational drama, allows ego-driven, and therefore fear-based thoughts to govern his behaviors and actions, and often focuses on those things that he perceives (often wrongly) will maximize the value of his personal financial rewards. The **enlightened** participant is self-aware, rises above organizational drama even when it may adversely affect his influence in the short-run, transcends the ego and its fear-based illusions, and focuses on those things that he empirically knows will enhance the value creation efforts of the enterprise (for which he will be rewarded eventually).

Navigating the Terrain of the Day-to-Day

There is no question that the enlightened participant in the commercial or social enterprise is a powerful source of positive energy and value creation. The energy field of the organization is, in a way, the aggregate of the energy fields of individuals. But this is an oversimplification. As an entity, a self-regulating, open system, the organization as a whole also plays a significant role in the creation of its energy field, and as explored earlier in this book, often generates energy sinks that can be local, regional, or systemic. The conscious participant is well-equipped to avoid these sinks, and over time, can influence (i.e., reduce) the strength of these sinks and decrease the forces of entropy and increase the frequencies of positive energy to eliminate them.

Yet, from a participant's perspective, there is a more subtle landscape that exists in the realm of organizations that reflects a grey zone between the obvious energy sinks and clear energy sources of the enterprise. This landscape is defined by the everyday meetings, conference calls, conversations, program roll-outs, project updates, brainstorming sessions, and so on, that are *not always easy* to characterize as emitting or originating positive or negative energy; rather they are memes that over time aggregate to create and sustain the culture of the organization, and in some cases, gather momentum to become a strong sink or a source. It is in this *seemingly* innocuous day-to-day where the conscious enterprise participant must be most aware, and where self-empowerment can be most effective, in successfully navigating the shadowy terrain.

Consider how many policies, programs, processes, procedures, protocols, and practices the typical participant encounters in one way or another in a single week within an organization. And further, consider how these memes shape and influence how interactions occur, how work gets done, how decisions get made, and how the cultural fabric of the organization is woven. This complex dynamic raises critical questions that the conscious participant should explore, such as:

- What tacit messages do I receive each day from the organization that I overlook or may not even be aware of?
- How is the nature and culture of the organization conditioning me, and how does this affect my thinking, behaviors, and actions?
- How many things are "done to" me with an inherent expectation of compliance, but with little to no explanation as to why?
- To what extent am I programmed to act or react in certain ways that are unconscious, passive, or even submissive?
- To what degree do I participate in activities that are harmless on the surface but may impact positive or negative energy creation more than I realize?

SUTRA LESSON ***The Silent Killers***[22]

In *Increasing Employee Productivity*, Robert Sibson offers simple, timeless wisdom about how organizational practices can be silent, invisible, and even insidious, but also very destructive:

"Organizations of almost all types have imposed upon themselves a variety of unproductive and restrictive practices. Self-imposed unproductive practices are frequently procedures, programs, or traditions: the way a company does business."

With these questions in mind, it is helpful to examine several common scenarios and storylines that often occur in organizations, even in those that are somewhat conscious and high performing, and further explore how the conscious participant plays his informal role with greater awareness and attention, without fear, and in a more proactive or pre-emptive capacity than others. Consider the following situations:

- **The Scenario:** Business process reengineering, restructuring, and downsizing/ rightsizing—*beware, the consultants are coming!*—often result in only a fraction of the desired impact these initiatives always promise, and moreover, they cause extensive counter-productive activity and unintended energy sinks.
  The Storyline: The *unconscious* participant typically works in constant fear of these kinds of initiatives, distrusts the intent behind them (and often the decision-makers who decide to do them), and demonstrates frustration, cynicism, and in some cases direct or indirect opposition to anything that is treated as transformational. In contrast, the *conscious* participant does not live in fear of these initiatives, since he continuously strives to improve his performance, expand his influence, and contribute greater value. He does not view his situation through the lens of self-preservation or "keeping his job" in a steady state, and is therefore able to detach in a way from the distracting drama these initiatives often cause. Rather, his view of the world is one of constant change and co-evolution, and fully expects transformational activities to constantly occur, however misguided or off-the-mark they may be. In fact, he is surprised when these kinds of activities do not occur, and pleasantly surprised when they actually make sense. Moreover, he is proactive and takes initiative in getting involved in these efforts as a way to shape their direction, improve their effectiveness, and influence their outcomes, again, not for survival, but to help ensure the greatest impact for the organization. In those cases where these initiatives are poised to do significant damage to the enterprise, he will openly and directly challenge them in a constructive way that is consistent with the true nature and values of the organization.
- **The Scenario:** A long-term emphasis on quality, productivity, and value creation is often replaced with a short-term emphasis on across-the-board cost reduction in challenging economic times or when there is competitive disruption in a particular commercial sector or industry.
  The Storyline: The *unconscious* participant typically views this as inevitable and does not invest much psychic energy into the lack of wisdom that accompanies a retrenchment strategy during difficult times. Again she retrenches in her own way, looks to cut costs that do not really matter (in a mode of compliance), and attempts to fly under the radar due to fear of losing something, a portion of her operating budget or perhaps her job. The *conscious* participant directly challenges this philosophy and will openly question how cost-cutting initiatives help

value creation and the long-term health of the enterprise. She applies her understanding of co-evolution and continuously works to pre-empt these situations by influencing other leaders (formal and informal) to proactively plan for downturns and difficult cycles, so that the enterprise can grow and flourish when other organizations are struggling.

- **The Scenario:** Budgeting, planning, and resource allocation discussions and decision-making often take too long and result in sub-optimal decisions that make sense in the rarified air of the executive suite but not on the ground where things actually happen.
  The Storyline: The *unconscious* participant typically complains about this lack of understanding and insight and then begrudgingly complies with the decisions that have been made, doing what she can with what has been allocated. In contrast, the *conscious* participant proactively develops her own scenarios regarding the requirements of her role and/or functional unit along with potential outcomes. She provides quality, fact-based information up-front to decision makers in a non-threatening manner, in the spirit of open information sharing, and then begins her own planning for how to best prepare for and execute the solution set of potential decisions. She uses her true power to influence these entirely predictable and often sub-optimized processes.
- **The Scenario:** Performance expectations are developed, performance reviews are conducted, and compensation decisions are made using processes that often rely too heavily on judgment rather than observations and facts, and rely too much on transactional, on-line tools rather than on strategic, personal conversations.
  The Storyline: The *unconscious* participant typically complains about this process and its administrative burden and subjective, poor quality outcomes, and is inevitably dissatisfied in its outcomes. In contrast, the *conscious* participant understands that formal pay-and-performance processes are rarely very effective, despite all of the misguided attention paid to them by organizations. He therefore invests significant energy in both informal feedback and more formal performance conversations on a regular basis with co-workers, customers, team-members, supervisors, etc. Moreover, he is rigorous, diligent, and fact-based in conducting periodic self-assessments that easily replace any organizational tool or form due to the rigor and quality he applies. Finally, he demonstrates honesty, integrity, and a strong willingness to improve when discussing and assessing his

performance, rather than going through the motions to minimize effort and maximize pay increases. Simply put, he is a role-model for the objective review and assessment of performance.

- **The Scenario:** Succession planning, traditional career-pathing, vertical promotions, and job re-evaluation practices are often too prominent in organizations, focusing too much hierarchical activity, organization energy, and financial investment on too few people, and placing too much emphasis on the rewards that come with getting "promoted."
  The Storyline: The *unconscious* participant invests way too much psychic energy in these areas, worrying about things like how long she has been in her current job or job grade, whether her pay grade is correct for her job, and how she can position herself for participation in succession planning and the next promotion (and of course, a pay raise). The *conscious* participant invests little psychic energy in these distracting and usually unproductive activities, and instead focuses her own personal development activities on increasing her value contribution to the organization. At times, this *does* involve job/role changes, promotion opportunities, and compensation review, but these do not drive her behavior. Outside of the job evaluation and promotion arena, she is comfortable (and will proactively undertake) having discussions with her mentors, coaches, and/or managers about her trajectory and her financial rewards opportunities as part of her overall value proposition and her personal, meaningful, co-evolution with the enterprise. In summary, value creation and not personal gain drives her activity with the wisdom that with improved value contribution increased personal rewards will come.

SUTRA LESSON *Power over Force* [23]

In his striking and persuasive book, *Power vs. Force: The Hidden Determinants of Human Behavior*, David Hawkins shares important insight on the nature of power:

"Force always moves against something, whereas power doesn't move against anything at all. Force is incomplete and therefore has to be fed energy constantly. Power is total and complete in and of itself and requires nothing from the outside."

The enlightened participant is extraordinarily successful in almost any type of organization. Of course, the spirit, values, and culture of some organizations will be a better fit for certain individuals than others. But the enlightened participant understands this and will eventually find the organization with which he or she can maximize meaning, fulfillment, enjoyment, and value contribution in the long run. To be clear: those participants who are aware, awake and self-less (and who are able to transcend their egoic mind) are the most effective, productive, and successful people *in any organization that creates positive value*. Those participants who are not aware, who are asleep and self-ful (and who allow their ego to sabatoge their work effectiveness), are the least effective people in an organization, *over the long term*, unless their organization is in the business of creating negative energy.

There is no question that in many organizations, and in many situations, there are ample short-term financial rewards (promotions and pay increases) and non-financial rewards (ego-stroking recognition) for those people who are highly unconscious, listen to the deceiving voice of their ego, and use politics, control-tactics, and hierarchy or other sources of artificial power to "get ahead." But even in organizations who are very young in the process of their awakening, those who choose to stay asleep will eventually leave too many "dead bodies laying in hallways" and too many "old skeletons hiding in closets," and the conscious participant will ultimately emerge triumphant in true spirit, true power, and true success.

The enlightened participant attracts success by welcoming it everywhere and with everyone. And this is especially true of the enlightened leader. She influences reality through her attention to how the world actually works, how everything is connected to everything else, and how the transcendental spirit is the universal language of success. She role models inclusivity (not exclusivity), proactive engagement (not reactive opposition), openness to a broad field of possibility (not conditioning to narrow belief systems), and collaborative activity (not self-centered separation and control). Through self-empowerment, informal authority, compassion, courage, and humility, the conscious participant is a powerful energy source within any enterprise and will provide the leadership needed to help our organizations awaken to their destiny: a new reality of creating superior social and economic value.

Staying Grounded and Self-Empowered

Each day billions of people around the world go to work and each day the vast majority of us experience many of the challenges explored in this chapter and in previous chapters regarding how we interact and get work done. The more healthy we are physically, mentally, emotionally, and spiritually, the more effective we are in navigating the terrain and transcending the drama of our day-to-day through consciousness, self-empowerment, and grace. Each day is a journey itself, and each day we must *practice* the art of mindful being and doing. The great poet, Walt Whitman, once wrote about his own journey, "Afoot and lighthearted, I take to the open road, healthy, free, the world before me, the path leading wherever I choose." Whether literal or metaphorical, Whitman's personal philosophy is one each of us can embrace each day, if we free our mind from the clutter and nonsense of modern life.

To set each day up for success, it is wise to carve out fifteen minutes first thing each morning, perhaps on the train into work, or the walk from the parking lot, or even in one's office or at one's workstation, to briefly meditate in a focused manner on the keys to creating positive energy and remaining grounded in the "middle way" of self-empowerment. In starting this daily ritual, the enterprise participant might recite something like the following:

- I quiet my mind and observe my thoughts. I do not judge my thinking and easily let go of unproductive thoughts.
- I am here right now. Yesterday is gone and tomorrow does not exist. The quality of today determines the quality of tomorrow.
- I am grateful to be a part of this organization. I am thankful for the opportunity to contribute. I have the power to create my day.
- Today I will do my work with discipline, acceptance, enjoyment, and enthusiasm. I will be positive and help others be positive too.
- Today I will take care in what I say, how I say it, and how I work with others. I will let the integrity, humility, and dignity of my spirit shine through.
- I am not a prisoner of my ego. I can observe its cleverness and smile. But I know that others are prisoners, and that they are suffering because of this.
- I will not allow the unconscious behaviors and actions of others to deter me from doing my best work and achieving excellence.

- In my work I will seek first to understand, cease to pass judgment, honor opinions but utilize facts, share information, and search for common ground.
- Today, as I do every day, I will not fear, fight, fly, or freeze when challenges arise. Rather, I will flow with presence and have faith in my own power.
- I am here right now, ready for a great day. I detach from other people, places, and things in my life. They are not real at this moment in time.
- I have the power to help my organization in many ways and make this day a great day. I am ready to get started.

THE TAO: Walking a New Path

In getting started on the path toward conscious participation in and contribution to the enterprise, consider the following diagnostic questions:

- ***To what extent are you becoming a conscious participant through the development of self-empowerment?*** Consider how your personal and professional lives align with and enhance the other through healthy practices involving your body, mind, emotions, and spirit. Consider the extent to which you carefully monitor, assess, and increase the positive energy that you create through the wellness that comes from a balanced, grounded, and mindful lifestyle.

- ***How would you characterize the levels of proficiency that you possess and demonstrate with respect to the competencies of consciousness?*** Consider how well your skills, knowledge, and abilities align with the needs of the organization. Consider how well these skills, knowledge, and abilities align with those demonstrated by highly successful and influential people within the enterprise Consider how specific and rigorous you are in focusing on these competencies in development planning and professional growth activities.

- ***How attentive and realistic are you in understanding the degree to which you are actually aware and conscious in your role, your performance, and your contribution?*** Consider the state of your health and well-being and your ability to create positive energy. Consider the state of alignment and satisfaction with the external and internal value propositions of the organization. Consider the state of your performance, competencies, and value contribution relative to organizational needs.

- ***How well do you navigate, influence, and transcend various memes, forces, and energies that affect the dynamics of the enterprise?*** Consider your degree of awareness relative to those things that are programmed and conditioned to influence behavior. Consider your ability to detach from, mitigate, and transcend the ego-driven politics, drama, and control-oriented activities of everyday organizational life. Consider the degree to which you are grounded, balanced, centered, and dignified in your daily activity within the organization. Consider the frequency with which others in the organization seek you out based on your wisdom, insight, serenity, and tolerance.

NINE

The Currents of Consciousness

Imagine that you are at the annual, dreadful holiday party at a downtown hotel where everyone there wishes he or she were not, including you. You have a made a pact with yourself this year that you will not over-indulge in lousy wine to find relief from the pain of this tradition. You know from experience that when relief is required, you can either medicate, or meditate, so you find yourself alone in a corner trying to be conscious in the moment and be grateful that you are in fact breathing. A stately gentleman happens to walk by and notices you alone, so he introduces himself as a board member, and congratulates you on some of the good things the organization is doing to stay alive and thrive during difficult economic times. For some reason he comes across as more tuned into things than most board members, and so you ask him about the board's perspective on the future of the enterprise, given its challenges. You will never forget his response, which he delivers with an elegant ease that is as compelling as it is simple. He says to you: "Life is consciousness. The organization may live or it may die. The important thing to understand is that to alter your outer life's experience, you must first change your inner life's consciousness. When you, and others in your organization, awaken to this true reality, together you will prosper." He then smiles and walks into the crowd. When you later make inquiries to find out more about this mystical director, no one has ever heard of him before. **This is satori.**

In this chapter we will explore important concepts about the power of the collective awareness, summarized by the following principles:

- **The enlightened enterprise demonstrates a level of consciousness that enables it to influence its own reality.**
- **The enlightened enterprise understands the fabric of the organization is defined by the quality of intangible energy flows among participants and with its environment.**
- **The conscious and enlightened enterprise transcends the traditional definitions of success and strongly believes in the broader mission of its role in the world as an enduring source of value.**
- **The enlightened enterprise walks its own path learning along the way how to expand its consciousness to achieve higher levels of performance.**

The enlightened enterprise is a high performing organization that consistently achieves superior results through conscious co-evolution with its environment. In the vast realm of organizational research and study, there is a wide variety of definitions of high performance relative to internal goals, metrics, scorecards, and benchmarks. Some organizations define performance strictly in financial terms, while others define success much more in operational terms. Some balance both in describing good or great performance. In non-commercial organizations, defining high performance can actually be more difficult and nuanced. For example, how should a hospital, university, or government agency define high performance?

In the case of a large public university with a medical system, which includes staff, faculty, students, researchers, doctors, patients, administrators, trustees, alumni, the community, and the state legislature among its stakeholders, asking this question would result in many different and perhaps even conflicting definitions. Defining great performance is not always as easy as it seems.

The conscious, high-performing organization views and defines performance in the context of value creation for its members/participants, owners, investors, customers, community, network partners, and other constituents in a way that expands traditional definitions of performance to include the dimensions of people, community, and the environment.

In achieving success, the conscious organization invests more in cooperation than competition. It does not oppose, confront, exclude, control, or coerce. It does not take. It does not act as if it is entitled. Rather, it employs an expanded definition of value creation that transcends narrow descriptions such as stock appreciation (for the publicly traded organization) or the financial value of the enterprise (for the privately held organization) or revenue or membership (for the social sector organization). As a review from an earlier chapter, in the enlightened organization, the expanded view of value creation reflects the whole continuum, including:

- The social and economic impact that enterprise products and services have on its customers, customer organizations, and other constituents.
- The economic impact that the enterprise has on its external networks, network partners, and their organizations.
- The financial impact that the enterprise achieves in terms of its profitability and associated return on assets and/or invested capital.
- The financial gain from invested capital for owners in the form of stock and other equity-type appreciation.
- The social and economic impact the enterprise has on its participants, their families, and communities with respect to education, wellness, growth, and overall standard of living.
- The environmental impact the enterprise has in its communities and anywhere it has operations with respect to conservation, preservation, restoration, and sustainability.

SUTRA LESSON *What is High Performance?*[24]

In *Good to Great and the Social Sectors: A Monograph to Accompany Good to Great*, Jim Collins provides a compelling definition of greatness for both businesses and social organizations:

"A great organization delivers superior performance: In business, performance is defined by financial returns and achievement of corporate purpose. In the social sectors, performance is defined by results and efficiency in delivering on the social mission."

He goes on to say:

"A great organization makes a distinctive impact and achieves lasting endurance."

The conscious organization is a strong source of positive energy over the long-term, having awakened to the ideal of its shared destiny with the world. To achieve lasting impact, and deliver enduring value, the enterprise transcends narrow and rigid definitions of success (which are often highly destructive memes that originate in the financial and investment community), influences its socio-economic ecosystem to accept its distinctive view of value creation, and delivers *net* social and economic benefits to its stakeholders.

Creating Our Shared Reality

The conscious organization begins with the conscious participant. As spiritual beings that create organizations and participate in their activities, each of us actively participates in influencing our individual and shared realities. Whatever we call reality emerges from an active construction we in part create and in which we participate. In this sense, we do not see true reality; we see our construction of reality. We have real experiences, but this does not necessarily mean we experience true reality. As we see reality, we act, and as we act, we shape our reality. Reality is constantly being created out of the realm of possibility through our thoughts, behaviors, actions, and interactions.

In the quantum world, matter and energy become one and the universe can be thought of as a field of energy where all energy is in a constant state of vibration and interaction. Everything is connected to, or entangled with, everything else. This suggests that we are all affected by what everyone else is thinking, feeling, and experiencing.

At the end of the amazing film, *Being There*, on a cold and overcast winter day, the President of the United States is giving a eulogy for a dear friend and successful industrialist. At the same time, the mysterious main character of the film, Chance, decides to leave the gathering and go for a walk through the woods where he finds a pond that has not yet frozen. We can hear the distant echo of the President closing his eulogy with a quote from his dead friend, that, "Life is a state of mind," while Chance serenely and confidently begins to walk on water out toward the middle of the lake.

As spiritual beings in human form making our way in the chaotic and commercial world of "modern" society, do we truly believe that life is a state of mind? Are we ready to walk on water, or at least walk a new path? Are we ready in this new millennium to believe that we are not just actors but actually creators? And do we believe that spiritual and psychological concepts and principles are of practical value in the world of organizations? In the words of one of the great spiritual thinkers of the previous century, Ernest Holmes, *nothing is more practical!* Spiritual life *is* daily life. Spiritual mind *is* ordinary mind. Nothing more or less. Extending this concept, one might argue that the most successful organizations are those that succeed by simply being and doing, not by searching and attaining. And they measure their being-ness and doing-ness in both tangible and intangible ways, using both social and economic measures.

The enlightened enterprise understands that stability and permanence can only come through consciousness, creating value through harmony and diversity, simplicity and complexity, integration and differentiation, while letting go of form and structure. This consciousness represents an awareness that the organization does not need to confront its reality, but rather create it. There is no illusion of identity and therefore there is no attachment. Where there is no attachment, there is no suffering. What does attachment and suffering mean in an organizational context? Only when organizations are attached to their own mythology, their own elegant strategy, and their own "superior and unique" identity can there be failure, the enterprise version of suffering. But the conscious organization knows that failure does not exist. Failure is not a person, place, or thing. Failure and the fear of failure are illusions of the ego, the collective org-ego of the enterprise, with all of its unwanted and unhelpful defense mechanisms and distortions. In creating its own reality, therefore, the conscious organization creates its own success.

Transcending Fear and Awakening

Because of the power of ego among individuals and groups, many organizations inadvertently create cultures of fear, including fear of failure, fear of the competition, fear of change, fear of upsetting the boss, and fear of over-stepping boundaries or breaking rules and policies. At the individual level, all thinking comes from the ego which thrives on fear. As astutely explored and described by Eckhart Tolle in his insightful teachings, the egoic mind wants to be separate, special, and in-control. But it also feels that it is constantly under threat and understands that all form is subject to entropy and inherently unstable. It therefore exists in a constant state of fear of change and impermanence. The organization is no different. The org-ego also see itself as constantly under threat and in fear of entropy and dissipation as an open system at the mercy of the dangers of its competition and its broader environment.

Throughout this book, we have explored how most organizations behave in stunningly ego-based and unconscious ways that reduce or drain energy, weaken the fabric of their culture, diminish their ability to create value, and threaten their existence. These practices are grounded in ego-driven fear and want. An awakening is needed, an elevation of the collective mind into a higher level of consciousness. With this in mind, consider the primary challenges that organizations face and *what is involved in this transcendence* (in part as a review of the key issues outlined in the first chapter but now as a broader and richer examination):

- **Organizations overemphasize objects, structure, and hierarchy as sources of stability and proofs of permanence.** Organizations need to shift from defining their identity using objects to demonstrating their true nature based on value. They need to elevate their purpose into a broader and more conscious mission of value creation that goes beyond traditional (and artificial) limitations. This involves transcending the world of form, allowing the spirit of the enterprise to flow freely through it and out into the environment, with positive energy attracting more positive energy. For a medical system, for example, this might entail shifting from an emphasis on its luxurious facilities, state of the art technologies, and world class Ph.D./MD staff members, to more of an emphasis on how the institution has improved the health of the community through the extraordinary quality of care and its preventive and holistic health and wellness activities. How refreshing it will be when in the future, hospitals are viewed as sources of healing and wellness as opposed to their current status as simply a place where people go to "get treated" or have requisite surgery and where it seems most people will tell you that they left the enterprise sicker than when they walked (or got wheeled) in.
- **Organizations are obsessed with short-term results at the expense of long-term effectiveness, the health and well-being of people, and the preservation of the environment.** Organizations need to shift away from reporting and rewarding short term goal achievement and quarterly financial results, and move toward a more robust and longer-term view of measuring and assessing performance. They must broaden their vision to understand what is truly important in the

process of co-evolution, leading to sustainability and sustained success. This includes using metrics that go beyond the "four walls" of the enterprise in looking at the performance of networks and the socio-economic ecosystem as a whole. This also includes the use of *lead* indicators (as opposed to just using *lag* indicators) that reflect how performance *today* will affect value creation two to three years *down the road*. In the case of a telecommunications firm, for example, this might entail assessing the efficiency and quality of the telecommunications infrastructure of society as a whole, and then working with other upstream and downstream firms to increase their collective value contribution to all consumers. It might entail measuring the diversity of entry-level talent pools that help predict the potential pools of future leaders, or tracking progress in developing new reconditioning processes for obsolete hardware, impacting future environmental sustainability.

- **Organizations apply two sets of values: the *actual* values demonstrated through actions and the *spoken* values described through words.** Organizations need to constantly monitor the degree of alignment—and close alignment gaps as needed—between their written values and their values-in-action, their true nature. They need to constantly monitor destructive memes that slowly infiltrate the enterprise and eliminate or change them to preserve the purity of the value system. For a social service agency, for example, where there is constant pressure from state funding sources for the organization to show "hard" results and prove financial viability, there can be a tug-of-war between doing the right thing for the individual and proving a cause-and-effect result from the service provided. The agency will not be true to itself if it talks about doing the right thing but sacrifices service quality for efficiency in the actual mental health care provided.
- **Organizations believe they are the best at everything, can do no wrong, require little outside expertise, and do not need to collaborate with other network entities.** Organizations need to shift from the ego-driven "go-it-alone" strategy to a more collaborative and specialized model. Innovation and value creation in the future will require both deeper specialization and broader integration of activities. Organizations will increasingly compete as well as cooperate in their co-evolution with the environment. This will involve transcending the org-ego of the enterprise with the awareness that

the health of the socio-economic ecosystem as a whole is critical for long-term sustainability. In the case of a community college, for example, survival may require a whole new paradigm of success where the enterprise must engage with other area schools, private training programs, and local employers to create a curriculum that meets the needs of the community, but also enables the school and its "partners" to deliver value in a creative and financially feasible way.

- **Organizations believe that their participants' behaviors can be shaped and controlled through policies and programs that require obedience and compliance.** Organizations must shift from a compliance orientation to a commitment orientation in engaging their workforce if they wish to achieve substantially higher levels of productivity and value creation. In the context of a seller's market for talent due to long-term demographic trends, people will have choices and will gravitate to work environments that are more meaningful and rewarding. In an increasingly complex and interconnected world, the enterprise cannot control the drivers of its success. It must enable and flow with them. In the case of a high performing retail organization, for example, the vast majority of policies regarding work hours, work location, and time or off/time away (for corporate employees) have been eliminated or significantly relaxed, and replaced with a philosophy of total flexibility coupled with a very strong results-orientation.
- **Organizations are overconfident from current and historical success, and over-confident in their understanding of what makes the enterprise effective.** In most cases it is in the best interest of organizations to be very careful in applying traditional assumptions of what works, what makes people work hard, and why there always has to be a right answer. This kind of dualistic thinking is more and more out-of-step with our interdependent, interrelated, and nuanced world.

  Past success is not a condition for future success, and especially not for sustainable value creation. In fact, the whole concept of success is changing, taking on a broader definition as our social and community networks evolve. In the case of a metropolitan police organization, for example, the world is getting more complex and diverse, and people in the community have less patience and tolerance for "old-school" police behavior. And while the law is often clearly black and white, law enforcement professionals will still need to break-down old practices, focus more on preventive safety and protection, and build awareness and tolerance for the grey areas they encounter and that inevitably arise more frequently in a more complex society. In short, police organizations must renew their vision of what it means to "serve and protect" in a way that is better aligned with the values and needs of a more sophisticated community. Some are showing the courage to try. This can be seen most recently in how some police departments around the country are changing the way they conduct suspect lineups and engage eyewitnesses, after increasing evidence showing a high number of wrongful convictions due to mistaken identifications.

- **Organizations believe that management is the key to enterprise success, and focus too much on formal leaders and managers as the sources of success.** Organizations need to shift from the belief that management is the most important group in an organization to a more enlightened view where the very concept of a hierarchical management structure begins to fade away, and is replaced by a network of key roles with clear accountabilities and seamless communication channels. Highly successful organizations do not manage *people*, they manage *work activity*. And in the future, traditional criteria like *span of control* will be replaced with new concepts like *scope of network responsibilities* and *potential for impact on value creation*. In the case of a research and development organization, for example, the enlightened enterprise might value more highly those roles that have a deep and specialized scientific orientation versus those roles that have a "management" emphasis. Management will no longer be equated to leadership that assumes a higher level of responsibility or impact. The roles that carry out the work that directly creates value, based on a broader and more enlightened definition of success, will be valued most highly from an economic investment and return perspective.
- **Organizations reward senior executives beyond market competitive levels or out of alignment with the performance of the enterprise, while tightly managing the rewards of the rest of the workforce.** Organizations must move away from the belief that since management is the key to enterprise success (not the case, as described above), managers should be paid at much higher levels *relative* to others and/or the market, or even worse, relative to the results they achieve. There is no question that senior management/leadership type roles demand higher salaries in the marketplace for talent than, say, a financial analyst or public relations role. However, in the future, organizations

will determine reward strategies based less on level and more on the potential for direct impact that the role has on the drivers of value creation. In the case of a global airline, for instance, it is not far-fetched to envision a situation where the role that is responsible for optimizing the efficiency of plane routes worldwide using highly complex, mathematical models is deemed to have a greater potential for impact, and therefore a greater compensation opportunity, than a senior executive role responsible for marketing.

Letting Go and Unleashing

The key to joy, success, and prosperity, for both individuals as well as organizations, is through the act of *letting go* of the self. The art of awakening is not a matter of adding or attaining something, it is a process of ridding something, often many things. Organizations can begin to walk their own path toward a greater level of consciousness not by acquiring something, but by discarding something, probably many things. Our enjoyment as social beings does not come from finding something positive from the external world, but by creating the absence of something inside ourselves: negative energy. Rather than searching for the silver bullets, the "best practices," the smartest consultants, or the coolest technologies, organizations can walk their own path through simple acts of *unlearning*, *deprogramming*, and *unleashing*. Our collective true nature is a world without boundaries that is not found through more thinking, but through less, un-cluttering our collective mind and de-conditioning our learned views of reality.

Consider the inherent power of positive energy that is unleashed within the organization that decides to improve the effectiveness of its slow, bureaucratic, and hierarchical decision-making and problem solving processes by simply not creating many of the decisions in the first place, or by dissolving problems rather than solving them. For example, do organizations really have to spend so much energy deciding who gets to participate in certain discussions or attend what meetings? Consider that *being more inclusive is a lot easier than being more exclusive*. Do organizations need to green-light so many projects and initiatives through planning committees, approval meetings, budgeting discussions, and hyper-detailed project plans? Consider that *being more trusting of people is a lot easier than being less trusting*. Do organizations need to spend so much time on the development of rules, policies, and guidelines for everything from size-of-office to how many shares of stock someone is granted to specific terminology that can or cannot be used in external communication? Consider that *believing in the power of good judgment is a lot easier than trying to engineer "good" behavior.* Do organizations need to spend so much time and energy on developing complicated compensation strategies and systems that over-emphasize precision and segment people from the unified whole? Consider that *rewarding people sensibly for their contribution to value creation is a lot easier than copying the compensation practices of other firms.*

MY SAMADHI *A Personal Hope*

As an organization effectiveness consultant for over two decades, I have witnessed and studied the evolution of commercial and non-commercial organizations. I have seen how the transformative technologies of the past twenty years, such as personal computing and the internet, have influenced how organizations do their work. I have seen how the economic cycles, with their dramatic ups and downs, have affected how organizations manage and invest their financial capital. I have seen how globalization has increased the complexity of many organizations and their strategies and operations. I have seen entire industries disappear and new ones emerge, and I have seen their business models change, transform, and even come full circle.

I have seen many trends come and stay or go, including reengineering, total quality management and ISO 9000, high involvement work systems, just-in-time operations, total reward systems, teams and team effectiveness, kaizen and six sigma, customer relationship management, enterprise resource planning, activity-based costing, open-book management, chaos theory and management, outsourcing, off-shoring, and authentic leadership. How many hundreds of other trends have I missed on this list?

I have also seen, and have been a part of, the explosion of an industry that is intended to help organizations do work and perform better: the consulting industry. When I completed my undergraduate degree it seemed that everyone either wanted to go into investment banking or consulting. I don't know if that is true today, but I do know that, while the industry has been hit hard over recent years due to economic cycles and the resulting fiscal conservatism of many organizations, there remains an awful lot of consultants and other "advisors" walking around pounding on doors or dialing for dollars.

Is there a correlation between all these trends and all these consultants? I'm not sure. Perhaps the question is not even relevant. Organizations will always look for and need external support and guidance. In fact, as I have argued in this book, those organizations that do not think they need quality help, advice, and counsel are probably suffering from the org-ego, limiting their field of possibility and sub-optimizing their performance. However, I would argue that most consulting firms add less value than they should and have not adequately evolved with their external environment. While the world of organizations has fundamentally changed, the world of consulting has not.

Consultants still spend too much time (and cost their clients too much money) collecting unneeded data, crunching irrelevant numbers, filling binders with too much paper, developing overly-complicated strategies, force-fitting off-the-shelf programs, over-promoting cool technologies, and spending too much time with executives and not enough time with the rest of the workforce (to get the real picture of how the organization works). And in a mystifyingly unregulated industry, consultants still avoid measuring their impact or being held accountable for the value they have (or have not) delivered.

Consider the consulting firm that chartered a small team to develop a client satisfaction and impact measurement process. Objectives of the user-friendly process included gathering information that would help the firm improve its consulting performance, demonstrate a commitment to client value creation, and yield a fact-base that could be used in firm marketing efforts. The process was reinforced at every single partner meeting and conference call for two years and yet less than ten percent of client relationship managers used the tool. When one partner was asked why he did not use the tool, he responded by saying "*I'm anxious about what the results might show; what if they are not good?*"

Within our society's enormously vast network of social and business organizations, there is a need and there always will be a need for quality consulting services. At the same time, there is also a need for an entirely new business model of consulting, where consultants must increase their own levels of consciousness, unlearn many of the old and current patterns of consulting work, and commit to a whole new way of thinking about the nature of reality, change, and value creation within their own organization and with their clients.

It is my dream that this reflects a co-evolutionary process, a collaborative path where consultants and clients can walk together and consciously improve the performance of entire networks of organizations and the socio-economic ecosystems in which they participate.

Summarizing the Currents of Consciousness

In the side-splittingly hilarious film *This Is Spinal Tap*, a "rockumentary" of a fictitious heavy-metal band of the 1970s (the era of great heavy metal music, of course), the filmmaker interviews the band's lead guitar player, Nigel Tufnel, in his guitar shrine in one of the film's many epic scenes. Nigel is talking about his special amplifier that goes to "11" and which is louder than other amplifiers that only go to "10." In deadpan delivery, the filmmaker asks why the loudest setting is not the standard 10 on the amp's dial, and the guitar player responds once again that the amp *goes to 11 to give it that extra boost*. The interviewer presses further and suggests that the amp could just as easily be the loudest at the setting of 10, but could be louder than the 10 of other amplifiers. Mr. Tufnel looks quizzically at him and says very seriously in his most proper English accent *but this one goes to 11*. The interviewer then ends the conversation, dumbfounded and confused.

This silly exchange is a fun metaphor for the enlightened enterprise as an "amplifier" of performance. Through greater consciousness, the organization is able to go beyond traditional definitions of high performance but in ways that, at times, may be hard to define or pinpoint, but that definitely result in something exciting and extraordinary (as an aside, note there are actually eleven chapters in this book!).

There are strong and positive energy fields that are currents in our ocean of existence. These currents of consciousness that apply especially to organizations and that have been explored in depth throughout this book, in many different ways (not necessarily using the labels assigned here) include: courage, caring, coherence, capability, collaboration, community, and co-evolution. They represent a set of potential *values* for the enterprise that desires to break through to whole new levels of performance and sail on the sea-currents of success, even if normal performance dials only go 10! The seven "C"-currents of consciousness are summarized as follows:

- **Courage:** The enlightened organization is highly committed to an elevating purpose, optimistic about its ability to achieve its goals, and resilient in the face of setbacks. The enlightened organization creates the conditions that foster and unleash courage among its participants, and in turn demonstrates courage as a leader in the networks, communities, and ecosystems within which it participates as a value-creating entity. It demonstrates daring, boldness, and fortitude in creating the reality that will ensure its mutual success and survival within its broader environment. It understands that courage is the foundation for creativity, innovation, and constant transformation in a chaotic and dynamic world. It values courage across its networks of value creation and realizes that this quality may be the most important driver of endurance and sustainability in a world that has for too-long been dominated by the illusion of safety that comes from fear- and control-driven phenomena.
- **Caring:** The enlightened organization understands and shows empathy for the perspectives and feelings of its internal participants and external constituencies. It has a clear sense of the ebbs and flows of the emotional climate within the organization and how the climate is affecting the performance of individuals, groups, and networks. It is aware of its own potential blind-spots that can cause dissatisfaction and disengagement among its members. As part of its true nature, the enlightened enterprise believes more in *caretaking* than in *controlling*. It cares about people and their health and well-being. It does not invest vast amounts of resources in "proving" the ROI of investing in the wellness of its participants; it simply does it, with the awareness that with a multiversity of people comes a wide array of needs. The organization is absolutely not responsible for the health of its people, nor is it responsible for their life-situations, but it is responsible for actively *supporting* their health improvement activities and overall experience and fulfillment at work.
- **Coherence:** The enlightened organization understands that its values-in-action and passion for value creation define the day-to-day reality of its participants and shapes the culture of the enterprise. It is aware that culture is developed and supported over time by establishing and reinforcing the conditions that foster an optimal work experience and coherent environment for its people. It invests a significantly greater amount of effort and resources in establishing and aligning these enabling conditions—the antecedents if you will

to productive behavior and action—relative to much less effort establishing policies and programs that attempt to coerce behavior through compliance and consequences. It builds a value creation culture *as it goes about its business*. This is characterized by clear expectations of high performance along with the freedom in the workplace to accomplish them with acceptance, enjoyment, enthusiasm, and unity, without fear or concern for failure. It does this in part through helping its people unlearn some of their beliefs, assumptions, and attitudes, and then learn new ways of thinking that are more congruent with the strategic intent, desired culture, and emerging consciousness of the entity.

- **Capability:** The enlightened organization continuously develops, nurtures, enhances, strengthens and refreshes its strategic and operational capabilities on an ongoing basis. It understands that its capabilities are the single most important sources of productive energy for creating value in the long-term. It understands that the most critical capabilities are not those that reside in a single person or group, but those that reflect a unique mix of skills, knowledge, relationships, and processes created across groups, within and across networks, as well as at the enterprise level, making them impossible for competitors or imitators to replicate or acquire. The enlightened organization understands that both learning and unlearning are critical capabilities in and of themselves. Moreover, it pays close attention to the capabilities that are critical to its successful co-evolution with its ecosystem and sustainability with the broader environment.
- **Collaboration:** The enlightened organization builds an environment of healthy relationships by fostering highly collaborative and productive activities and interactions. It understands the importance of maintaining a collaborative climate through trust and integrity within the organization as well as with other entities in its external environment. The enlightened enterprise knows that healthy collaboration is the foundation for many of the other conditions that lead to sustained and superior value creation. It continuously seeks to enhance the conditions within the organization for both formal and informal collaborative activities to take place. In addition to trust and integrity, the enlightened enterprise understands that openness, information sharing, limited hierarchy, distributed decision-making, and the power of multiversity are the current and future keys to ever-increasing productive collaboration.

- **Community:** The enlightened organization creates the conditions for building highly productive groups, networks, and communities. The principles that guide all interactions are grounded in the values of the organization. These values are consistent with the fundamental conditions of humility, curiosity, integrity, honesty, authenticity, diversity, creativity, and simplicity. There are constant opportunities and few barriers for people to interact, converse, exchange ideas and information, and form new relationships. The enlightened enterprise understands that in a healthy and meaningful work environment, informal and positive norms of behavior are more powerful than formal rules and policies. As technology more and more allows work to be done within a virtual workplace or across cyberspace, the enterprise actually invests more, not less, in establishing the conditions and supporting the organic emergence of meaningful and productive communities.
- **Co-evolution:** The enlightened organization has full awareness that it co-creates its reality with the external environment. It understands that its evolution as an entity is interdependent with the evolution of the broader social and economic ecosystem and natural environment within which it exists. In its awakened state, it embraces chaos and disequilibrium as fundamental sources of positive energy that lead to transformation and innovation. It knows that the degree to which it can conceive and shape its reality will determine its future success and survival. This success is dependent on unleashing the creativity of participants within the enterprise to drive innovation and develop new ways of creating enduring value.

Sutra Lesson *The Ecology of Community*[25]

In *The Web of Life: A New Scientific Understanding of Living Systems*, Fritjof Capra touches on many aspects of the currents of consciousness and the conditions for enterprise success:

"All members of an ecological community are interconnected in a vast and intricate network of relationships, the web of life ..."

He goes on to say:

"These, then are some of the basic principles of ecology—interdependence, partnership, flexibility, diversity, and as a consequence of all those, sustainability."

Reading the Pathmap to Consciousness

There is no single path to achieving greater levels of consciousness and value creation. Each enterprise is unique and must walk its own path, increasing its awareness and improving its performance along the way. There is no final destination on this walk, no Shangri-la at its end or pot of gold. And there is no Zen master waiting in the lotus position to confirm the organization's attainment of enlightenment, since enlightenment cannot be "attained" as a thing. Unfortunately, it cannot be described either. It can only be experienced. The end, therefore, does not really exist; it is the quality of the walking path that is created that matters. Throughout this book there have been many examples of what enlightened organizations do or do not do, and in this way, we can get a sense for what enlightenment, as spirit-consciousness, the path of awareness, can bring to any organization. *So how does an organization go about walking its own path?*

Every organization is at a specific point in its evolution. Those organizations that are very young have the opportunity to create an enterprise that walks a path of consciousness from the beginning. Those organizations that have been around for a while and that have implemented strategies, built structures, engineered processes, and developed a culture with specific beliefs, behaviors, and norms, have the opportunity to refresh, revitalize, and reinvent the enterprise by walking a new path. Regardless of the life-situation, or life-stage, of an enterprise, there is a basic map for walking *the first few steps* in the right direction and in a highly practical and productive way. This roadmap, or pathmap to consciousness if you will, has the following steps (and please note, these are presented in a practical logic flow, but there are many ways to walk this path):

- Develop/describe the true nature—its mission and spirit-in-action—of the enterprise.
- Develop/describe the values and values-in-action of the enterprise.
- Develop/describe the external and internal value propositions of the enterprise.
- Identify/describe the value networks of the enterprise and its current and desired role(s) within those networks.
- Identify/describe the value creation drivers and capabilities of the enterprise.

- Develop/describe the overall value creation strategy and culture of the enterprise.
- Develop/describe the co-evolution strategy and framework of the enterprise.

Each of the steps in the pathmap to creating and building a more conscious and high-performing enterprise is further defined in more detail as follows:

- **True Nature:** *Describe the true nature of the organization.* Begin by using words, phrases, stories, images, symbols, people, objects, and any other thing that conveys the organization's true nature. Keep in mind that true nature reflects the purpose and spirit of the enterprise. It is elevating and enduring, and transcends traditional ways of thinking about success and value. As you describe true nature, make sure that you are clear on whether it reflects the current state or the desired state of the organization, and if there is a gap, characterize the gap, form hypotheses as to its source(s). Then begin developing a strategy for creating or renewing the enterprise mission.
- **Values:** *Describe the values of the organization.* Begin by capturing stated values, perceived values, informal cultural norms that demonstrate values-in-action, and formal operating norms and other artifacts such as policies and programs that provide insight into the organization's actual value system. As you describe values and values-in-action, make sure you are clear on whether there is a difference between stated values and actual values, and if there is a gap, characterize the gap and form hypotheses as to its source(s). Then begin developing a strategy for creating or renewing and refreshing enterprise values.
- **Value Propositions:** *Describe the value proposition of the organization.* Begin by reviewing the elements of the external value proposition and the internal value proposition, and then study available sources that reflect concepts of vision, mission, strategy/strategic intent, and strategic imperatives. Also study external marketing, advertising, and public relations messages and materials. With respect to the internal value proposition, study employee communications and materials regarding compensation, benefits, other reward programs that people value. Describe development and growth opportunities, employee perceptions of interactions and relationships, and other things that are offered to people as employees or members of the enterprise. Keep

in mind that value propositions, whether internal or external, are clear, compelling, and distinctive. As you describe the value propositions, make sure that you are clear on whether it reflects the current state or the desired state of the organization, and if there is a gap, characterize the gap and form hypotheses as to its source(s). Then begin developing a strategy for creating or renewing the enterprise value propositions.

- **Value Networks:** *Describe the organization's value networks and its role within those internal/external value networks.* Begin by identifying the key internal processes of the enterprise (at a high level of altitude) that carry out most of its important work in creating value, and identify the participant roles that are directly involved in these processes as well. Once you have described the key processes in a general way (you do not have to do detailed process mapping to do this sufficiently, so do not fall into that abyss!), expand your perspective by describing the interactions and interdependencies between the key processes themselves, and between the key processes and other, perhaps less critical processes and entities within the organization. Once again, identify the roles that are involved in this expanded web of activity. Finally, expand your perspective further by describing the interactions and interdependencies between the internal networks and outside networks and entities, along with any additional roles that are important to the expanded web that now crosses the organization's permeable boundaries. Analyze your work to get a deep and broad understanding of the fullness of the interacting networks, the key nodes where significant value creation takes place, and the key roles that are involved. Then begin developing strategies for supporting and/or improving enterprise network effectiveness.
- **Value Creation Capabilities:** *Describe the organization's value creation drivers and capabilities.* Based on the integration of your work in describing the organization's value proposition(s) and your understanding of its value networks, brainstorm the strategic and operational capabilities that are important in "driving" the achievement of the external value proposition and the value creation activity within the various networks. Keep in mind that a capability represents a combination of things, such as processes, practices, interactions, and competencies, that are integrated and synchronized in a way that reflect a critical—and often unique—proficiency of the enterprise. Once capabilities are determined, a potential next step is to

assess their relative importance by segmenting them based on the degree to which they are strategic or operational, directly or indirectly driving value creation, and directly or indirectly linked to competitive advantage. As you describe the value creation capabilities, make sure that you are clear on whether they reflect the current state or the desired state of the organization, and if there is a gap, characterize the gap and form hypotheses as to its source(s). Then begin developing strategies for prioritizing, building, strengthening, and sustaining critical capabilities.

- **Value Creation Culture:** *Describe the organization's overall value creation culture*. Begin by reviewing all the work you have done to this point. Next, begin brainstorming, using words, phrases, stories, images, pictures, graphs, charts, data, and other ideas and artifacts that convey the value creation strategy and culture. Also review how individual and group performance expectations, goals, feedback, assessment, and development occurs and how these activities are blended into (or not) the day-to-day work activities of the enterprise. Develop draft statements from this brainstorming work that best characterize the value creation strategy and culture. As you describe culture, make sure that you are clear on whether it reflects the current state or the desired state of the organization, and if there is a gap, characterize the gap and form hypotheses as to its source(s). Then begin developing a strategy for supporting, strengthening, and/or renewing the enterprise value creation culture.
- **Co-evolution Strategy:** *Describe the organization's co-evolution strategy and framework*. Begin by identifying and studying current enterprise activities that are focused on interacting with, cooperating with, and influencing the external world. Utilize this information to begin to create a more robust, and rigorous approach to the process of co-evolution. Segment potential activity into enterprise (internal), ecosystem (internal/external), and environmental (external) categories. If the organization is already using a co-evolution strategy or framework, review the enterprise, ecosystem, and environmental activities that comprise the framework. If possible, study the evolution of the framework itself, and the degree to which there has or has not been disciplined use of the framework, including the consistent organizational review of activity, the collection and analysis of needed data, the incorporation of findings and learnings into the strategic and operational activities of the enterprise, and the periodic

refinement of the strategy and capabilities over time. Keep in mind there should be a process and set of indicators for assessing the effectiveness of the organization's overall ability to evolve successfully. As you define or refine the framework, make sure that you are clear on whether it reflects the current state or the desired state, and if there is a gap, characterize the gap and form hypotheses as to its source(s). Then create or continue to improve an effective co-evolution strategy and framework.

The pathmap to consciousness and high performance is a powerful way to get started on the journey. There is, however, another dimension to building enterprise consciousness and that is through the *daily practice of conscious behaviors and actions*. Greater enterprise wisdom and enlightenment are further developed and sustained through regular, ongoing practices that organizations can undertake to ensure they do not revert back to old unconscious and destructive ways of doing things. Consider how powerful it would be if an organization were to routinely do some or all of the following (these are just a few ways, among an infinite number of ways, to practice and solidify new, more positive patterns of conscious behavior):

- Offer thirty-minute morning yoga and meditation sessions for participants in the mornings and afternoons.
- Consistently communicate internally and externally a broad definition of value creation and implement simple lead and lag metrics that focus on *both* social *and* economic value.
- Replace all artifacts and memes in the organization that represent structure as a vertical hierarchy (with boxes and solid/dotted reporting lines) with an enterprise network model (with nodes and webs of internal and internal/external value creating activity).
- Provide weekly forums that focus on mental, physical, or spiritual health issues and wellness activities (and give benefits-related incentives for participating in these events and activities).
- Conduct monthly interactive training sessions that focus on improving the productivity of interactions and replacing cognitive distortions with more positive, and less ego-driven, thinking patterns.
- Sponsor and support study groups around the enterprise that focus on applying positive action-schemas in daily work activities.
- Apply a 15-minute breathing and centering exercise at the beginning of key meetings for creating a collective *presence* in the room.

- Conduct quarterly large-scale community conferences to explore, simplify, and improve innovation, information sharing, and decision-making processes and practices.
- Weave into the strategic planning process the co-evolutionary framework and process for determining internal, ecosystem, and environmental activities that support strategy execution.
- Conduct annual workshops among leaders and influencers from across the enterprise network to explore and address the degree to which strategic, positive memes (rather than entropic, negative memes) are taking root.
- Develop sustainability imperatives, key initiatives and projects, and progress assessments that are presented annually to the external community (with distributed responsibility across the enterprise web for doing this work).

THE TAO: Walking a New Path

In getting started on the path of experiencing the flowing currents of consciousness, consider the following diagnostic questions:

- ***How does your organization define high performance?*** Consider the measures that the organization uses to *analyze* performance. Consider the yardsticks and benchmarks that are used to *assess* performance. Consider the degree to which the organization consistently falls below, meets, or exceeds expected and desired levels of performance. Consider the degree to which the organization uses external/competitive benchmarks to assess performance.

- ***How does the organization demonstrate fear-based behavior?*** Consider how the organization uses policies and programs to influence behavior. Consider how the organization responds to internal crises and external threats. Consider the degree to which the organization is motivated by excellence and winning versus being motivated by *not* underperforming and *not* losing.

- ***How does the organization demonstrate ego-driven behavior?*** Consider the degree to which there is a gap between how the organization perceives itself and its overall performance. Consider how the organization uses policies and programs to influence behavior. Consider the degree to which hierarchy, status, and title affects the culture and day-to-day work activities, interactions, and decision making. Consider the degree to which the conditions of openness, trust, and inclusiveness are present (or not present) in the workplace.

- ***How are the seven C-currents of consciousness similar or not similar to your organization's values?*** Consider the degree to which your organization's actual values are consistent with the nature of courage, caring, coherence, capability, collaboration, community, and co-evolution. Consider the extent to which there may be differences between your organization's actual value system—its values-in-action—versus its stated values. Consider how the current value system influences day-to-day work activities and interactions.

- ***What steps is your organization taking to walk a more conscious and enlightened path?*** Consider how the organization acts and behaves today in conscious and unconscious ways. Consider what might indicate that the organization is ready to walk a different path. Consider the degree to which current or future efforts to walk a new path should be formal or informal in terms of the effort and activity to walk a new path. Consider what is needed to successfully do so.

Closing—
A Collective Opportunity

THE OPENING SEQUENCE OF THE BRILLIANT FILM *CONTACT* places the viewer in orbit above the earth. The breathtaking imagery is exquisitely balanced by the random noises, sounds, and voices that emanate from our planet, a cacophony of radio waves that to an alien observer in space, could easily represent the voice of our world, that is to say, the voice of Gaia, the life giving energy-consciousness of our planet. As humans and as inhabitants of this planet, we know that this is in fact not the case. The true voice of Gaia is not the chatter that its material form—the physical earth and all of its structures—emits; it is something deeper, richer, and beyond description. This is not unlike mistaking the incessant voice in our individual as well as collective egoic mind as our own spirit, our true nature. We know our spirit transcends this distorted, clever, and deceiving voice. So it is the case with our organizations. As we have left the most unconscious century in history (it is interesting to note that in the film the first radio waves to reach an alien intelligence originates from the most unconscious, ego-driven, and pathological regime of all time), we are hopeful that we are entering a more conscious one, and organizations will play an incredibly important role in this pendulum swing in our ongoing evolution.

To use a recently popularized term, the turn of the millennium can be viewed as a tipping point, a moment in time when the momentum of our collective consciousness is shifting from the stunning unconscious behavior of our recent past to a new realm of consciousness, where the confluence of scientific, psychological, spiritual, social, and organizational ideas (and *ideals*) are beginning to create an enlightened critical mass, a powerful collective energy, that has the virtue and capacity to change the nature of our reality and our future for the better.

In this book we have explored the socio-economic systems we create in the form of organizations, and we have imagined the potentialities that are open to us collectively when we can act and interact more effectively and consciously to create a more enlightened enterprise. As an organization explores the realms of true nature, energy creation and flow, the laws of productive and sustainable co-creation, and the power of healthy interactions and relationships, it becomes more self-aware. The organization that is more aware, walks its own path, lets go of unnecessary and negative attachments, forms a greater understanding of who it is and what its possibilities are, and creates a stronger bond with its internal participants and the external environment.

It consciously reinforces timeless, values-based behaviors to build and sustain an enduring culture, reinforce its guiding strategic intent, and successfully drive strategy execution. It understands that control-based and fear-based management practices generate paralyzing negative energy while inclusive and collaborative management practices generate liberating positive energy. It understands that it must define a much different and broader vision of success to ensure its long-term survival, and that its survival, its destiny, is one that is shared with its collaborators, competitors, customers, and communities.

Most organizations today are still asleep at the wheel. They have a sense of what direction they wish to be driving in, but have not yet awakened to a new, more conscious view of reality. Some will be able to stay on the road for years to come, primarily in survival mode (and much of it due to entropy's sibling, inertia), but many will veer off course and end up in the proverbial ditch. However, more and more organizations around the world across commercial as well as social sectors are becoming more enlightened. They are walking a more conscious path. They are paving a more intentional road. They are applying many of the principles outlined in this book. They act more like organic systems than artificial organizations. They are breaking down centralized structures in favor of distributed networks. They are more enabling than controlling. They are building new social networking and collaborative arrangements. They are more connected than isolated. They are more sensitive to and embracing of the multiversity of humanity. They care about their people and believe in the productive power of compassion and empathy. They realize that cooperation and competition can and actually must coexist. They understand their success is intrinsically tied to the success of their communities and surrounding environment. And they are fully aware that their future is dependent upon and inseparable from the consciousness out of which their actions originate.

My Samadhi *A Personal Urging*

Each organization is at its own place on the continuum of consciousness. Each organization is at its own stage of awakening to the realities of this new millennium. And each organization has the opportunity right now to take a critical look at itself and determine how ready and willing it is to undertake the journey of enlightenment and create the conditions for achieving superior levels of performance and value creation.

Each chapter in this book closes with a set of questions and considerations for walking a new path, helping enterprise participants and leaders to diagnose organizational readiness for the journey. In my consulting work, I consistently found that one of the most powerful strategies for supporting transformation was conducting a broad and deep diagnostic study of current issues and challenges, threats and opportunities, and strengths and weaknesses, of the organization. This type of effort creates a rich fact-base and strong platform from which to identify obstacles and enablers, assess readiness, map potential new directions, and begin planning for new strategic imperatives and their aligned initiatives. With this in mind, I would urge you to consider using this book as a resource in exploring, designing, and implementing a robust study for taking a critical look at your own organization to determine its readiness and willingness to walk a new path of consciousness and high performance.

In addition to the frameworks, tools, continuums, and diagnostic question sets found throughout the book, here are a few "reminder" questions for you to consider and address in your strategic endeavor:

To what extent is there a shared view among leadership that the enterprise is underperforming relative to its potential?

To what extent is there agreement throughout the enterprise that its business model is not well aligned with the new realities of our world's social, economic, and environmental challenges?

To what extent is there an emerging desire to move beyond financial statements and annual reports to explore a broader definition of success, one that includes how the enterprise contributes to the social good of our world?

To what extent is there a sense that the culture of the enterprise is not effectively co-evolving with the networks and communities within which it operates and serves its constituents?

To what extent are there indicators that the workforce of the enterprise is not as present, engaged, and productive as it might be in creating value?

And to what extent are the values of enterprise participants evolving to include a much greater desire for meaning and personal fulfillment in the workplace, one that includes a broader sense of social value?

It is my hope that you will use this line of questioning in your diagnostic work. They will help shine the light on the best path for your enterprise.

In this book we have explored many diverse concepts of and conditions for increasing enterprise consciousness and improving organizational results. We have seen how the enlightened enterprise understands that the fabric of the organization is not defined by the quality of tangible, yet unstable, objects, products, structures, or services, but by the quality of intangible, invisible, and yet powerful energy flows among participants within the enterprise and across its boundaries. The enlightened enterprise walks its path of superior value creation fueled not by the controlling forces of policies, protocols, and programs, but by the positive energy harnessed from healthy participants, strong interactions, lasting relationships, powerful capabilities, collaborative communities, effective networks, and enduring, sustainable practices.

Our collective current reality is the realization that our personal and professional lives are innately interconnected and inherently meaningful. And that we have an opportunity to clear away the contaminated clouds of fear, separation, and control and, through the uniquely human constructs we call organizations, create a future reality of enduring socio-economic prosperity. Each organization will walk a unique path, but each path will be linked to each other path on this collective journey. This does not require a new generation of leaders to emerge from top ten business schools; rather it requires the current generations of people to transcend our own patterns of thinking and doing, and awaken from our sleep. Now is our time. The good news is this awakening has already begun.

ENDNOTES

1 Barbara Marx Hubbard, *Conscious Evolution: Awakening Our Social Potential* (New World Library, 1998), 71.

2 Jason Jennings, *Less Is More* (Portfolio, 2002), 122.

3 Fritjof Capra, The Tao of Physics: An Exploration of the Parallels Between Modern Physics and Eastern Mysticism (Shambhala, 2000), 225.

4 Lynne McTaggart, *The Field: The Quest for the Secret Force of the Universe* (HarperCollins, 2008), xxiii.

5 Ervin Laszlo, and Jude Currivan, *CosMos: A Co-creator's Guide to the Whole World* (Hay House, 2008), 102.

6 Marco Iansiti, and Roy Levien, *The Keystone Advantage: What the New Dynamics of Business Ecosystems Mean for Strategy, Innovation, and Sustainability* (HBS Press, 2004), 8.

7 Wheatley, Margaret, *Leadership and the New Science: Discovering Order in a Chaotic World* (Berrett Koehler, 2006), 101.

8 Peter Schwartz, *The Art of the Long View* (Doubleday Currency, 1991), 186.

9 Mihaly Csikszentmihalyi, *The Evolving Self* (New York: HarperCollins, 1993), 155.

10 Felix Salmon, "The Quote of the Week," *The Week*, April 23, 2010, 14.

11 Peter Senge, Bryan Smith, Nina Kruschwitz, and Joe Laur, *The Necessary Revolution: How Individuals and Organizations are Working Together to Create a Sustainable World* (Doubleday, 2008), 44.

12 Robert E. Sibson, *Maximizing Employee Productivity: A Manager's Guide* (AMACOM, 1994), 2.

13 Marvin Weisbord, *Productive Workplaces Revisited: Dignity, Meaning, and Community* (Jossey-Bass, 2004), xxii.

14 Jeffrey Pfeffer, *Competitive Advantage through People: Unleashing the Power of the Workforce* (HBS Press, 1994), 41.

15 William A. Pasmore, *Designing Effective Organizations: The Sociotechnical Systems Perspective* (John Wiley & Sons, 1988), 2.

16 Frank LaFasto, and Gary Larson, *Teamwork: What Must Go Right/What Can Go Wrong* (Sage Publications, Inc., 1989), 85.

17 M. Scott Peck, *The Different Drum* (Touchstone Simon & Schuster, 1987), 84.

[18] Jeremy Rifkin, *The Empathic Civilization: The Race to Global Consciousness in a World in Crisis* (Tarcher/Penguin, 2009), 529.

[19] Sandra Seagal, and David Horne, *Human Dynamics: A New Framework for Understanding People and Realizing the Potential in Our Organizations* (Pegasus Communications, 1997), xviii.

[20] Eckhart Tolle, A *New Earth: Awakening to Your Life's Purpose* (Plume, 2005), 295.

[21] Thich Nhat Hanh, *The Art of Power* (HarperOne, 2007), 42.

[22] Robert E. Sibson, *Increasing Employee Productivity* (AMACOM, 1976), 64.

[23] David R. Hawkins, *Power vs. Force: The Hidden Determinants of Human Behavior* (Hay House, 1995), 132.

[24] James Collins, *Good to Great and the Social Sectors: A Monograph to Accompany Good to Great* (Jim Collins, 2005), 8.

[25] Fritjof Capra, *The Web of Life: A New Scientific Understanding of Living Systems* (Anchor Books, 1996), 298, 304.

INDEX

A

Acceptance, 224
Accountability, absence (organizational energy sink), 79–80
Action, ineffectiveness, 192–193
Activity, 52
Activity-based costing, 257
Actual values, demonstration, 253
Adapting, competency, 231
Agreement
  areas, 198
Agreement, active focus, 195
Argyris, Chris, 139
Association, 50–51
Attachment, absence, 251
Attracting, competency, 232
Auberdene, Patricia, 7
Authority orientation, nature, 202
Awakened doing
  example, 208
  modalities, 207
Awakening
  art, 256
  transcendence, 251–256
Awareness, 28–29, 235–236
Axelrod, David, 175

B

Balance (achievement), harmony (usage), 111–113
Bateson, Gregory, 7, 101
Behavioral psychology, knowledge, 23–24
Being, resonance, 78
Best practices, 62, 256
  usage, 145
Biodiversity, protection/preservation, 122
Biological systems, evolution, 99
Blaming/personalizing, replacement, 195
Boundless/natural curiosity, 234
Brache, Alan, 63
Brainstorming sessions, 238
Brand logo, meme, 116
Broad-based business literacy, development, 138
Broad-based incentive compensation program (meme), 114–115
Business
  acumen, 150
  ecosystems, 98
  incentives, creation, 120
  models, 118–119
  organizations, network, 258
Business processes, 55–56
  redesign, 62

C

Capabilities
  extension, 149–151
  mix, group/team condition, 168
Capabilitiy, consciousness current, 261
Capra, Fritjof, 262
Career-pathing, 242
Caring, consciousness current, 260
Cause-and-effect organizational behavior model, 26
Change
  continuity, 179
  degree, 3
  event-driven activity, 106
  initiatives, sub-optimization/failure, 106–107
  true nature, understanding, 106–109
Chaos
  control, 86–87
  theory/management, 257
Classroom training, 159
Co-evolution
  chaos, 95
  consciousness current, 262
  constituencies/networks, 235
  framework, development, 124–128

koan, 101
process, 253
strategy, description, 266–267
Cognitive distortions, existence, 194
Coherence, consciousness current, 260–261
Collaborating, competency, 230
Collaboration
conditions, 165
consciousness current, 261
forms, 166
Collaborative activity
effectiveness, 218
incenting, 180–184
Collaborative model, 179
Collaborative orientation, nature, 202
Collective activities, cost allocation, 120
Collective opportunity, 271
Collective spirit, potency (prevention), 25–26
Collins, Jim, 249
Command chains, dissolution, 30
Commercial organizations, profitability, 19–20
Commercial sector organizations, questions, 8
Common ground, finding, 205
Communication competencies, 150
Community, 21
building, 177
consciousness current, 262
ecology, 262
effectiveness, exploration, 176–180
experiences, involvement, 178
power, leverage, 121–122
Compassion, power (practice), 92
Compensation decisions, 241–242
Competencies, 237
exploration, 225–233
extension, 149–151
framework, pre-fabricated models (adoption), 149
list, 227–233
model, development, 226
Competitive landscape, trends, 113
Competitor secrets, discovery, 44
Complexity (koan), 108
Compliance, requirement, 254
Conscious behavior
actions, daily practice, 267
positive patterns, 267–268
Conscious behaviors/actions, daily practice, 267
Conscious enterprise, creating/building, 264–267
Conscious interactions, practice, 223
Conscious interdependence, 192
Consciously intelligent organizations information, understanding, 105
Consciously intelligent organizations, awareness, 103
Consciousness
currents, 247, 259–262
summary, 259–262
defining, 235–236
emergence, self-diagnosis, 235–237
koan, 189
levels, 226–227
roadmap/pathmap, reading, 263–268
self-cultivation, 212
Conscious organization, success (achievement), 248–249
Conscious participant, questions, 239
fear, absence, 240
Conscious participation, 225
Constituent base, understanding, 113
Constructive feedback, 4
receipt, 234
Consumer-based intelligence, capture/synthesis, 57
Contribution levels, group/team condition, 168
Control, span, 255
Control-based behavior, 222
Control-oriented organizational behavior model, 26
Control-oriented policies/practices, usage, 114
Convergence
power, 26–27
revelation, 21–27
Corporate financial reporting, accuracy/clarity (increase), 6
Corporate social responsibility, dilution, 42–43
Corporate stewardship, 56
Courage, consciousness current, 260
Creating, competency, 150, 227–228
Creativity
enabling, 213–215
organizational repression, 214
organizational support, 214–215
Critical thinking, 150
Csikszentmihalyi, Mihaly, 112
Culture, definition, 65
Customer

behavior, control, 28
focus, 56
intimacy, approaches, 57
nature, understanding, 113
support, 206
Customer relationship management (CRM), 257

D

Daring, competency, 231–232
Data, capture/collection, 195
Dawkins, Richard, 114
Day-to-day terrain, navigation, 238–244
Decision approval processes, steps (elimination), 148
Decision making
activities, struggle, 148
avoidance, 194
ease, 146–149
effectiveness
improvement, opportunities, 148–149
struggle, 148
examination, 147
information, relationship, 147
processes, steps (elimination), 148
review process, implementation, 149
Decision-making tool, meme, 116
Decision rights matrix, development/syndication, 148–149
Demand, creation, 57
Deprogramming, 256
Design, coherence, 182
Development, 51
Dharma, 13
Diagnostic questions, 236–237
Disagreement, agreement (contrast), 195
Discernment/detachment, 103
Discipline
differentiators, 151–152
importance, 152
Disequilibrium, primary catalyst, 107–108
Displacement, impact, 84–85
Distributed leadership capability, development, 89
Diversity, 200–206
Doing, modalities, embracing, 224
Doing/being, contrast, 23–24
Duality, delusion (organizational energy sink), 81E
Ecosystem
activities, 126
intelligence, 126
Efficiency, achievement, 108
Ego
approval, 190
convenience, 191
experience, 78–79
fairness, 191
feeding, 80–81
illusions, 251
Ego-driven control orientation, 142
Ego-driven go-it-alone strategy, 253–254
Ego-driven mind, development/sustenance, 190–191
Ego-driven thinking, unconscious state, 192
Ego-driven thoughts, allowance, 238
Egoic mind, transcendence, 222–223
Einstein, Albert, 119–120
Electromagnetic radiation
creation, 74
detection, 75
Electromagnetic waves, characterization, 73–74
Emergent opportunities, advantage, 104–105
Emerging consciousness, self-diagnosing, 235–237
Emery, Marilyn/Fred, 175
Emotionally intelligent organizations, 103
Empowerment, term (overuse), 218
Energy
connection, 235
cosmic dance, 73
ebbs/flows, 85–86
exchange, experience, 48
flowing fields, 71
laws/forces, understanding, 22–23
sea, 75
sources/sinks, understanding, 76–87
Energy fields
alignment, 75
interaction, 73–76
strength, increase, 87–89
Engaging, competency, 229–230
Enjoyment, 224
source, 207
Enlightened enterprise
creation, 11
external environment, shared destiny, 120–121
positive energy, 87–88
purpose, 36, 40

spirit, 36
Enlightened leaders, communication, 88–89
Enlightened organization, 29, 34, 47
agility/flexibility/productivity, 135
distributed leadership capability, 89
form/structure understanding, 30
learning, constancy, 161
microcosms, 178
physical/mental disease, nondiscrimination, 213
purpose, definition, 35
Enlightened participant, 117
self-awareness, 238
success, 243
Enlightenment, concept, 210–211
Entanglement, 23
Enterprise
activity, 125–126
organization responsibility, 20–21
creating/building, 264–267
defining, 19–21
effectiveness, impact, 222, 254–255
formal/informal activities/processes, 158
for-profit organization, comparison, 20
initiatives, failure, 63
intelligence, 125–126
change, 106
internal/external value propositions, understanding, 221
leaders, behavior, 4
long-term viability, 40
mission, 35
open system, 20
org-ego, transcendence, 253–254
participants
perspective, 11
role, 142
phenomena, interpretation, 22
purpose-based social system, 18, 19–20
quality, 35–36
self-regulating system, 96
social responsibility, 43
spirit/values, demonstration, 221
strategic/operational activities, 266–267
success, 16
true nature, representation, 18
true spirit, 17
unified field, creation, 204–206
value creation processes/networks, understanding, 221–222
value network, principles (association), 59–60
wisdom, demonstration, 103–106
Enterprise resource planning (ERP), 62–63, 257
Enthusiasm, 224
Entropy, existence, 112
Environment
change, 108
complexity, increase, 144
open-system, interaction, 98
organization co-evolution, 46–47
preservation, 252–253
sustaining, importance, 121
Environmental activities, 127
Environmental analysis, 126
Environmental/competitive landscape, threats/challenges (openness), 46
Environmental dynamics, organizational response, 113
Environmental health and safety (EHS) employees, awakened doing, 208
Environmental intelligence, 127
Environmental leadership, 127
Equilibrium, open system (unnatural state), 107–108
Evolution
cause-and-effect, simplification, 101
laws, review, 98–103
natural selection basis, 99
tendencies, 112
Evolutionary effectiveness, 113
Executing, competency, 230–231
Executive accountability, increase, 6
Experience, 48
creation, 189
Experimentation, 90
External networks, 21
External value networks, interactions, 60
External value proposition, 48, 221
alignment/satisfaction, 236
clarity/distinctiveness, 49
creation, 47

F

Facilitating, competency, 150–151, 228
Fact-base, improvement, 197–198
Fear, transcendence, 251–256
Feedback
loop, 183
quality, improvement, 116
Financial incentive programs, 180

Financial indicators, 55–56
Financial measures, 182
Financial rewards program, 54
Force, power (contrast), 242
Formal teams/groups, unenlightened organization usage, 170
For-profit organization
  cross-section, examination, 181
  enterprise, comparison, 20
Full value exchange, defining, 47
Functional roles, impact, 142
Future, co-creation, 19
Future performance, determination, 68

G

Gaia, voice, 271
Geometric patterns, application, 23
Goals
  group/team condition, 168
  obstacles, removal, 196
sensibility, 182–183
Goleman, Daniel, 103
Grounding, 244–245
Ground-state energy, 74
Group-based incentive programs, 180–181
Groups, 20
  effectiveness
    conditions/elements, 167–170
    exploration, 167–171
  ideas/behaviors/actions, energy sources, 77
  involvement, 138–139
  metrics, 183
Growth, achievement, 57

H

Habitats/ecosystems, restoration, 123
Hagelin, John, 73
Hamel, Gary, 44–45
Hammer, Michael, 63
Hanh, Thich Nhat, 225
Hanna, David, 139
Harmony
  koan, 111
  positive energy, absence, 112
Hawkins, David, 78, 242
Health
  active practice, 220–221
  emphasis, 208–210
  preventive procedures, 27
Hierarchical behavior, 222
Hierarchy
  hubris, organizational energy sink, 81–82
  organizational overemphasis, 252
Hierarchy, observation, 9
High performance, defining, 249
High-performing organizations, 62
High quality interactions, achievement, 197–198
Historical-based constructs, usage, 189
Holmes, Ernest, 251
Horne, David, 192
Hubbard, Barbara Marx, 19
Human behavior, dynamics (understanding), 190
Human capital inputs, emphasis, 156
Human consciousness, beliefs/understanding, 24–25
Human constructs, impact, 18
Human enterprise, types, 20
Humanity, respect, 204

I

Iansiti, Marco, 98
Identity-driven organizational behavior model, 26
Impact, 48
Improvement infrastructure, 183
Impulsive responses/reactions, avoidance, 194
Incentive programs, implementation, 183–184
Individuals, 20
  health/wellness, 209
  mind, ego, 81–82
Individual thoughts/behaviors/actions, energy sources, 77
Informal leadership, 226–227
Information
  acquisition/sharing, 157
  decision making, relationship, 157
  flow, middle management conduit, 109
  intelligent organization, relationship, 105
  nonlocal transmission, 74–75
Innovation
  culture, requirements, 214
  fostering, 214–215
  organizational repression, 214
Integrating, competency, 151, 228–229
Integrative activity, group/team condition, 170
Intelligent organization, information

(relationship), 105
Interaction
assumptions/belief systems, 197
cognitive distortions, 197
harmony, 187
ineffectiveness, 192–193
nature, description, 197
norms, 172
quality, improvement, 198
topic/objective, 197
Internal conditions/activities, understanding/cultivation, 46
Internal dynamics, group/team condition, 169
Internal networks, 21
Internal value networks, interactions, 60
Internal value proposition, 221
alignment/satisfaction, 236
creation, 47
enlightened organizational investment, 53–54
viewpoint, 53
Involvement work systems, 257
ISO 9000, 257

J
Jantsch, Erich, 101
Job evaluation, 152
Job re-evaluation, 242
Just-in-time operations, 257

K
Kaizen, 257
Key capabilities, 125–126
Key relationships/interactions, 143
Key responsibilities, 142–143
Kinetic energy (active energy), 74
Knowledge management, 157
Koan, 13
co-evolution, 101
complexity, 108
consciousness, 189
culture, 65
harmony, 111
memes, 114
natural selection, 99
open system, 97
participant, defining, 20
productivity, 132
self-empowerment, 220
sustainability, 122
true nature, 28
value creation, defining, 42
value network, 59
value proposition, 48

L
Lag indicators, 56, 253
Large-scale initiatives, 179–180
Lattice, 219
Leadership, 257
development, unenlightened organization investment, 139
Learning, 234
conditions, 159–160, 173–174
experiences, 160–161
provision, absence, 219
management, 157
nature, reframing, 158–162
processes, 160
pursuit/monitoring, 223–224
Levien, Roy, 98
Living systems, cycle, 108
Logistics, management, 57
Long-term effectiveness, expense, 252–253
Long-term sustainability, impact, 6
Loyalty orientation, nature, 203

M
Magnetic attraction, 87
Management mania, organizational energy sink, 83–84
Market focus, 56
Matter, laws/forces (understanding), 22–23
Memes
concept, organizational unawareness, 115
evolution, 115
koan, 114
power, exploration, 114–117
proactive disabling, 195–196
Memetics, study, 115
Metrics
framework development/syndication, 100
meaningfulness, 182
Middle management, de-emphasis, 109
Mind/body/spirit, investment, 92
Mindshare, competition, 115
Mitigating harm strategy, 43
Motivational orientation, nature, 203
Multi-cultural enterprise, network activity (productivity), 204
Multiversity, 200–206

embracing, 204–206
management, 204

N

Natural selection (koan), 99
Nature
laws, embracing, 91
pure energy, 92
Negative energy
flows, 77
generation, 76–77
Negative memes, 117
Network-based solutions, 82
Networks, 21
activities, effectiveness (diagnostic information), 64
concept, embracing, 59
effectiveness, exploration, 171–174
entities, collaboration, 253–254
facilitation, 161–172
governance, 172
ideas/behaviors/actions, energy sources, 77
intelligence, 172–173
interfaces, 173
involvement, 138–139
management, 158
measurement/assessment, 174
participation, 126
responsibilities, scope, 255
Newtownian mechanics, application, 23
Non-judgmental communication, 206
Non-localized energy sources/sinks, occurrence, 86
Non-renewable natural resources, conservation, 123
Not-thinking, 25

O

Obedience, requirement, 254
Objective, non-judgmental curiosity, practice, 195
Objective data, application, 205
Objective observation, subjective assessment (contrast), 195
Objects, organizational overemphasis, 252
Off-shoring, 257
Ongoing learning, requirements, 159
Open-book management, 257
Open system
environment, interaction, 98
koan, 97
Open-system interactions, creative energy, 138
Operational capabilities, 145–146
Operational efficiency, 157
Operational excellence, 56
Operational organizational capabilities, 145
Opportunity, seeking, 90
Optimal productivity, key conditions, 143–144
Optimal work experience, enabling, 139–144
Order, enlightened enterprise creation, 114
Organizational behavior, models, 26
Organizational capability
concept, 55–56
positive energy source, 144
Organizational dynamics, viewpoint, 102–103
Organizational energy sinks, 79–85
Organizational initiatives, energy sources, 78
Organizational interactions, disruption, 192
Organizational leaders, role, 88
Organizational learning, social process, 159
Organizational literacy, gaining, 222
Organizational needs, pay opportunities (impact), 152–153
Organizational practices, destructiveness, 239
Organizational processes, energy sources, 77
Organizations
chains-of-command, 81–82
challenge, summary, 6–10
co-evolution, 109
collective ego, feeding, 80–81
communication, 7
consciousness, emergence, 54
creativity/innovation reduction, 214
diagnostic questions, 236
direction, 272
effectiveness, 190
convergence, 18
improvement, 1
ego (org-ego), impact, 24
energizing, positive action (usage), 89–92
energy, ebbs/flows, 85–86
environment, co-evolution, 46–47

evolutionary point, 263
fulfillment, experience, 206–208
health, 236
historical success, 254–255
input transformation, 134
interaction, 4
interest, 2
internal climates, 104
internal/external ability/agility, 126–127
internal/external environments, prediction/direction/control, 9
life-cycle, 145–146
long-term success, reasons, 6–7
management, importance, 255
market power, achievement, 5
members/employees, disconnection, 4
mission, 224, 235
operations/financials understanding, 2
participation, 3–4
products/services/interactions, advantage, 49
qualities/conditions, continuum, 138–139
scenario building, usage, 110–111
scenario planning
strategic process utilization, 110
usage, 110–111
short-term results, 252–263
short-term success, 5
social systems, 3–4
societal influence, achievement, 5
strategies, progress, 8
strengths/capabilities, understanding, 46
structure, overinvestment, 58
structure/hierarchy/leadership, focus, 9
success, 5, 6
defining, 9
transformation, 27–28
true nature, description, 264
unconscious entities, action/behavior, 7
value
creation, defining, 9
description, 264
well-being, 236
work, 235
completion, 99–100
Organized labor, concept (importance), 41
Outsourcing, 257

P

Participant
behaviors, shaping/controlling, 254
defining, 20
expectations, 173
work enjoyment, 207–208
Participation, 181
composition, 173
norms (group/team condition), 169
Pasmore, William, 155
Patterns
breakdown, 22
pathology, organizational energy sink, 84–85
transcending, 205
Pay-for-performance, 180
Pay levels (grades/bands), 152
Peck, M. Scott, 177
People
assets/capital treatment, 9–10
consciousness, emergence, 54
management/control, 196
mental/physical health, 210
potential, unleashing, 190–196
role, understanding, 15
satisfaction/productivity, 140–141
trust, 89
well-being, 252–253
People, connection (increase), 3
Perfectly designed problem, 120
Performance, 237
development, 65
discussions, 2
excellence levels, 225
expectations, development, 241–242
feedback, exchange, 141–142
levels, attainment, 227
management, 64–65
processes, failure (reasons), 66
measurement processes, 179
orientation, 64
real-time conversations, 67
requirements, 45
standards/indicators, 144
targets/ranges, 45
tension, group/team condition, 169–170
Permanence, proofs, 252
Personality types, research, 191
Personal value propositions, 53
Pfeffer, Jeffrey, 147
Physical reality, 23
Physical sciences, discoveries, 22

Policies, paradox (organizational energy sink), 82–83
Porter, Michael, 44–45
Positive action-schemas, 89
Positive energy
  creation, 224
    ability, 236
  fields, 259
    creation, 204
  flows, 77
  generation, 76–77
  inherent power, 256–257
  power, enlightened enterprise understanding, 87–88
  source, 212–213, 250
Positive organizational memes, examples, 116
Positive/productive relationships, building, 198–200
Positive reinforcement, 4
Positive value, creation, 243
Power
  force, contrast, 242
  fostering, 225–233
Power-based organization, drama, 238
Prahalad, C.K., 44–45
Pritchard, Robert, 133
Problem solving, 150
  ability, 234
  usage, 195
Process
  blame, 91
  performance development, 65
Production employees, empowerment, 219
Productive activity, qualities, 131
Productive energy, source, 212–213
Productivity
  defining, 134–136
  determinants, understanding, 136–139
  examination, 134
  exploration, 133–134
  importance, 133
  koan, 132
  long-term emphasis, 240–241
  research, 135
  technology, driver, 156
Product testing, coordination/management (outsourcing), 57–58
Program performance development, 65
Program roll-outs, 238
Project/program management, 157
Project updates, 238
Psychic energy, investment, 242
Psychic roles, impact, 142
Purpose, 142
  clarity, 181
  group/team condition, 168

Q

Qi, universal energy, 72
Quality
  commitment, 91
  long-term emphasis, 240–241
  orientation, 201–202, 234
Quantum mechanics, application, 23

R

Random opportunities, advantage, 104–105
Reality
  perception, 250
  scenario-building, impact, 109–111
Real world, artificial construct, 26
Recognition, absence, 4
Reengineering, 257
Regulating, competency, 151, 229
Regulatory/legislative information, dissemination, 58
Relational-based solutions, 82
Relational energy, 74
Relational energy field
  positive/negative charges, 75
  power, 74–75
Relationship building, practice, 223
Relationship management, 158
Relationships, 51, 198–199
  elements/conditions, 199
  importance, 199
Relativity, principles
  application, 23
  demonstration, 96
Renewable natural resources, sustainable use, 122–123
Renewal, process, 211–212
Resources
  enabling, group/team condition, 168–169
  planning/acquisition/allocation technologies, 156–157
Responsibility
  group/team condition, 168
  scope, 154
Restructuring/redesign activities, energy

investment, 135
Results achievement, linkage, 67–68
Results area measure, 182
Results-based orientation, 67
Review, rigor, 183–184
Rewards, 52
linkage, 67–68
Rifkin, Jeremy, 179
Risk
orientation, nature, 202–203
taking, 90
Roles, group/team condition, 168
Rummler, Geary, 63

S

Salmon, Felix, 120
Samadhi, 13
personal challenge, 85–87
personal concern, 151–152
personal discovery, 31–33
personal examination, 233–235
personal experience, 117–119
personal hope, 257–259
personal journey, 210–212
personal memo, 13–16
personal perspective, 62–63
personal revelation, 175–176
personal urging, 273–274
Satori, 13, 39, 71, 95, 131
example, 17
Scanning technology, usage, 100
Scenarios
building, impact, 109–111
planning, 126
strategic process utilization, 110
Schwartz, Peter, 106
Seagal, Sandra, 192
Seeking, competency, 150, 227
Selective adaptation, tendency, 102
Selective attention, usage, 101–102
Self
experience, 78–79
separation, organizational energy sink, 79
Self-actualization, 219
Self-awareness, nonpractice, 238
Self-driven research, 222
Self-empowered confidence, 234
Self-empowerment, 226–227, 243
ability, 244–245
ascending, 218–225
koan, 220
process, 220–225
Self-maximizing organizations, impact, 102
Self-organizing systems, creativity (impact), 101
Self-regulation, self-sufficiency (equivalence), 100
Senge, Peter, 124
Senior leadership
observation, 9
role, 149
Service
ability, 90
orientation, 234
Shared goals, obstacles (removal), 196
Shared reality
creation, 250–251
exploration, 4–6
Short-term financial rewards, 243
Sibson, Robert, 133, 239
Six Sigma, 257
Skill-building, provision, 219
Skill development, linkage, 67–68
Social beings
enjoyment, 256
impact, 3–4
Social good strategy, creation, 43
Social organizations, network, 258
Social sector organizations, questions, 8
Socio-economic ecosystems, nature, 149–150
Socio-economic systems
dynamics, 125
exploration, 271–272
health, 253–254
Socio-technical systems, perspective, 155
Socio-technical work systems, concept, 155
Space-time, understanding, 23
Specialization, requirements, 100
Spirit-consciousness, 25
Spiritual beings, 188
human form, 250–251
Spiritual exploration, importance, 76
Spirituality, beliefs/understanding, 24–25
Spiritual orientation, nature, 200–201
Spoken values, description, 253
Sponsorship/guidance, group/team condition, 167–168
Stability, sources, 252
Staff statistics/analytics, 105–106
Star organizations, effectiveness, 5
Steward, Julian, 101
Stillness

degree, 28–29
practice, 25
Strategic alignment, 126
Strategic capabilities, 56
Strategic imperatives, value proposition (comparison), 45
Strategic organizational capabilities, 145
Strategic sustainability, 127
leading, 119–124
Structure
observation, 9
organizational overemphasis, 252
stranglehold, organizational energy sink, 82
Sub-elements, 125–126
Success, defining, 9
Succession planning, 242
Suffering, 233
absence, 251
Supply chains, management, 57
Survival, value creation (contrast), 40–41
Survival of the fittest, concept, 125
Sustainability
core capabilities, 124
enlightened organizations belief, 122
koan, 122
practices, 123–124
Sutra, 13, 72

T
Talent, 62
acquisition activities, 139
loyalty/commitment/contribution, 213
Tao, 13
new path, 36, 68, 93
Team effectiveness, conditions/elements, 167–170
Teamwork, 150
trust, relationship, 167
Technology
enabling, 172
investments, 156–158
power, 156
role, reframing, 154–158
Thinking
ability, 234
biased ways, 192–193
defensive ways, 194
exaggerated ways, 193
irrational ways, 193–194
usage, 195
Thought-patterns, prevalence, 194
Tiller, William, 73
Time, tyranny (organizational energy sink), 80–81
Time-based constraints, organizational creation, 80–81
Time orientation, nature, 201
Tolle, Eckhart, 78, 207, 224, 251
Top-down corporate-driven programs, focus, 14
Top-down model, usage, 138
Total quality management (TQM), 257
Transference, impact, 84
Transformation, event-driven activity, 106
Trist, Eric, 139
True nature, 264
koan, 28
leverage, 28–19
nature, exploration, 27–30
presence, 25
rediscovery, 30–33
True power, fostering, 225–233
Trust
collaboration condition, 166
teamwork, relationship, 167

U
Uncertainty, embracing, 110
Unconscious capitalism, 7–8
Unconscious entities, action/behavior, 7
Unconsciousness, awakening, 19
Unconscious participant
psychic energy, investment, 242
understanding/insight, absence, 241
Unconscious state, 233
Understanding, importance, 204–205
Unenlightened organization, 29, 34, 47
leadership capability, 89
restructuring/reorganization, 135
Unified energy, 74
Unifying, competency, 232–233
Union, positive change, 41
Universe
emptiness, 74
harmony, coherence, 96–97
sub-quantum level, 72
Unlearning
acts, 256
pursuit/monitoring, 223–224
Unleashing, 256–259

V
Value, 264

alienation philosophy, 41–42
capabilities, 55–58
chains, 58–64
contribution, 237
drivers, 55–58, 182
understanding, 206
growth, 56
networks, 58–64, 265
koan, 59
organizational links, 123–124
organizational application, 253
proposition, 224, 264–265
true nature, demonstration, 33–36
wealth, belief, 119
Value-based organization, 34
Value creation
activity, networks (examples), 61
belief, 119
capabilities
description, 265–266
usage, 144–146
culture, 65
description, 266
inculcation, 64–68
support, 64
defining, 9, 42
drivers, description, 265–266
enlightened enterprise understanding, 121
enterprise ability, 63
goals, 224
impact, potential, 255
key drivers, 143
long-term emphasis, 240–241
process/reason, organizational implicit/explicit beliefs/principles, 44–45
purpose, interaction support, 198
strategy, 125
survival, contrast, 40–41
values-based commitment, 40
view, enlightened organization expansion, 43–44, 249
virtue, 39
Value-creation strategy, development, 44–47
Value-generating processes, examination, 63–64
Value proposition, 45
creation, 47–55
koan, 48
quality, 50–53
strategic imperatives, comparison, 45
Values-in-action, 221
Variable pay, 180
Variances, reduction, 57
Vertical promotions, 242

W

Waste, reduction/elimination, 123
Watch-outs, 174
Wavicles, 72
Weisbord, Marvin, 175
Well-being, 236
emphasis, 208–210
Wellness
practice, 220–221
programs, return on investment clarity (absence), 209
Wheatley, Margaret, 101
Whole system
involvement, 175
methodology, effectiveness, 176
Work
characteristic, selection, 133
completion, 99–100
ethic, decline, 118
experiences, improvement, 141
key responsibilities, variation, 142
nature, defining, 132–133
participant enjoyment, 207–208
quality, improvement, 141
research, 135
valuation, 152–154
process, 152
strategic approach, 154
Work environment
evolution, 14
safety, creation, 42–43
Workforce
development, 139
mobilization, 177
planning, 139
process, implementation, 100
presence, 137
rewards, management, 255–256
Workplaces
diversity, 2
health issues, 213
safety, baseline requirement, 122–124
World, conditioned view, 26

Z

Zero-point energy, 74

ABOUT THE AUTHOR

As a management consultant and professional services executive for over twenty years, Christian Ellis has worked very closely with more than fifty organizations across a wide variety of commercial industries and social sectors to help them improve overall enterprise results. He was educated at Northwestern University, the University of Chicago, and Duke University where he focused his studies in the areas of industrial engineering, organization dynamics, and general management. He grew up in rural Minnesota, has lived in Illinois and North Carolina, and currently resides in Malibu, California. He can be reached at christianellis@theenlightenedenterprise.com.

To further explore the concepts found in this book, provide feedback or share personal insight, and access additional resources, such as the *Walking The Path Workbook* (supplements the text with over twenty user-friendly frameworks and diagnostic tools), please visit www.theenlightenedenterprise.com.